Organizational Behaviour
Reassessed

Tn

↑

Rl

0

R

Organizational Behaviour Reassessed

The Impact of Gender

edited by

Elisabeth Wilson

SAGE Publications
London • Thousand Oaks • New Delhi

SAGE Publications Ltd
6 Bonhill Street
London EC2A 4PU

SAGE Publications Inc
2455 Teller Road
Thousand Oaks, California 91320

SAGE Publications India Pvt Ltd
32, M-Block Market
Greater Kailash - I
New Delhi 110 048

British Library Cataloguing in Publication data

A catalogue record for this book is available from the British Library.

ISBN 0 7619 7092 4
ISBN 0 7619 7093 2 pbk

Library of Congress catalog card number available from the publisher

Printed in Great Britain by Cromwell Press Ltd, Trowbridge, Wiltshire

Contents

Preface

I first encountered Organizational Behaviour (OB) officially when I became a student on an MBA programme. How nice it was to learn about all the different bits of behaviour that happened in organizations, tidily chopped into bite size pieces, and how I as the manager could have some influence on them. All I had to do was to fit the right theory to particular people. It was illuminating, yet something was missing.

Of course this was not really my first encounter with organizational behaviour, as I had been working in organizations, as both employee and volunteer, for over 20 years. Even before that, I had experienced organizations as a school child, user of the UK National Health Service, and churchgoer from an early age, my father being the local minister. In almost all these organizations it appeared part of the natural course of events that men were in charge, with women in supportive and subsidiary roles. The exceptions were two all-female schools, which gave me some alternative role models, and in the second, some limited participatory structures and a sense of justice. I am of the post-war generation whose parents advised me to get a degree 'in case you are ever widowed', and have experienced my share of discrimination and setbacks.

It was only later when as a lecturer I started to read about gender and organizations that the scales fell from my eyes, and I felt some identification, a sense of authenticity, about what I was reading. All the 'other' organizational behaviour that I had met, the stuff that never made the textbooks, now had some explanation: the deference of women to men; the avuncular boss who put his arm round me; the sarcastic manager who ridiculed my inexperience; the pressure on men to conform; the difficult promotion path.

There are any number of standard OB textbooks, indistinguishable from each other, and almost all written from a male, managerialist, and often ethnocentric, viewpoint. They perform a certain function, but not one that I find satisfying, because they affirm the current order. This book grew out of a perceived need to challenge OB from the particular perspective of gender. I was tired of teaching OB topics without reference to gender, and wanted to gather together many of the insights that had emerged into one volume. Initially conceived as a book chapter, this book has survived two changes of publisher and the loss of a co-editor to emerge in its current form.

Happily things have changed since this book was first conceived, and OB appears to be undergoing a renaissance at the moment. I feel happy that this book is published at the same time as a number of other critical texts in the field. May the debate continue.

Elisabeth M. Wilson
Manchester, August 2000

Acknowledgements

I should like to thank my fellow contributors to this volume, both those who stuck with me when finding a publisher was initially difficult, and those more recently recruited.

There are a number of colleagues at the Institute for Development Policy and Management at the University of Manchester who demand particular mention: Bill Cooke encouraged me to persist; and Debra Whitehead and Karen Hunt helped order the manuscript.

I should also like to thank Rosemary Nixon and later Kiren Shoman from Sage for their patient support and guidance.

Contributors

Iiris Aaltio-Marjosola is Professor of Management in Lappeenranta University of Technology, Lappeenranta, Finland. Her research interests consist of organizational culture and its change, gender issues in management as well as entrepreneurial organizational cultures. Her background is in business administration and in organization psychology. She has formerly held academic posts as Associate Professor at the Turku School of Economics and Business Administration, Senior Scientist at the Academy of Finland, and Senior Lecturer in organization psychology at the Helsinki School of Economics and Business Administration. Her work on gender consists of both issues on femininity and masculinity and has been published in journals and book chapters in Scandinavia and internationally.

Yochanan Altman is Research Professor in International Human Resource Management at the University of North London. In 2000 he was also visiting professor at the University of Paris and the Hong Kong Baptist University. A psychologist and anthropologist by background, he is interested in the interaction between people and culture at the workplace. In addition to his academic career he has been consulting widely with organizations and individuals on careers, competence and inter-cultural awareness. This also brought him to the study of women at work and the role of working women in society.

Margaret Dale is an employment consultant and has written a number of books in the area of Human Resource Development and the use of competencies. She is a member of the Chartered Institute for Personnel and Development, is professional advisor to the Universities Competences Consortium, and acts as an expert witness in the assessment of earnings loss in personal injury and medical negligence cases. She carried out research into management style from a woman's perspective and developed a framework of competencies required for effective organizational management. She went on to explore why women 'chose' not to apply for management jobs for her MSc dissertation. With an extensive background in organizational and management development and the management of change in universities, the Health Service and Local Government, her particular concern is the way organizations impact on and treat people. She is a member of her local Community Health Council, and acts as a mediator in the National Health Service complaints process. Her recent research concerns informal learning at work and she is currently writing another book on this topic.

Judith Foreman is Programme Director of the Masters in Managing Organizational Change at Bradford College in the Department of

Management, Hospitality and Leisure Studies. Her research and teaching interests are in race, ethnicity, gender, sexuality and organization.

Mary Beth Gallagher began her business career with a major international airline in the United States. After occupying a variety of managerial positions in airport operations, she returned to school obtaining a Master of Arts degree in psychology from Antioch University in Seattle, Washington. After a brief career as a psychotherapist, Mary Beth relocated to the Los Angeles area where she worked as the Assistant Director of the Field Study Program at the Anderson Graduate School of Management at UCLA. Being in an academic environment and attending classes at Anderson re-ignited Mary Beth's interests in business. Looking to integrate her business and psychology backgrounds, Mary Beth enrolled in an Industrial/Organizational Psychology programme at the California School of Professional Psychology in San Diego, California. She will be graduating with her Master of Science degree in May, 2000. When not working or attending classes, Mary Beth is pursuing her passion for international travel.

Lorraine Green is a lecturer in Sociology at Sheffield Hallam University, previously having worked as a research fellow in the centre of Applied Childhood Studies, and a lecturer in Sociology and Social Work at the University of Huddersfield. Her research interests and publications are around issues of power, gender, sexuality, sexual abuse, residential care and childhood. Current research projects focused on sexuality and sexual abuse issues in children's homes, and on a cross comparative analysis of legalistic and therapeutic responses to sexual abuse in three European countries.

Jeff Hearn is originally from London. He studied at the Universities of Oxford, Oxford Brookes, and Leeds, and completed his PhD at Bradford. He has been teaching, researching and writing on gender relations in organizations since 1977. A special focus of this work has been co-writing with Wendy Parkin on sexuality in organizations. He has also conducted research on men and patriarchy, historical change, and men's violence to known women and children. This work was initially at Bradford University which he left in 1995 to join Manchester University where he is Professorial Research Fellow. His next book is *Unspoken Forces*, co-authored with Wendy Parkin, on violation in organizations. He is currently Visiting Professor and Academy of Finland Senior Fellow at the Swedish School of Economics and Business Administration, Helsinki, working on gender relations in transnational organizations, and men's practices in Europe.

Heather Höpfl is Professor of Organizational Psychology and Head of the School of Operational Analysis and Human Resource Management, Newcastle Business School, Newcastle upon Tyne, UK. Heather Höpfl is known for her original research in organizational culture, management development and organizational theory. She completed her PhD in Organizational Psychology at Lancaster University, UK in 1982 and has since worked in the theatre, in research and in teaching. She has undertaken research with a number of large organizations in the UK including British Airways, the Prison Service, the Department for Education and Employment, and also the Land Transport Authority in Singapore. She has a particular interest in the relationship between structures and processes and this has been an important part of her work on the design of systems environments both for the analysis of airline safety information and for the development of learning organization approaches for management development. She is married to Harro Höpfl and has two children, George and Max.

Anne Kovalainen is Professor in Gender Research, Swedish School of Economics and Business Administration, Helsinki, Finland and Docent in Economic Sociology at the Turku School of Economics and Business Administration, Finland. She has been a Visiting Research Fellow at London School of Economics and Political Science (2000, 1996) and the University of Bradford (1993). Her research interests are in economic sociology and gender, working life, methods, and gender theories. Her recent books have covered issues such as European Employment Systems; welfare, social care and gender, and neo-entrepreneurship in welfare services, as well as several articles in Finnish and English.

Beverly Dawn Metcalfe is Senior Lecturer in Human Resource Management in the HRM Department, Staffordshire University. Her background is in project management and management development in the defence and telecommunications industries and also the public sector. Her work experiences contributed to her decision to move into academia and stimulated her to research the broad areas of Human Resource Management and gender and management. Her research interests include the construction of gendered identities at work; International Human Resource Management, and gender; dress and identity; performance management; and gender and performativity. In addition to research and lecturing she also consults in the areas of Human Resource Strategic Development and Equal Opportunities.

Albert J. Mills is a Professor of Management in the Department of Management at Saint Mary's University. He incorporates race/ethnicity and gender in his teaching of organizational behaviour – drawing on 'Malcolm X' and 'Norma Rae' to educate and inspire students. His research centres on the impact of organization on people, focusing on organizational change and human liberation. These lifelong concerns were formulated on the shop floor of British industry and through involvement in the movements for social change that characterized the 1960s. Mills' early images of organization – images of frustration, sexually segregated work, power disparities, and conflict – were experienced through a series of unskilled jobs and given broader meaning through campaigns for peace, women's liberation, environmental survival and social change. Albert Mills has authored and co-edited several books, articles, and conference papers that hopefully contribute to more than tenure and promotion in the university system.

Sue Newell is Professor of Innovation and Organizational Analysis at Nottingham Business School, Nottingham Trent University. She is a Chartered Psychologist who has worked previously at Portsmouth, Aston, Birmingham and Warwick Universities. Her main research interest is in the area of innovation, knowledge and organizational networking but she maintains an interest in more general HR issues, including selection and assessment, management development and gender and work.

Wendy Parkin is a principal lecturer in Sociology and Social Work at the University of Huddersfield. Her research and publications are in the field of sexuality, gender, emotion and organizations. Her current research is on the relationships between sexuality, gender, violence and organizational worlds.

Elizabeth Sondhaus is currently an organizational consultant with the District Attorney's office, County of San Diego, San Diego, California, USA. She completed her PhD in clinical psychology at Washington University in St. Louis, Missouri, USA, in 1997. She has practised as a therapist working with families and individuals, specializing in women's issues and trauma. She has also worked as research coordinator on several projects, including the assessment of post-traumatic stress disorder in Vietnam veterans and developing an instrument for the assessment of the disorders of early childhood. Her current research interests include gender issues in organizations, cross-cultural organization development, and the use of narrative in organizational interventions. Her work has appeared in the *Journal of Behavioral Medicine* and in *Neuropsychology*.

Elisabeth Wilson's first career was in social work, and encountering discrimination, she sought to make herself more promotable by taking an MBA. This led to a career change, lecturing at Liverpool John Moores University, and an abiding research interest in gender and organization. She has published articles and book chapters in this field as well as on managing diversity, yoga and management, and public sector structure and culture. She now works in the Institute for Development Policy and Management at Manchester University, where she is happy to have found a niche where she does not have to argue daily the relevance of gender. She is married to Michael Taylor and has two adult children.

1 Organizational Behaviour and Gender

Elisabeth M. Wilson

Organizational behaviour

Organizational behaviour concerns the interface between the individual, other individuals and groups, and the organization. It has its roots in a number of social science disciplines: psychology contributes to the understanding of individual personality and processes such as perception and attribution; sociology explains phenomena such as roles and groups; and social anthropology offers awareness of organizational culture. Some areas of study borrow from more than one discipline, and additionally from less obvious disciplines such as philosophy and literary criticism.

Many authors, for instance Schein (1996), dislike the term 'organizational behaviour', pointing out that it suggests an anthropomorphic view of organizations. Organizations do not behave, although people associated with them demonstrate behaviour. 'Organization studies' might be a more appropriate term, but implies that only organizations, not the people in them, are studied. In addition the term 'organization studies' has tended to become associated with a subset of research in this area, generally ideologically critical of mainstream work. Notwithstanding these observations, in this volume for reasons of ease and comparability, the term 'organizational behaviour' (OB) will be used.

In this chapter the concept of gender is examined, looking first at distinctions that have been made between sex and gender, before examining the impact of gender on conventional views of OB and organizational analysis, including brief discussion of masculinity/ies, a topic on which OB is often silent. Next, some of the basic tenets of feminist research methodologies will be discussed. Lastly the contents of the remainder of the book will be previewed.

The concept of gender

Gender is often perceived unproblematically as synonymous with biological sex, a historical and highly normative category (Brewis et al., 1995), that is, a something which exists outside its current context and determines roles and behaviour. Therefore a person found to be biologically female would also have the feminine gender. This is biological essentialism (Garrett, 1987), a belief that everyone has a pre-determined inner essence, a view challenged, for instance by de Beauvoir (1949) who wrote about becoming a woman, rather than it being innate. Lorber and Farrell (1991) similarly assert that gender is a social construct, that is, gender is a category people collectively agree to subscribe to as a concept.

Kelly (1955) was the first to describe constructs, and he developed the idea of Personal Construct Theory (PCT), which is concerned with the concepts people use to make sense of the world (Gammack and Stephens, 1994), and are assumed to be unique to each individual. Some of the key points of PCT are as follows. It is assumed that each individual has his or her own construct system, and that these systems, which develop through life, give meaning to individuals, despite some inherent contradictions between constructs (Stewart et al., 1980). Meaning is managed through the personal construct system (Gammack and Stephens, 1994). Whilst individual construct systems are the basis of PCT, it is also acknowledged that there can be similarities between constructs employed by different people (Easterby-Smith et al., 1996). Constructs tend to be arranged hierarchically, that is, some are subordinate to others (Stewart et al., 1980).

Social constructs, those that may be shared between individuals, have become a commonplace concept within social science research. Despite variations in schools of social construction, some common features can be established. Social constructionists reject an epistemology (theory of knowledge) where there are 'real' objects out there, which can be discovered (Paalman, 1997). They consider that everyday objects can have different meanings for different people, so that in a sense, they construct different objects, a phenomenon known as multiple reality (Paalman, 1997). Thus people construct their own reality in social interaction, and through relations with others people can create or change their realities (Paalman, 1997). In their everyday lives, people are involved in different settings, which the social constructionists describe as multiple inclusion, and there is no necessary congruence between the norms of behaviour or beliefs in different settings (Paalman, 1997). This means that people have a series of realities which can influence each other (Paalman, 1997). Whilst concluding that constructs shape our reality, there is a degree of fluidity implied by the social constructionist argument that does not explain the strong and widespread repeated patterns of, say, gender role expectations and stereotyping which will be discussed later in this volume (see Mills and Wilson).

Social constructionism explains gender in terms of ideas or concepts. However, some writers go further and insist that gender is constituted through interaction, rejecting the idea of gender as traits, variable or role (West and Zimmerman, 1991). Gender then becomes an active output of the social structure of organizations, not merely a passive attribute of individuals. This is the view that is commonly known as 'doing gender', where gender is seen as processual rather than as a given characteristic (Gherardi, 1994); thus reference may be made to the production and reproduction of gender within organizations (Acker, 1990). This also means that actions, events and organizations may be referred to as 'gendered', that is partially formed on the basis of gender constructions. Gherardi (1994) contends that gender is not merely 'done', but also thought about beneath the level of the conscious mind. The notion of male and female, and masculine and feminine, depends of course upon bipolar constructs and it has been pointed out by many writers (e.g. Spender, 1985) that one of the pair is always privileged. In the case of male and female, it is the male that is privileged. This is accentuated by the (largely unconscious) pairing of groups of binary opposites, such as men and rational, women and emotional. If what is attributed to one gender is denied to the other, then the way people do gender increases or decreases sexual inequality (Gherardi, 1994). For instance, rationality is a prized ability within organizations; however, if men are perceived as rational, then women as their opposites cannot be, and are therefore less worthy of organizational recognition and reward. Lorber and Farrell (1991) suggest that gender is an integral part of structures of domination and subordination with women in a position of inequality.

If however male and female are viewed as a continuum rather than bipolar opposites, (Oakley, 1972, cited in Garrett, 1987), then the dualism of masculine and feminine can be seen as an oversimplification (Alvesson and Due Billing, 1992). It is also questionable in the light of cross-cultural studies indicating that gender roles vary widely (Garrett, 1987). Some writers go further in their criticism of gendered binary concepts, asserting that 'the male/female dichotomy has no intrinsic biological or other essential reality' (Cornwall and Lindisfarne, 1994a: 9). Bem (1974) challenges the conceptualized divide between masculine and feminine by suggesting that some individuals may have characteristics commonly associated with the other, that is they are androgynous. By laying stress on the differences between men and women, both similarities between them, and also differences among each category can be overlooked. For instance, female employees can be old, young, better or worse educated, have domestic responsibilities or not, and be in different industrial sectors. All these differences may contribute to very different experiences of what it is to be a female employee. A number of chapters in this volume take the view that gender is primarily a social construct.

A further way of conceptualizing gender, which builds on the idea of gender as process, is to see it as discourse (Burrell, 1989). The word discourse was described by Foucault to encompass both a particular area of knowledge or social practice, and also the way that knowledge is constructed (Hardy, 1994). To put it another way, a discourse can be described as a self-referential area of assertion or discussion with prescribed limits. Discourse, by privileging certain topics and excluding others, acts to reproduce organizations in a particular way, and imposes parameters on acceptable types of identity. Culture can thus be seen as a discursive product (Harlow and Hearn, 1995) and is rarely sex-neutral (Watson, 1992). For instance Watson (1992) described the UK Civil Service 'sensible chap' discourse, which privileged a certain group of candidates for 'Fast Track' promotion by virtue of their class, education, and gender. A 'discourse of masculinism' was found in the UK financial services sector, privileging men above women, and supporting the maintenance of masculinity (Kerfoot and Knights, 1993: 659). There are of course alternative discourses (Mills, 1988), as evidenced by volumes such as this, and these can be seen as resistance to the dominant discourse (Mills, 1988). (It should be noted that in strict terms Foucault envisages discourse as involving resistance that is hence not extra-discursive.) Mills and Murgatroyd (1991) suggest that within the world of work there are two basic gender rules:

1. It's a man's world
2. It's a man's work

They do however point out that there are competing rules, different ways of looking at things, and different discourses, instanced for example by women in positions of authority, and legal constraints. Thus gender rules are outcomes of interaction, and not immutable (Mills and Murgatroyd, 1991). Cockburn (1991) similarly suggests that there is a social contract operating in men's favour that has two clauses. The first of these is a domestic clause, that every man has authority over a wife/housekeeper/child minder/sexual partner. The second clause concerns the workplace, that men guarantee each other rights over women (Cockburn, 1991).

Within this chapter for the sake of clarity, male and female will be taken to refer to biological sex, and masculine and feminine to socially constructed gender. The understanding that gender is processual rather than essentially determined will guide what follows. After this initial discussion of gender, the next section looks at the impact of gender on organizational analysis.

Gender and organizational analysis

For a long time, organizational behaviour and organization studies were regarded as gender neutral and took no account of gender (Rothschild and Davies, 1994). Another way of putting this is that the bulk of organizational theorizing has been gender blind, that is, it has not taken gender into account in any way: first and most straightforwardly as a variable; second, as a process; third, as gendered power relations (Marshall, 1995), and fourth, as an influence on academic means of production (Spender, 1990).

Early studies looked at gender as a variable; for instance Bartol (1978) posed the question as to why organizations are structured along gender lines, which she observed as a ubiquitous phenomenon. Mills (1988) comments on the famous Hawthorne studies, where gender as a variable was not properly taken into account in interpreting results. Tancred-Sheriff and Campbell (1992, republished from 1981) reviewed the work and influence of female organizational sociologists, which included pioneering work from writers who were generally closely allied to management, researchers who were concerned with oppression, and those who optimistically explored alternative forms of organization. One strong influence on a number of social sciences was Gilligan (1982), who wrote about a 'woman's voice'. Gilligan (1982) was an advocate of essential differences between the genders and focused attention on the lack of attention to women in research. As an example of this, the sexual division of labour is something that has long been noted (Mills and Murgatroyd, 1991) but was taken for granted for many years. Mills and Tancred (1992) criticize the gender blind nature of most organizational analysis, which they contend leads to error, and their edited volume *Gendering Organizational Analysis* is a corrective to this state of affairs. Including gender in organizational analysis may help comprehension of otherwise incomprehensible outcomes, such as why the best person did not get the job, and thus it has been described as a 'grid of intelligibility' (Gray, 1995: 46).

Recent critical comment about gender in organizational theory takes a number of forms, including links with critical studies in general in the field of organizational studies, and also analyses of gendered power relations (Marshall, 1995). Critical studies in management take the view that the proper role for management research is not for managers, but rather the critique of management as an activity (Johnson, 1996). For instance many writers question the notion of the rational organization (e.g. Roper, 1994), and see this as a self-serving social construction of management.

Gendered power relations have been commented on as the exercise of male power in relation to personnel processes and interpersonal relationships in organizations (Wells, 1973), and these will be discussed more fully in Green et al. (in this volume). The concept of patriarchy is often used to explain gendered power relations in the workplace, but not all contributors to this volume find it helpful. Patriarchy may be seen as too all-encompassing. It implies women are helpless victims, does not explain phenomena such as female sexual harassment of men (Merrick, 1995), and elides some of the nuances of gendered organizational life.

Despite the interest in gender shown by the writers in this volume, gender has been ignored in much of organizational analysis (Mills and Tancred, 1992; Marshall, 1995), has been silenced as an organizational topic (Harlow and Hearn, 1995), or been treated in a biased manner, by assuming all gender is male, reducing it to a variable only, or dealing in stereotypes (Burrell, 1989; Hearn, 1994). Calas and Smircich (1990) draw attention to the (male) gendered nature of organizational theorizing. They suggest as corrective measures that there are three approaches which can be taken: revising, reflecting and re-writing. Surveying several academic disciplines, they state that revising includes completing/correcting the record, assessing gender bias in current knowledge, and making new organizational theorizing. Reflecting includes questions of epistemology; they raise the question of who does theory in whose interests, and question the gendered nature of traditional epistemology. They suggest an iterative, reflective process looking at the relationship between 'knowledge' and 'the ways of doing knowledge' (Calas and Smircich, 1990: 240). They describe re-writing as an operation in which the politics of a text can be demonstrated by indicating what they describe as the strategies of 'truthmaking' (Calas and Smircich, 1990: 244). They propose deconstruction as one technique for undertaking this, demonstrating that a text may be gendered even if this is not part of the content (Calas and Smircich, 1990).

A cursory glance at some recent OB textbooks (e.g. Bartol and Martin, 1994; Buchanan and Huczynski, 1997; Jackson, 1993; Mullins, 1999) indicates that attention to gender is becoming more evident. No longer can all textbooks be described as gender blind, although many remain gender myopic. Consideration of gender tends to be concerned with particular topics, such as stereotyping and leadership, rather than being a consistent critical thread. Jackson (1993) limits his contribution to consideration of what is associated with masculine and feminine in different cultures, particularly using Hofstede's (1991) framework. Bartol and Martin (1994) have a similarly limited menu. However Buchanan and Huczynski (1997) and Mullins (1999) manage to integrate research on gender into a number of topics, particularly leadership and management style.

Although a number of writers are exercised on the topic of gender, as is obvious from this review of some of the literature, nevertheless it remains a minority interest (Hearn et al., 1989). Marshall (1995) contends that those writing from a reformist perspective are more likely to find their work accepted by others. The author accepts the contention that OB has tended to neglect gender as a powerful force shaping behaviour and outcomes. However, Alvesson and Due Billing (1992) advise that not everything can be explained by reference to gender, and warn against 'gender reductionism' (p. 87). Often the interrelationships with class, age, race (Cornwall and Lindisfarne, 1994a), and sexuality are ignored.

Masculinity/masculinities and male cultures are a recent addition to the OB literature. Criticisms have been made of the fact that only one type of masculinity tends to be discussed in general terms (Cornwall and Lindisfarne, 1994a), and in relation to organizations (Alvesson and Due Billing, 1992). This has been described as 'hegemonic masculinity'. As such it has a normative function (Cornwall and Lindisfarne, 1994b), that is, it provides a template or pattern for what 'proper' masculinity should be. A number of writers have sought to deconstruct masculinity to demonstrate that there are different masculinities in different locations (Cornwall and Lindisfarne, 1994b), at different levels of the organization (Mills and Murgatroyd, 1991), at different times (Kerfoot and Knights, 1993), and at different life stages (Collinson and Collinson, 1989). More examples can be found in Roper (1994), Kerfoot and Knights (1993), and in the recent popular constructs such as the 'new man', and 'the lads'.

Although the work on masculinities is interesting, what is noteworthy is that within OB there is no comparable body of work on femininities. Within OB gender has tended to be taken as referring to women's interests. For a comparable focus on women to that of masculinities one would have to explore women's studies. The reasons for this imbalance can only be conjectured, but could be related to the dominant position of men within academic OB and organizational research. For instance, publications on women in management outnumber studies of men and masculinities in organizations: thus women managers rather than male managers are problematized (Hearn, 1994). One criticism of the 'women in management' approach is that it ignores theorizing on gender in management prior to the advent of women managers (Calas and Smircich, 1990), and a great deal of its current output suffers from this. Another criticism is that it privileges the concerns of a narrow group of female workers, mostly white, middle-class women, who by virtue of their background and education may already have considerable advantages over other female workers. This volume therefore goes beyond studies focusing on men and women managers, and looks more broadly at the interaction of gender with and within organizational life.

Although this section has established clearly that gender encompasses more than the concerns of women, it seems apposite in the next section to consider feminist research methodology, as it challenged established methods and outputs of research.

Feminist research methodology

Research about gender and organizational analysis leads to methodological considerations of feminist research methodology. A survey of the literature (e.g. Harding, 1987; Eichler, 1988; Stanley and Wise, 1993; Stanley, 1990; Roberts, 1990) indicates that there is no one paradigm holding sway, but rather a series of overlapping conceptual fields, feminist research methodologies. Indeed some variants (e.g. Stanley and Wise, 1993) repudiate the idea of paradigmatic approaches to research.

Writing on feminist research methodology uses definitions integral to all discussion of methods. The following definitions are derived from Stanley (1990), Stanley and Wise (1993) and Harding (1987). Method is defined as a technique for gathering evidence, or a specific set of research practices, such as interviews or surveys. Methodology is described as theories of how research should proceed which give a perspective or theoretically informed framework. Epistemology concerns the theory of knowledge, and tells us who can be a knower, what can be known, and what constitutes and validates knowledge. Thus it gives guidance on what counts as an adequate theory, and how research findings are to be judged. Ontology is a way of being, and is a theory of reality.

Feminist research methodology encompasses non-sexist research methodology (Eichler, 1988), and has concerns which overlap with humanistic approaches to research (Reason, 1988; Coleman, 1989). It concerns itself with ethical considerations (Oakley, 1990; Stanley and Wise, 1993) and with the significance of the gender of the researcher in fieldwork (Warren, 1988). Above all, it is concerned to undertake good research, as is any methodology, albeit with different parameters of validity (Stanley and Wise, 1993; Roberts, 1990; Oakley, 1990). Roberts (1990) raises the question as to what extent 'good' research in the past has represented scientific validity and reliability, and to what extent it has been instead a social construct of one half of the population, men.

Feminist research methodology has links with intellectual antecedents which include the women's movement and feminism, humanistic approaches in their broadest sense in the social sciences and helping professions, and postmodernism and deconstructionism. Feminism questioned the status quo in many fields of life, whether the under-representation of women in certain occupational groups, discriminatory legislation or, in the research field, the disregarding of gender as an important variable (Eichler, 1988). Researchers identifying themselves as feminists promote the idea of research for women, rather than on women (Stanley and Wise, 1993) bringing a political and ethical perspective to the conduct of research. The aim is not merely to redress past under-representation of women as the subjects of research, but also to undertake research that will directly help women. Feminist research methodology does not, however, have a monopoly of concern for the subjects of research, as humanistic approaches to research have similar concerns.

Stanley and Wise (1990) chart the history of feminist research methodology. They describe how originally it had three main strands: first, it was on women, for women, second, it was overtly political, and third, it espoused qualitative methods. From these beginnings methodologies have become more elaborate. To try to encapsulate what seems to be the essence of feminist research methodology/ies, there follows discussion of three distinctive areas, philosophy, ethics and practical advice on methods.

First looking at philosophy, Harding (1987) identified one philosophical strand of feminist approaches to research as feminist empiricism, which she describes as the main feminist response to bias in social sciences concerned with redressing the balance. The second approach is feminist standpoint which is promulgated by committed feminists, and is concerned with women's experiences of oppression (Harding, 1987). Researchers with this viewpoint view emancipation as a goal of research and criterion of validity (Hammersley, 1992). A third approach is feminist postmodern epistemology which has a scepticism about essentialist universalizing claims, and therefore does not accept that all women share experiences (Harding, 1987).

One pair of concepts extensively challenged is the dualism of objectivity and subjectivity. Many feminist writers challenge or reject the concept of objectivity, contending that all knowledge is socially constructed (Eichler, 1988; Stanley and Wise, 1993). Thus 'knowledge' should be treated as situated and competing knowledges (Stanley and Wise, 1993). The rejection of objectivity also stems from postmodernism and deconstructionism, which posit that all knowledge is partial, that one person's objectivity is another's subjectivity, and that all research is affected by the position, outlook, and experience of the researcher. One objection to the concept of objectivity springs from a moral objection to treating people, particularly women, as objects of research (Oakley, 1990; Stanley and Wise, 1993). If objectivity as a concept is rejected then acceptance of the validity of personal experience leads to the inclusion of emotional responses. Fox Keller (1980) contends that subjectivity/objectivity, like masculine/feminine, are patriarchal concepts.

Second, ethical considerations include a rejection of hierarchy in the research relationship. In relation to this, Hammersley (1992) contends that conventional researchers claim the right to define the topic, decide how and what data is collected, conduct an analysis, and write up the results. Hammersley's (1992) statement appears to be a description of the status quo rather than a considered answer to the criticism of power relationships in the research relationship. It is contended that all research is political (Cook and Fonow, 1986), and thus the great majority is framed in the dominant ideology (Eichler, 1988). The perspectives of men and women are seen as differing in general (Eichler, 1988) and in particular (Stanley and Wise, 1993). Writers such as Stanley and Wise (1993) propose that there should be no hierarchy between researcher and researched, and discuss some of the difficulties of implementing this. It is these considerations that lead the feminist researcher to deconstruct previous research proposals and outcomes, and in turn to frame hypotheses of a radically different kind.

Having looked at some of feminist research methodology's distinguishing features, three particular aspects that challenge traditional ways of researching and give practical advice on research methods will be examined.

An important area is non-sexist research methods, which are comprehensively described by Eichler (1988). Non-sexist research methodology is a subset of feminist research methodology, in that it identifies some of the ways in which research may be flawed, and which should be eliminated in the interests of good bias-free research, whether or not the researcher identifies him or herself as a feminist researcher. Eichler (1988) gives a clear account of this. She identifies seven sexist problems: androcentricity, overgeneralization/overspecificity, gender insensitivity, double standards, sex appropriateness, familism, and sexual dichotomism.

Androcentricity is the world seen from a male point of view (Eichler, 1988). Some of the origins for this can be seen in the fact that the academic world is predominantly male, particularly at the higher echelons that control research proposals and funding. The male culture of academic research is described by Morgan (1981: 101) writing about 'academic machismo'; he draws attention to the military metaphors used for academic debate. Overgeneralization/ overspecificity occurs when a study only concerns itself with one sex, but then generalizes the conclusions to both (Eichler, 1988). This can be seen in much current theory on organizational behaviour, which is largely based on generalizations derived from studies of men. Overspecificity, the counterpart to overgeneralization, occurs when it is impossible to tell from a study whether it applies to one or both sexes (Eichler, 1988). Many problems of sexist language are an outcome of overspecificity, such as when managers are referred to as 'he'; it may be unclear whether this is a linguistic convention or a study of male managers only.

Gender insensitivity consists of ignoring sex as a social variable (Eichler, 1988), and again this can be seen in much organizational behaviour theory. Marshall (1984) asserts that women may be motivated by social rather than individual needs, thus challenging the claimed universal validity of Maslow's hierarchy of needs. The next sexist problem identified by Eichler (1988) is double standards, where identical behaviours, traits, situations are evaluated by different standards. A much-quoted phenomenon is when identical behaviour by male and female managers is perceived as assertive or bossy respectively. Sex appropriateness (Eichler, 1988) occurs when human traits and attributes are assigned only to one sex. Thus there is a general assumption that women are caring, and thus more suited to certain types of jobs, leading to extensive job segregation by gender.

Familism happens when the family is treated as the smallest unit of analysis (Eichler, 1988). Familism is likely to be relevant when assumptions are made about the personal relationships and domestic commitments of male and female employees. Sexual dichotomism is an exaggeration of differences at the expense of recognizing similarities between sexes (Eichler, 1988). This can be seen in the debate about the differences between the management style of male and female managers.

Eichler (1988) gives a thorough analysis of the sins of commission within research and a checklist on how to avoid them. Criticism has been made (Stanley and Wise, 1993) that this contribution towards research method is necessary but not sufficient. It aims on removing the negative, systematic error, but does nothing to promote the positive. This would identify Eichler as a feminist empiricist (Harding, 1987).

Another second consideration is the significance of gender (Eichler, 1988; Hammersley, 1992). Warren (1988) points out that male and female are categories that everyone uses to classify others, and states that people, both male and female, respond differently to others of the same or opposite sex. The female researcher may be seen as low status, that is, endowed with a number of stereotypes held by men about women (Warren, 1988; Oakley, 1990). Hammersley and Atkinson (1995: 92) point out that the researcher cannot manufacture or reach a position of 'genderless neutrality'. In summary, the gender of the researcher is significant, because it is a defining and delimiting factor in the eyes of respondents. There are additional issues of power and status such as the immediately visible differences of class, race and ethnicity, which can affect personal attitudes and stereotypical responses, as can initially invisible differences such as professional background and sexuality. All this points to the researcher being situated in time and place.

A further theme in relation to research methodologies is the use of reflexivity within the research process (Cook and Fonow, 1986). This is also used in the humanistic tradition (Reason, 1988), and is also suggested by mainstream researchers such as Schein (1992). Stanley and Wise (1993) suggest that the researcher should reflect on her own position, and include emotion as a source of data. Whilst the rejection of the objective/subjective divide leads to acceptance of subjective experience as data (Stanley and Wise, 1993) it should not be understood as an abandonment, but rather a widening of method. Fox Keller (1980) for instance accepts objectivity within the research process in so far as there is a quintessential goal and search for truth, but she sees this as a process rather than a state or condition at which to arrive.

The implications of feminist research methodology/ies for this volume are that contributors have a wide choice of approaches to use in their gender analysis of mainstream OB topics. Each chapter covers one or more of the principal mainstream OB theories, before critiquing these and suggesting alternative ways of understanding the topic. Authors' preferences range between applying some of Eichler's (1988) strictures, for instance using gender appropriately as a variable, to wider applications of feminist research methodology. Varying epistemological stances are adopted, which in turn leads to different methodologies.

However all contributors to varying extents reject the positivist idea of one reality out there waiting to be discovered, and many adopt instead a social constructionist view of shared meanings. The aim of this volume is to investigate and deconstruct the many commonly used OB topics in order to explore their gendered connotations. Readers will find that a number of chapters touch on the question of power. Although Chapter 10 focuses on this topic solely, the pervasiveness of gendered power relations means investigation is apposite for a number of OB topics.

The contents of the book

In Chapter 2 Iiris Aaltio-Marjosola and Anne Kovalainen take a wide-ranging approach to the examination of personality, noting that gender is always a feature. Whereas a functionalist approach uses personality characteristics to make decisions about employee behaviour, an interpretative understanding of personality is more inclined to contextual and cultural understandings, incorporating gender in critique. Noting that the male personality is seen as norm, with the female as deviant, they challenge the assumed bipolar construct. They also discuss emotion and sexuality in organizations, and the contribution of psychoanalysis towards understanding personality, concluding that we should move towards a more fluid notion of personality.

Albert Mills and I examine perception, attribution and stereotyping in Chapter 3, noting how they work in concert to promote and maintain particular constructions of masculine and feminine. Conventional stereotyping of the roles of men and women outside the workplace, as breadwinner and carer/housewife respectively, influence perceptions within the workplace, affecting both men and women, generally to the detriment of women, and leading to gender segregation both horizontally and vertically. We discuss the pervasiveness of these gendered processes and their asymmetrical effects, postulating that what is detrimental for women must be helpful to (some) men. These phenomena are widely acknowledged in the literature, but as we observe, this appears to have limited effect on their prevalence and persistence.

In Chapter 4 Sue Newell starts by reviewing early models of communication, which she describes as linear and mechanistic compared with later, more fluid metaphors. Noting the extensive writing on communication differences between men and women, she critiques 'two cultures' theories, where women are perceived to communicate differently to men, as reductionist, ignoring power and status differences. She thus criticizes the assertiveness bandwagon as an unreflective outcome of essentialist thinking, based on an attribution error. Rejecting a male/female dichotomy, Newell instead proposes a social constructionist view, where language reflects asymmetrical power, and discursive practices create a subordinate status for women. The key question for research thus becomes how communication processes contribute to systems of domination. Newell notes that communication networks within organizations have differential impact on men and women, because of their different positions within the hierarchy.

Noting that accounts of motivation in textbooks are ostensibly gender neutral, in Chapter 5 Heather Höpfl focuses on organizational commitment, proposing that men's commitment is assumed, and women's regarded as deficient. This is because women do not subordinate their life outside to work. Using a dramaturgical metaphor, she suggests that commitment to an organization requires the 'suspension of disbelief'. Women are much less likely to be seduced by the corporate definition of reality, and therefore represent a threat to men's construction of identity, which is closely tied to work. Höpfl therefore proposes that the regulation of women in the workplace is to enable men to avoid facing their own ambivalence, and thus exposing the illusion on which their identity depends.

Beverly Metcalfe and Yochanan Altman in writing about leadership in Chapter 6 note how highly prized it is in organizations. Although conventionally portrayed as gender neutral, leadership has strong assumptions of masculinity, as can be seen in the gendered nature of trait, behavioural and contingency leadership theories. Sexual role spillover affects the perception of female managers and leaders, and combined with homosexual and homosocial reproduction of male management, leads to a disproportionate number of men in influential organizational positions. Metcalfe and Altman suggest that there are strong links between management, masculinity and militarism, and they question the feminization of management as based on an essentialist fallacy.

In Chapter 7 Elizabeth Sondhaus and Mary Beth Gallagher discuss the implications of the current business trend towards team-based organizations from a feminist perspective. They criticize the flawed implementation of teamwork, citing persistent systems of individual reward, the lone manager model at the top of organizations, ambivalence about empowerment, and antithetical structures and cultures. They argue that team-based organizations have fallen short of their potential for reducing organizational hierarchy and redistributing power, and propose instead a model of non-hierarchical organizations based on collaboration. A feminist implementation of teamwork would, they suggest, see hierarchy change to inclusiveness and connection, a decrease in pay differentials, and a new leadership model. This would demand a collaborative organization, which is relational rather than hierarchical, which values a diverse workforce, explores process not just task, challenges homeostasis, and demonstrates systemic change.

Margaret Dale looks closer at the subject of organizational design in Chapter 8, which includes a historical account of the evolution of the organizational form. She observes that the traditional organizational model, predominantly moulded by men, is linear, compartmentalizing and hierarchical. However its public face of accountability and rationality hides secret machinations that exist in a men-only domain. Alternative organizational forms such as the matrix, despite its apparent flexibility, do not challenge the hegemonic form, and newer manifestations such as flatter organizations and the virtual organization rely on the same paradigm. Even women-led organizations have to compromise for acceptance in a male dominated business world. Nevertheless Dale sees some hope in less formal, more fluid structures based on networking, and the increasing questioning by men of traditional work demands. She ends with a plea for organizations to acknowledge the values of both men and women.

In Chapter 9 on organizational culture I start by outlining the substantive difference between a functionalist and symbolic approach, noting that the latter is more sympathetic to a gender perspective. Some well-known writing on organizational culture is critiqued, and variously found to contain gendered language and limited gender awareness. However, only one major writer reviewed, integrates a gender perspective into his work. Corporate culture, which can be thought of as an extreme manifestation of functionalism, is described as taking a unitarist, management-centred approach, advocating a singleness of purpose and identity that cannot be sustained under a gender analysis. Gendered cultures are perceived as ubiquitous, from societal culture through to departmental and other subcultures. Thus gender is seen as a key organizing principle of organizational culture, integral to understanding.

Lorraine Green, Wendy Parkin, and Jeff Hearn in Chapter 10 note the evidence of men in powerful positions in organizations, and suggest that it is helpful to consider power as a relational phenomenon, only observable when used, rather than as a possession or resource as usually conceptualized in textbooks. The culturally dominant model of masculinity in organizations is hegemonic masculinity, and forms of masculinity that deviate from this are seen as subordinate, as well as femininities. Thus women find themselves in a double bind: those who take up men's jobs as managers or in traditionally male manual work are derided, but if they attempt to behave like men they are also rejected. In addition women are expected to undertake sexual and emotional labour which is unrecognized and unrecompensed. Power in organizations rests on the fact that it is not merely that culturally dominant men use their power, but also that women are dissuaded from resisting.

Judith Foreman in Chapter 11 states that the management of change literature rarely addresses gender, and corporate strategy is portrayed as gender neutral. However gender is central to the reproduction of organizations over time, and it is impossible to treat restructuring, for instance, as conceptually separate from gender. Foreman details the gendered consequences of flexible work, downsizing, new management practices, and private sector provision of publicly funded services. At the same time, equal opportunity departments can fail to understand the gendered outcomes of structural change, and may even disappear as a result of cost cutting. Descriptions of change agents use masculine imagery, and women's roles as change agents may be limited or unacknowledged. Foreman brings together a number of observations that give a new perspective on change.

References

Acker, Joan (1990) 'Hierarchies, jobs, bodies: a theory of gendered organizations', *Gender and* Society, 4 (2): 139-58.

Alvesson, Mats and Due Billing, Yvonne (1992) 'Gender and organization: towards a differentiated understanding', *Organization Studies*, 13 (12): 73-103.

Bartol, Kathryn (1978) 'The sex structuring of organizations: a search for possible causes', *Academy of Management Review*, October: 805-15.

Bartol, Kathryn and Martin, D.C. (1994) *Management.* 2nd Edition. New York, London: McGraw-Hill.

Bem, Sandra (1974) 'The measurement of psychological androgeny', *Journal of Clinical and Consulting Psychology*, 42 (2): 155-62.

Brewis, Joanna, Hampton, Mark P. and Linstead, Stephen (1995) 'Unpacking Priscilla: subjectivity and identity in the organization of gendered appearance', paper given at the Standing Conference on Organizational Symbolism, *Self and Identity in Organizations*, Turku, Finland, 29 June - 1 July.

Buchanan, D. and Huczynski, A. (1997) *Organizational Behaviour: An Introductory Text.* 3rd Edition. London, New York: Prentice Hall.

Burrell, Gibson (1989) 'The sexuality of organization', in Hearn, Jeff, Sheppard, Deborah, Tancred-Sheriff, Peta and Burrell, Gibson (eds) *The Sexuality of Organization.* London, Newbury Park: Sage. pp. 1- 28.

Calas, Marta and Smircich, Linda (1990) 'Re-writing gender into organizational theorizing: directions from feminist perspectives', in Reed, M. and Hughes, M. (eds) *Rethinking Organization: New Directions in Organizational Analysis and Research.* London: Sage. pp. 227-53.

Cockburn, Cynthia (1991) *In the Way of Women: Men's Resistance to Sex Equality in Organizations.* London: Macmillan.

Coleman, Gillian (1989) *Investigating Organisation: A Feminist Approach.* Bristol: School of Advanced Urban Studies, University of Bristol.

Collinson, David and Collinson, Margaret (1989) 'The domination of men's sexuality', in Hearn, Jeff, Sheppard, Deborah, Tancred-Sheriff, Peta and Burrell, Gibson (eds) *The Sexuality of Organization.* London, Newbury Park: Sage. pp. 91-109.

Cook, Judith and Fonow, Mary (1986) 'Knowledge and women's interests: issues of epistemology and methodology in feminist sociological research', *Sociological Inquiry,* 56: 2-29.

Cornwall, Andrea and Lindisfarne, Nancy (1994a) 'Introduction' to *Dislocating Masculinity: Comparative Ethnographies.* London: Routledge. pp. 1-10.

Cornwall, Andrea and Lindisfarne, Nancy (1994b) 'Dislocating masculinity: gender, power and anthropology', in Cornwall, Andrea and Lindisfarne, Nancy (eds) *Dislocating Masculinity: Comparative Ethnographies.* London: Routledge. pp. 11-47.

de Beauvoir, Simone (1949) *The Second Sex.* London: Pan Books.

Easterby-Smith, Mark, Thorpe, Richard, and Holman, David (1996) 'Using repertory grids in management', *Journal of European Industrial Training*, 20 (3): 2-30.

Eichler, Margrit (1988) *Non-Sexist Research Methods: A Practical Guide.* London: Allen and Unwin.

Fox Keller, Evelyn (1980) 'Feminist critique of science: a forward or backward move?', *Fundamenta Scientiae*, 1: 341-49.

Gammack, John G. and Stephens, Robert (1994) 'Repertory grid technique in constructive interation', in Cassell, Catherine and Symons, Gillian (eds) *Qualitative Methods in Organizational Research.* London: Sage. pp.72-90.

Garrett, Stephanie (1987) *Gender.* London: Routledge.

Gherardi, Sylvia (1994) 'The gender we think, the gender we do in our everyday organizational lives', *Human Relations*, 47 (6): 591-609.

Gilligan, Carol (1982) *In a Different Voice: Psychological Theory and Women's Development*. Cambridge, MA: Harvard University Press.

Gray, Chris (1995) 'Gender as a grid of intelligibility', *Gender, Work and* Organization, 2 (1): 46-50.

Hammersley, Martin (1992) 'On feminist methodology', *Sociology*, 26 (2) May: 187-206.

Hammersley, Martin and Atkinson, Paul (1995) *Ethnography: Principles in Practice*. 2nd Edition. London: Routledge.

Harding, Sandra (1987) *Feminism and Methodology*. Milton Keynes: Open University.

Hardy, Virginia (1994) 'An exploration of management development discourses', paper given at the British Academy of Management Conference, Lancaster, 12-14 September.

Harlow, Elizabeth and Hearn, Jeff (1995) 'Cultural constructions: contrasting theories of organizational culture and gender construction', *Gender, Work and Organization*, 2 (4): 180-91.

Hearn, Jeff (1994) 'Changing men and changing managements: social change, social research and social action', in Davidson, Marilyn and Burke, Ronald (eds) *Women Managers: Current Research Issues*. London: Paul Chapman. pp. 192-209.

Hearn, Jeff, Sheppard, Deborah, Tancred-Sheriff, Peta and Burrell, Gibson (1989) 'The sexuality of organization: a postscript', in Hearn, Jeff, Sheppard, Deborah, Tancred-Sheriff, Peta and Burrell, Gibson (eds) *The Sexuality of Organization*. London, Newbury Park: Sage. pp. 178-81.

Hofstede, Geert (1991) *Cultures and Organisations: Software of the Mind*. London: McGraw-Hill.

Jackson, T. (1993) *Organizational Behaviour in International Management*. Oxford: Butterworth Heinemann.

Johnson, Gerry (1996) 'The debate begins', *BAM News, The Newsletter of the British Academy of Management, 6*.

Kelly, George (1955) *The Psychology of Personal Constructs*. New York: Norton.

Kerfoot, Deborah and Knights, David (1993) 'Management, masculinity and manipulation: from paternalism to corporate strategy in financial services in Britain', *Journal of Management Studies*, 30 (4): 659-77.

Lorber, Judith and Farrell, Susan A. (1991) *The Social Construction of Gender*. London: Sage.

Marshall, Judi (1984) *Women Managers: Travellers in a Male World*. Chichester: Wiley.

Marshall, Judi (1995) 'Gender and management: a critical review of research', *British Journal of Management*, 6 (special issue): S53-S62.

Merrick, Neil (1995) 'Survey discloses harassment of men at work', *People Management*, 1 (5-9): 10.

Mills, Albert (1988) 'Organization, Gender and Culture', *Organization Studies*, 9 (3): 351-69.

Mills, Albert J. and Murgatroyd, Stephen J. (1991) *Organizational Rules: A Framework for Understanding Organizational Action*. Milton Keynes: Open University Press.

Mills, Albert J. and Tancred, Peta (1992) 'Introduction', in Mills, Albert J. and Tancred, Peta (eds) *Gendering Organizational Analysis*. London: Sage. pp. 1-8.

Morgan, D. (1981) 'Men, masculinity and the process of sociological enquiry', in Roberts, H. (ed.) *Doing Feminist Research*. London: Routledge. pp. 83-113.

Mullins, Laurie M. (1999) *Management and Organizational Behaviour*. 5th Edition. London, San Francisco: Financial Times Pitman Publishing.

Oakley, Ann (1972) *Sex, Gender and Society*. London: Maurice Temple Smith. cited in Garrett, Stephanie (1987) *Gender*. London: Routledge.

Oakley, Ann (1990) 'Interviewing women: a contradiction in terms', in Roberts, Helen (ed.) *Doing Feminist Research.* London: Routledge. pp. 30-61.

Paalman, Lisbeth (1997) 'A journey through social construction', paper given at the European Institute for Advanced Studies in Management and the Catholic University of Leuven, Belgium Conference on 'Organizing in a Multi-Voiced World: Social Construction, Innovation and Organizational Change', 4–6 June, Leuven.

Reason, Peter (1988) 'Introduction', in Reason, Peter (ed.) *Human Inquiry in Action: Developments in New Paradigm Research.* London: Sage.

Roberts, Helen (1990) 'Ten years on', in Roberts, Helen (ed.) *Doing Feminist Research.* 2nd Edition. London: Routledge. pp. xiii-xxi.

Roper, Michael (1994) *Masculinity and the British Organisation Man since 1945.* Oxford: Oxford University Press.

Rothschild, Joyce and Davies, Celia (1994) 'Organizations through the lens of gender: introduction to the special issue', *Human Relations*, 47 (6): 583-90.

Schein, Edgar (1992) *Organizational Culture and Leadership.* 2nd Edition. San Francisco: Jossey-Bass.

Schein, Edgar H. (1996) 'Culture: the missing concept in organization studies', *Administrative Science Quarterly*, 41: 229-40.

Spender, Dale (1985) *Man Made Language.* 2nd Edition. London, Boston and Henley: Routledge and Kegan Paul.

Spender, Dale (1990) 'The gatekeepers: a critique of academic publishing', in Roberts, Helen (ed.) *Doing Feminist Research.* 2nd Edition. London: Routledge. pp. 186-202.

Stanley, Liz (1990) *Feminist Praxis: Research, Theory and Epistemology in Feminist Sociology.* London: Routledge.

Stanley, Liz and Wise, Sue (1990) 'Method, methodology and epistemology in feminist research process', in Stanley, Liz (ed.) *Feminist Praxis: Research, Theory and Epistemology in Feminist Sociology.* London: Routledge. pp. 20-60.

Stanley, Liz and Wise, Sue (1993) *Breaking Out Again: Feminist Ontology and Epistemology.* 2nd Edition. London: Routledge.

Stewart, Valerie, Stewart, Andrew and Fonda, Nickie (1980) *Business Applications of Repertory Grid.* London: McGraw-Hill.

Tancred-Sheriff, Peta and Campbell, E. Jane (1992) 'Room for women: a case study in the sociology of organizations', in Mills, Albert J. and Tancred, Peta (eds) *Gendering Organizational Analysis.* London: Sage. pp. 31-45.

Warren, Carol (1988) *Gender Issues in Field Research.* London: Sage.

Watson, Sophie (1992) *Is Sir Humphrey Dead? The Changing Culture of the Civil Service.* Bristol: SAUS Publications, School for Advanced Urban Studies.

Wells, Theodora (1973) 'The covert power of gender in organizations', *Journal of Contemporary Business*, Summer: 53-68.

West, Candace and Zimmerman, Don H. (1991) 'Doing gender', in Lorber, Judith and Farrell, Susan A. (eds) *The Social Construction of Gender.* London: Sage. pp. 38-59.

2   Personality

Iiris Aaltio-Marjosola and Anne Kovalainen

Introduction

Personality as a research subject has lately become topical again in contemporary organizational behaviour literature and in management studies. Although personality was a focus of study earlier, the way of approaching the topic has changed. What can be termed contextual and cultural approaches have had an impact on theorizing questions about personality, and as a result the way questions of individual personality are related to organizational analysis has altered.

The earlier approach to gender in organization theories was to a large extent based on the ideas of sex roles and ideas of difference between genders, whereas the contemporary approach in organization theories when personality is discussed broadens the perspective to that of gender.

Literature in the area of organizational behaviour is usually focused towards students of management and organizational issues. In addition, there is literature that identifies itself under the theme of organizational psychology. In many cases both of these areas deal with the same kind of questions, like the relation between individuals, groups and leadership, but there are also differences coming from the differing basic orientations and the roots of research that are applied. There are definitions like:

> ...personality is the characteristic way or ways in which the individual thinks and acts when he or she is adjusting to the environment (Tyson and Jackson, 1992: 10).

> Personality is the combination of stable physical and mental characteristics that make up an individual's identity and give consistency to the person's behaviour (Weiss, 1996: 30).

> An individual's personality is the combination of psychological traits we use to classify that person (Robbins, 1992: 31).

> Personality is manifested in the behaviour, manners and attitudes of individuals. Personality theory is a field of science that has to do with the search for those attributes of people which are relatively enduring and which help define some important aspect of their individual identities (Hosking and Morley, 1991: 7).

The idea that personality characteristics are stable, and the idea of individual identity that they support, seems to offer a common ground for these definitions.

Gender is an integral part of individual identity. It can also be said that gender constitutes identity and embodies it. Bodies always convey a gendered identity, even if sometimes a false one, as is the case for transsexual identities. Gender identities are formed and moulded in public and in private, in society, in culture, in families, at work and in social life. The patterns and processes of socialization are not constant and rigid, but vary over time, culture and other factors.

The reasons why personality has always been popular in the organizational behaviour literature are manifold. One reason might be that managers benefit from personality theories, particularly on those that can be measured, tested and used for feedback to improve, adjust, train and make decisions about employee behaviour. Performance is, after all, based on behaviour. Managers are interested in personal dynamics as they affect behaviour and therefore performance (Weiss, 1996). Personality assessments are most commonly made through self-report questionnaires, projective tests and behavioural measures.

This type of approach can be described as functionalist, when the purpose of understanding personality is in order to find methods of applying knowledge to organizational situations and for managerial purposes. In this chapter the approach is more interpretative. We explore organizational behaviour literature and its theoretical cornerstones critically, using gender as a lens, a category that has been significantly neglected.

We will focus on the concept of gender identity in relation to organizational behaviour questions, using gender as a mirror to supplement and particularize understandings about organizational life. Personality is seen as one of the basic theoretical structures when individuals are described in organizational contexts. Whereas in a functionalist perspective it is argued that personality is something that exists 'as such', in this approach we see it as a concept that is theoretically constructed and dependent on particular ways of defining and measuring it. Issues raised by the cultural approach towards organizations are used as a frame to understand the complex relations that occur between gender and organizational behaviour. The aims of this chapter can therefore be summarized by the following six questions:

1. How does personality evolve in organizational behaviour studies?
2. How does this relate to gender and gendered organizations?
3. What are the nature and substance of gender belief systems in organizations?
4. What are the interconnections between gender and personality in the context of organizations?
5. What is the meaning of organizational language as a carrier of gender images?
6. What are the key elements in the questions of how organizations change in terms of gender related behaviour in organizational cultures?

Gender, personality and organizational behaviour: theoretical background

This section will present some theoretical cornerstones for understanding the relationship between gender and personality in the organizational context. We will take up some historical developments of how and why this understanding has evolved. To understand individuals in their work and activities in organizations, we need to know why some things are manifested the way they are in behaviour, and what components are usually categorized as gender components.

The concepts under discussion

What lies at the core of the gender personality? Can we think of a personality without gender? Would that mean a personality without a body? What about when the body is included? Would there be female and male persons, unchanged and derived from biology? Are the categories of female and male unchanging and stable, or are they culturally and socially constructed, and thus problematizing the actual contents of the gendered personality? If the latter is true, it might perhaps be more correct to speak about multiple gendered personalities and identities. People can be classified, at least most often by simple appearance, into females and males. Does that division by appearance tell us everything about the gender as a conceptual frame of reference and gendered identities, or does it tell us merely about the biological differences between sexes?

The differences between women and men seem to be self-evident and thus it may be difficult to see how the concept of gender can be constructed as a social institution or social category as such. 'Talking about gender for most people is the equivalent of fish talking about water' (Lorber, 1994: 13). As discussed in Wilson (in this volume) the concept of gender is usually assumed to be dichotomous and equivalent to our biological sex and genes. That is the major reason why some people may find it difficult to accept that gender is socially constructed, and constantly created and recreated out of human interactions in organizations and cultural and societal structures.

How could we define gender as a concept without the usual notions of a bipolar approach and stereotypical attitudes? One way of defining gender is to look at it with the help of examples that enable us to see the layered and changing nature of the concept. Thus gender is not a constant, unchanging, 'natural' category with two opposite poles. Gender is first and foremost a socially constructed, relational concept. Becoming a girl or a boy, a woman or a man, a boss or a secretary, is a result of a long process within various cultural and societal structures which shape the formation of individuality, personality and the gender identity. We are all familiar with the situation where we cannot be certain of a baby's biological sex. Judith Lorber (1994) gives a lively account of a small baby she saw being pushed in a stroller by her father. The baby was wearing a dark blue T-shirt and dark blue pants plus a Yankee baseball cap. Ah, a boy, she thinks, for a while, but then she notices the gleam of tiny earrings and lace-trimmed socks and little flowered sneakers. Not a boy after all? Gender done, she concludes (Lorber, 1994). Gender is thus not merely a biological category, but it is also actively 'done' by us in everyday life situations such as the one described here.

Just as the assumptions of the little baby's biological sex are knitted closely to the clothing and colours worn by her/him, the assumptions about the personality and gender are usually tightly linked with each other. The development of personality during the socialization process is related to the normative ideals of gendered personalities, how girls and boys, women and men are supposed to be. In this chapter we are focusing particularly upon questions of gender and personality in organizational settings. Many features in organizational behaviour are related to personality and identity, as well as the assumed differences between genders that are often taken for granted. Dichotomies of sex, sexuality and gender are built deeply into organizations, as in all social institutions, as well as into everyday life practices and processes. They partly reflect those historically abstracted dualisms in Western society, such as family/economy, male/female, public/private. However, these rigid divisions have been strongly criticized by feminist theorists, since to a large extent they are based on classical theories that have not taken gender into account.

Even if the content of gender is 'infinitely variable and continually in flux, the salience of gender is persistent' (Marshall, 1994: 171). To be able to distinguish personality and gender analytically from each other is impossible: even if gender does not have to be dominating, or not necessarily even the most prominent factor in the personality, it is always present. Any analysis from the gender perspective means that we not only take into account the socially constructed categories of feminine and masculine, but also that we constantly create the definitions and contents of these categories through various activities.

Gender in organizational studies

After the 1980s a growing number of studies were published where gender is taken into account, embodied in the frames and findings of organizational studies (for an overview, see Calas and Smircich, 1996; Knights, 1997). The perspective of gender has widened from an initial focus on women, into relations between genders, and then to men, who generally have been quite invisible in the social sciences, although for a different reason than women (Hearn, 1993). In a broader context, this debate is surrounded by the ideas and discourses that stem from the cultural approach to organizations, as well as from the postmodernist approach.

The rejection of universalistic ideas in management studies and the adoption of diversity in the analysis of management studies were not only restricted to postmodern approaches in social sciences and humanities. The meaning and importance of language and constructions that we create in cultural and social settings, and the interpretations we offer for these constructions, became important in many ways. Even though postmodernism was developed under the influence of literary theory and philosophy, its influence has been strong in many social sciences' ways of understanding and analysing their objects and the world in general. The gender perspective in organization theory and management has much in common with postmodern ideas of rejecting grand narratives and emphasizing fragmentation as an important part of the interpretations offered.

Female and male have for long been seen only as rigid dichotomies, categorizing all organizational behaviour into sex-role related stereotypes. This leads to simplistic attitudes in questions related to gender. It also leaves unnoticed the reality that the idea of gender-related stereotypes are often rigid and stem from the male norm, that is, regarding man as norm and woman as a deviation from the norm. This as such does not help in trying to analyse the complex reality of organizational life, and leads to a rejection of the idea that gender can be considered as a relation between sexes, not merely a concept with bipolar opposites. Even when many questions relate to gender, for instance similarities and differences between genders have been taken up as an issue, this still remains primarily a preoccupation of feminist organizational analysis, not one of mainstream organizational analysis to any great extent.

There are different ways of analysing gender in organizations ranging from gender differences (Chodorow, 1978; Gilligan, 1982) to gendering processes (Connell, 1987). Recent research has acknowledged the importance of gender, for instance in the communication and network relationships between managers and subordinates. Gender identity is an important, and inseparable, part of individual identity. We need to feel at home with our gender in the workplace and we need to be able to work in various networks with members consisting of men and women. As organizational members we use images of gender that are also rooted in the organizational culture. At the same time we are actively doing gender at the workplace; we are gendering work and organizations. From these standpoints we will explore the issues discussed below in this chapter.

Mainstream theories on personality in organizational behaviour literature

What about gender and personality within mainstream theories of organizational behaviour? The questions of gender and personality defined above have not so far been adopted in mainstream theorizing. Even the question of personality was neglected in organizational analysis for some decades. After a period of theoretical silence, personality issues in organizations and management have been brought into the research focus again. If organizational behaviour (OB) is defined as the systematic study of the actions and attitudes that people exhibit within organizations, personality issues are evidently at the core of this discussion. Personality theories are usually defined as concerned with the search for those attributes of people that are relatively enduring, and that help to define some important aspect of their individual identities. They also search for personality variables that apply to a large number of people and that are relatively stable over time.

The classical approaches on personality

The 'trait' approach was seen as the most influential one up to the late 1940s in the organizational behaviour literature, and is still used in managerial and leadership studies and literature.   Indeed, as Bryman (1994) argues, trait research enjoyed a renaissance in the late 1980s.   Over the years it has had enormous impact on our way of imagining managers and leaders as persons. There is further discussion of trait theory in Metcalfe and Altman (this volume).

  Nowadays there is a growing consensus amongst trait theorists that there are five fundamental dimensions of personality, the so-called Big Five (Digman, 1990).   There is more agreement on the number of traits than what the traits actually are, but probably the following are quite widely accepted (Arnold et al., 1995: 25-26):

1. Extroversion (sociability, assertiveness)
2. Emotionality (anxiety, insecurity)
3. Agreeableness (conforming, helpful to others)
4. Conscientiousness (persistent, organized)
5. Intellect (curiosity, openness to experience)

Additional classical trait approaches are for example Eysenck's Personality Questionnaire with three measured personality characteristics: extroversion, neuroticism (or emotional stability) and psychotism; Cattell's Sixteen PF with 16 personality factors and the Occupational Personality Questionnaire with 30 personality dimensions (Arnold et al., 1995).   The personality traits are measured by personality questionnaires.   Personality tests, as with other kinds of psychological measures, need to satisfy various well-established psychometric criteria before they can be considered to be acceptable measuring instruments.   They have to meet the criteria of validity (the test measures what it is intended to measure) and reliability (the consistency of measurement that the test achieves).   They are supposed to be objective and neutral in terms of gender, race, and social status, and other differences.

  In situations where social rules are strict and widely understood, personality will influence behaviour less than in unstructured situations, which lack clearly defined 'do's and don'ts'.   The attraction of the trait approach for managers is that it brings an aura of stability and predictability to employees' behaviour that all too often seems changeable and confusing.

  Although it is used quite frequently in personnel selection, in career planning procedures, and in other areas of current human resource management, the trait approach is also widely criticized.   To make a brief summary, linking personality dimensions to organizational behaviour issues is a complex matter, and making generalizations about the fit between organization and personality traits should be done cautiously.   The unreliable nature of personality testing in managerial selection is largely recognized, as the ability to predict future performance from the results of personality tests is demonstrably marginal (Dakin et al., 1994).   The extent of the benefits of trait theory appear to be to use it as a preliminary diagnostic tool for evaluating individual differences in work settings (Weiss, 1996).

After the trait approach failed to list consistent and coherent traits that would be universal and applicable to everybody, the focus was redirected to the style of individual behaviour, instead of personality. The style approach in organizational behaviour theories was prevalent up until the 1970s (see Metcalfe and Altman, in this volume). With the notion of personality as being culturally and socially defined, the style approach gave way to the more contextually oriented approaches.

The contingency approach redirected interest from the personality and its construction and focused on the situational interplay between individual and organization. Kurt Lewin (1951) asserted that behaviour is a function of the person and environment. Since then, interactional psychologists have extended Lewin's ideas by stating that human behaviour can best be understood by explaining the person, the situation and how the two interact.

A further research area that arose in organizational behaviour research during the 1990s is the meaning and existence of emotions in organizations. The irrational side of organizational life, as the emotional aspects of life are sometimes called, is closely related to the questions of personality within organizations, human factors and their dark side. There are many approaches that can be classified under the label of this theme, however the most intensive efforts can be found in the field of clinical approaches to organization, or in studies of dysfunctionalism of organizational life.

These approaches have some common ground with trait approaches, but there are also distinct differences. Whilst earlier there were attempts to find the ideal features of leaders, more recently the focus has been more on the dysfunctional impact that managerial personalities have on the shared fantasies and patterns of action in the organization (as one of the first, see Kets de Vries and Miller, 1984). Clinical approaches towards management continue the long-range research tradition of combining the ideas of psychoanalysis with questions about organizations (Bion, 1959). Broadly, these approaches relate to a psychodynamic theory of organizational behaviour. This school of thought accounts for individual differences by arguing that people deal with their unconscious, fundamental drives differently. Personality and how it changes is a core question in the theory of psychoanalysis. Gender has played a major role in critiquing psychoanalysis.

Applying psychoanalytic understanding to questions of OB, both the childhood experiences and past experiences of managers are reflected in the daily life of organizations and managerial work. One of the basic psychoanalytic concepts used is the transference mechanism, which means that past emotions tend to be evoked, and transferred to present, real-time situations. Thus managers' individual fantasies, based on past experiences, may transfer into shared organizational fantasies, and impact on the culture and behavioural patterns of the organization and on its strategies. This may be an advantage or disadvantage to the organization. For instance narcissistic behaviour displayed by managers and entrepreneurs is seen to produce many disadvantages in the organization (Kets de Vries and Miller, 1984). The absence of gender is a major problem in these approaches as well.

Recent developments

Organizational culture is a concept that helps us to understand the dynamic interplay between organizations and organizational behaviour, as well as the impact of organizational practices over individuals and personalities. Organizational culture does not merely concern the dress code in the company, but deeper levels of behavioural models, organizational practices and norms for behaviour. Handy (1993) among others has presented a typology for organizational cultures, which all call for special personality characteristics in members of organizations. Handy's typology is further critiqued in Wilson (Chapter 9 in this volume).

To build a bridge between the cultural approach and classical theories on personality, situational theories appear to offer a good fit with the basic ideas of a cultural approach. The unique culture of the organization can be seen to form a special, individual context, the 'situation' for experiences of organizational members, which are dependent on the values and basic assumptions of the organization that they inhabit. The organizational context therefore gives emphasis to certain features of personality; entrepreneurial cultures call for entrepreneurial types of personalities, bureaucratic cultures specialists, and so on. Not only do organizational cultures select suitable individual personalities, also personalities search for organizations where they will fit well. This explains the power of organizational practices in relation to individuals.

To sum up the developments of personality issues in organizational behaviour literature, it seems as if understanding of the individual and personality has shifted from the rigid essentialist notion of personality traits and categories, into a more flexible and fluid definition of the contents of personality, with its meanings in organizational dynamics and structure. The place of the gendered personality in these theories is the question we turn to in the next section.

Critique of the mainstream theories from a gender perspective

Differences between various approaches can include, among other things, the definition and importance they give to the concepts and categories of gender, individual and society, and particularly the meaning of personality in this context. As a general criticism of mainstream theories, it can be unequivocally stated that the experience of women has not been crucial or important. This is especially clear in research on organizational behaviour, where the subject in question has often been male, representing the mainstream. Thus this means that theories about and of organizations and organizational behaviour are inevitably gender biased. Even though there is now a substantial literature on gender and organizations (e.g. Calas and Smircich, 1992; 1996), there are still many signals to females that they are not regarded as full organizational members. The separation of the 'female-question' from the mainstream organizational text can be found even in the newest textbooks, where the feminist critique of the mainstream theorizing has been put into one chapter, and the rest of the book can thus forget the question of gender (e.g. Clegg et al., 1996).

Organization as a special context for behaviour

It is surprising how often in OB textbooks women-at-work issues come together under the general label 'minority groups at work', although it is recognized in this literature that women in society are more and more likely to work full-time and pursue careers in the same manner as men. In a cultural sense however, women's points of views are still seen as tangential to the mainstream body of organizational knowledge. Labelling women-at-work issues as those of minority groups tends to continue the tradition of cultural subordination in questions of management and organization.

It is a well-known fact that the vast majority of managers of today's organizations are still men. The work force is highly segregated according to gender both horizontally and vertically (Acker and van Houten, 1992; Reskin and Padavic, 1994). This means that in management positions there are more men than women, especially in higher management. The difficulty women experience entering top management positions and board memberships is a global phenomenon.

There have been studies of how the male emphasis is present in some of the basic studies of OB literature (Mills, 1988). For instance, in the research design of the Hawthorne Studies a group of males and females were separated, but the findings were presented as an explanation of the behaviour of employees per se. Very often, men's statements of dissatisfaction are recorded as valid expressions of alienation from their working conditions. Women's discontent on the other hand has been explained by reference to their 'weaker physical stamina' and 'family commitments'. That is, men's attitudes were interpreted as primarily job related, and women's as being primarily related to their gender (Feldberg and Glenn, 1979). It is also notable that researchers in classical studies of OB were mostly men, and that women entered the field later.

There is a wealth of empirical evidence that to think managers is to think male. This is a global phenomenon, as found in the study of Schein et al. (1994), who compared stereotypes about managers in Japan, China, USA, Great Britain and Germany. The normative ideals of the relevant and suitable personality are strongly related to the normative ideals of each culture: in addition to women, ethnic and sexual minorities do not tend to correspond to ideas of 'the best characteristics' of any manager.

The idea of heroism is not gender-neutral either (Aaltio-Marjosola, 1994; Kovalainen, 1995). To be a hero as a woman is a paradox itself, since heroes are, by definition, men. Heroism and charisma have always been a part of leadership and organizational behaviour studies. In organizational life this kind of polarization between female and male roles is also apt to occur. Being female is most often seen to mean being gentle, moral, pure, family-oriented, emotional, weak and delicate, while being male means, of course, being worldly, success-oriented, aggressive, pragmatic, rational, tough and strong (Gerzon, 1992). Different qualities develop which identify 'manhood' and 'womanhood'. Male gender has always been seen more in the context of individualism, compared to female gender that is seen in the context of relatedness.

Organizations and especially business enterprises are communities where success to a large extent determines the values and norms adopted by the culture. Ideals about how to act, about how to do successful business, and how to be successful in one's career are important in this process of creating cultural values. Heroism, and the individualism on which heroism is based, are important in attempting to understand how ideals are born in the organizational culture. Success stories that remain in the organizational memory and that circulate round the company often contain elements of heroism. In this way heroism may become an inherited part of organizational culture and its values. Heroism and charisma have many close resemblances to the masculine stereotypes in the organizational settings (Steyrer, 1998).

Organizations may create understanding about 'core' personality, that is, which kind of personality attributes are relevant and primary, versus which kind of traits are in the background and not as important. Achievements and success are a big part of this process of creation. If women are not involved in the success stories of the organization, if they stay at the margins, their voices become silent, and the personality traits that are usually related to women's ways of behaving become secondary in the culture. In many companies such women's subcultures exist. Sub-cultures are women's way of coping within a complex, male type of organizational culture, and a way of giving and receiving social support from other members of the sub-group. At the same time the organizational culture may become dichotomized between stereotyped male and female subgroups. This is the starkest example of work segregation between men and women (Aaltio-Marjosola, 1994).

In personality research connections were sought between psychological traits and motivational factors, to try and establish the combination of traits and motivations associated with certain kinds of success or certain positions. The models were almost without exception based on white, middle-class, male samples but presented as universal results. The omnipotence of psychological traits and factors was recognized for a long time, but gender was not acknowledged by including women in empirical research settings. The diversity and inconsistency of personality traits led to research into managerial styles, again without considering women or gender (Kovalainen, 1995).

The cultural categories often presented about organizations, such as the classical division by Handy (1993) may themselves be gendered by nature. What Handy did not take into account was that men are by and large in power positions and also select others to power positions among themselves. As well as power culture, other cultural models in organizations appear male by definition: task culture is often based on competition and male bonding, and role culture itself has often been characterized in male terms only (Itzin and Newman, 1995).

In clinical studies of management, often based on psychoanalytic theory, gender has not been raised as an issue (for the relationship between feminism and psychoanalysis in general, see Mitchell, 1974 and Chodorow, 1978). For instance, narcissism and other dysfunctional personality features could be studied in relation to gender, not as general managerial attributes as they usually are studied. Some research indicates that successful female leaders have good relationships with their fathers (Henning and Jardim, 1976). This relationship may increase the daughter's possibilities for identification and pave the way to an independent choice of profession and career (Jörstad, 1996). It is also stated that women in their careers often feel to be pushed to tone down their femininity during the career and play by male rules. At the same time the whole issue about career is questioned by the feminist critique. Women often tend to see their work and their career as happening accidentally (Marshall, 1989), not as the result of a conscious effort with climbing up the ladder.

In psychoanalytical literature the impact of fathers has been recognized as having impact on entrepreneurial careers (Kets de Vries, 1995). The childhood of many male entrepreneurs is portrayed as a very disturbing experience. Their fathers are often accused of having deserted, manipulated or neglected the family, whereas the mother usually comes across as a strong, decisive and controlling woman. This pattern seems to belong to entrepreneurial mythology. However, the question is not asked in reverse: the parenthood of male managers with regard to their own children has been largely neglected. Mythology about fatherhood, masculinity and leadership may have a similar kind of background (Aaltio-Marjosola and Lehtinen, 1998). Psychoanalysis as an analytical tool has been criticized broadly in this sense. It seems to work as an analytical tool to make mothers feel guilty and does not question societal practices that make private life the appropriate domain for women. It does not generally accept the idea of women in work-life or women as managers, or in general, challenge current societal practices.

We may end by briefly commenting on recent developments that have taken place in gender studies which focus on the maleness of management (Hearn, 1993). Some of them challenge the whole idea of personality as a unique concept in terms of masculinity. Sometimes these approaches seem to form alternative approaches, rejecting feminist critique and writing about the 'real nature' of men that is oppressed in society with many female norms, perpetrated in schools where there are more female than male teachers. The remainder of the approaches start from the same standpoints as female studies, with critics of the power relationships in society that are more favourable to men (or certain qualities/types of men) than to women.

Summary

To sum up the critique of OB studies from the standpoint of gender, the mainstream paradigms of OB literature have left gender out of the analyses to a very large extent. Gender appears only as a variable, as men and women. However, using our frame of reference, gender is seen as a critical concept in organizational analysis that can break the boundaries of generalizability, and reveal that generalizability and mainstream theorizing may support gender bias. Even when differences have been explored, much of the research has focused either on similarities or differences between these two groups and consequently created ideas of generalized 'women' and generalized 'men'. At the same time gender is seen in these theories as something that enters the organization without there being a responsibility to consider the practices, values and norms that may support gender biased structures. The question of organizations as producing gender is seldom addressed.

The original idea about categories of personality traits were to do with functionality. Because of its relative stability it is no wonder that management hopes to gain benefits out of its use in personnel selection and other human resource management practices. Stability and predictability go hand in hand. It is safe to have pilots who are able to work in crisis situations, and so on. The gender approach challenges the generalizability of the concept of personality. There are other perspectives like race, societal status and age that can do the same. To be able to move beyond dichotomous thinking, be it situational and context related, or generalized knowledge about men and women, it is necessary to focus on gender as a theoretical concept which has a larger focus than the biological bodily appearance admits. In the following we are looking for alternative approaches that give more space to various interpretations and uses of the concept of gender.

Alternative theories

The earlier period could be defined as characterized by studies of sex differences and sex roles, given and fixed contents of femaleness and maleness, and femininity and masculinity. However it can be argued, as Lorber (1994) does, that there is no essential femaleness or maleness, femininity or masculinity, womanhood or manhood, however, once a gender is ascribed, the social order constructs and holds individuals to strongly gendered norms and expectations. This process has been called socialization into a gender and existing gender roles. Organizations are one context for socialization processes in terms of gender. This viewpoint in the definition of gender has been widely adopted during the recent period in women's studies and feminist research, and as such, reflects a development in the understanding of the concepts of sex, gender and identity.

Challenging organizational analysis

Organizations do play a fundamental role in establishing and maintaining gendered hierarchies that favour men over women (e.g. Reskin and Padavic, 1994; Wilson, 1996). The hierarchies are invisible, yet measurable in the percentages of women and men at rungs of the organizational ladder, however they are not easily 'revealed' or changed since they are not the only institutions that are gendered. Society and its organizations produce, reproduce and maintain gender differences through various kinds of social processes.

Women's studies and feminist research has impacted on many of the basic conceptual categories used in organizational studies, to such an extent that changes in the theoretical constructs are not only allowing gender into the original theoretical premises, but gender as a theoretical construction is itself actively processed and embedded into the theoretical starting points. This comes out clearly in relation to the basic assumptions held earlier on first the concept of personality as a stable rigid constellation; and second managerial styles, where heroic behaviour was clearly masculine, and a highly valued behavioural model. The feminist critique of personality, in stating that gender is an analytical concept and can be seen as social construct, has eroded the basis of essentialist thinking, and thus changed the basic assumptions made about stable, and also male and female, personalities.

Since leadership may be regarded as 'a management of meaning', we can also see how meanings are created, privileged or marginalized, often by managerial efforts, and how they come to define organizational reality. In this organizational reality, men may be considered more 'real' than females, who may become a marginalized, silent and invisible part of the culture. Organizational talk, the special language evolved in an organization's culture, is a way of carrying, producing, and reproducing sex segregation in the organization (Garsombke, 1988; Wilson, 1992). This segregation is seen in the divisions between men and women within organizational structures: horizontal divisions mean that men and women work in different occupational groups and economic sectors, and vertical divisions mean that men work in higher managerial positions. The glass ceiling phenomenon describes the fact that even if in many cases women work in management positions, it can be shown globally that they are missing from higher managerial positions, still generally held back by their male counterparts.

Organizational language is related to the power structure of the organization in many ways. Power is identified as a pervasive characteristic of organizational life, and discourse is conceived as a medium through which power relations are maintained and reproduced. Discourse in organizations may systematically privilege or marginalize different organizational experiences in the eyes of the dominant culture. Women's voices may be systematically left out of the dominant discourse or women may become linguistic 'outsiders' in an organization. Language and communication are discussed further in Newall (in this volume).

The shape of the organization's culture comes from the organizational past, where the shared understanding about the ways to act and think in the company were created. How this happens, and the social and psychological factors behind the process, are illustrated in the work of Schein (1985). The ideal personality characteristics favoured in the organization are shaped in this kind of process. Awareness of these mechanisms as well as of their relationship with gender issues offers a way of avoiding gender bias in interpretations about organizational cultures.

Sexuality in organizations

Even if it is not possible to distinguish personality and gender from each other, it is possible to distinguish the cultural and societal outcomes of gender. These are more often unfavourably related to women than to men in social settings. One of these 'outcomes' is sexuality in organizations.

Sexuality in organizations can be related to power dimensions, which are associated with problems such as sexual harassment, unwanted or repeated verbal or physical sexual advances; or remarks or behaviour that are offensive to the recipient and cause discomfort or interfere with job performance (Reskin and Padavic, 1994). In general, people usually see sex as an extremely individual and private matter. The closer we come to the body, sexuality, feelings related to the body, motherhood and pregnancy, the more unimportant it is in terms of the 'formal' organizational system. It seems that only extreme incidents such as sexual harassment within organizations will break the perceived neutrality of the body (Korvajärvi, 1998). A clinical approach to organizational behaviour issues may be fruitful in trying to understand incidents such as sexual harassment in an organizational context. Moreover, dysfunctionalism of organizational life, discussed earlier in this chapter, acts at the background and the need to connect gender issues into its theorizing shows up here clearly.

In addition, erotics and sexuality between men and women are part of work-life and workplace relationships in general and they may lead up to marriages and establishing families. Discourse on sexuality in organizations easily faces moral issues, even if it is difficult to put definite standards by which to judge what is right or wrong and to use the same ethical measure from one case to another. Organizational cultures frame the experiences of people in relation to sexuality in the workplace and create behavioural patterns that people obey. Some organizational cultures tend to encourage inequality, like sexual harassment or the habit to present sexist jokes that undervalue women, while others are more favourable to professional kind of behavioural patterns in work and support equality between men and women.

Sexuality can also be evident in organizational settings where no power dimension is included. This aspect of sexuality is sometimes voluntarily displayed, ranging from flirting and courtship to consensual seduction. Sexuality in organizational behaviour can even take on some features from domestic life, such as calling a secretary an 'office wife' (Pringle, 1989: 158-77). Sexuality as linguistic and social practices as well as in relation to political discourse has nowadays been the focus of a variety of studies (see McFadden and Sneddon, 1998: 82-95 for an overview). This requires us to move beyond its biological, 'natural' and destiny-like nature towards seeing it as a contextualized, socially determined affair.

Female sexuality in organizations is sometimes denied, seen in dress-codes that avoid any seductiveness as well as in other areas of behaviour. Gherardi (1995: 65) emphasizes the need to see women as subjects in organizations instead of objectifying them, and states that the discourse on sexuality which constructs women as victims forces them to desexualize themselves in order to enter organizations. Women then continue to be constructed as objects, and there is a silencing of female sexuality and women's capacity to be the subject of pleasure.

Sexuality has to do with bodies and their physical appearance and visibility. We suggest that as well as standards for core personality being created in the organization, as was discussed earlier, core body becomes a part of its understanding as well. Organizational culture implies a set of standards that every community expects their members to obey, and they include things related to the body. Managers in organizations often face quite strict dress codes and as male managers can even create these codes intentionally, alternative feminine managerial dress codes are needed. This is an example of the symbolic nature of management in organizations in general and of the way it is presented and encouraged for instance in the media.

Summary

With the increasing criticism of sex-role research, which assumed certain abstract and constant roles existing across situations, cultural variations and life cycles (Hess and Ferree, 1987), research turned to more complex questions: for instance, whether biological and social sex relate to each other, and whether socialized sex exists outside of biological bodies, in cultural and societal settings. The concept of gender was soon seen as a principle that organizes social contracts, societal structures, individual behaviour, and existence. The gender order can be defined as a mode of interpretation through which individuals construct their subjective identity and their social identity. It is through this interpretation of gender and gender order that the subjective attains importance in the analysis of organizational behaviour. However, within organizations we can sketch out different gender belief systems, which refer to a set of beliefs and opinions about males and females and about the qualities and contents of masculinity and femininity. Gender order is not a natural order, and thus it is constantly under renegotiation and reconstruction, and subject to tensions in the change process (Kovalainen, 1999).

However, organizational theorizing has so far avoided, to any large extent, practising self-reflection in relation to these questions. Gender and sex have been used more as variables in its analysis, not as something that are products of organizations as well. 'Doing gender' in organizations (as discussed in Wilson, Chapter 1 in this volume) is a perspective that implies challenging, comprehending, and being able as well as willing to change some of the essentialist understanding in organizational practices. We may also finish by saying that, as we see it, what is definitely not needed is a substitution of OB theories that are meant either for men or women in the place of theories that aim to suit both. Instead of alternative theories, what is needed is a constantly critical attitude towards organization theorizing from a gender perspective.

A case study: personality and cultural ideals

As described earlier, organizational theory develops in close connection with organizational and management research. Instead of trying to be an alternative, new organizational theory, a gender perspective can present a more critical approach inside organization theory, challenging its main tenets. The case presented here describes a research project that demonstrates how descriptions of core cultures, core competencies or core values easily leave gender out of the analysis, and thus support gender biased explanations.

The research project collected longitudinal, ethnographic data from an enterprise, focusing on its organizational and cultural change. In order to study change, it is necessary to find out some pertinent dimensions by which to demonstrate that the change has occurred over the time described. The categories used in this particular study were risk-taking, innovativeness, sense of togetherness, and entrepreneurship.

When looking at the organization more closely a high level of work segregation, both hierarchical and vertical, was found between men and women. The company was a high-tech company, with male engineers working in the field. Women worked there mostly as secretaries, in cleaning, and in the restaurant serving lunches for the rest of the employees, as well as in the packing department.

When stories and anecdotes were gathered by ethnographic means for cultural analysis, it was found that women had their own 'sub' stories, often with no connection to the 'core' stories that talked about success, failures and funny occurrences that happened during research projects in the organization. The stories were, in a way, segregated into men's and women's stories. Men (in men's stories) were figures that made the firm succeed, by risk-taking, spontaneous behaviour, and sometimes by doing funny, unexpected things. Personalities that fitted these values of the core culture were similar to commonly described stereotypes of men: being expressive, heroic and success-oriented. Women in these stories occurred as passive side-figures in the successful research and marketing projects. Their role was to help men, without a very strong professional identity of their own. 'Those women, they surely don't want anything to change at all', said one of the supervisors.

Maija, a salesperson in the company, tried to get promotion to sales manager in her department. She had extra good results in her work, she did well with the customers and her sales records were high. However, she did not get the job, and it was given to a man from another department. Maija was told she was difficult, which was odd because she had no problems with the customers, and she seemed to have very good relationships with the female secretaries in the department. It seemed to be difficult for her to get into the core networks of the company, inhabited by her male counterparts.

This can be understood by suggesting that men in the company fitted well with the core ideal values of experimentalism, risk-taking and innovativeness. These values were needed for success in the projects. Being separate from the male networks, Maija did not have a chance to get involved in them and to show her competence as a manager. She was in a way stuck within the sub-culture of women who criticized, without making a lot of noise, the male emphasis of the core values and the accompanying ignorance of the female secretaries' professional abilities.

Success stories stored in organizational memory describe success in simple ways. A heroic story recounts visible, dramatic and successful organizational actions. As we have seen, they tend to reinforce cultural simplicity as regards to gender. When men and women work separately on different levels in the organizational hierarchy as well as in different positions, values relating to that reality easily become rigidified. This works as a kind of cumulative process in the production of gender values and stereotypes: if women work in positions where there is not a lot of power to change things, they easily become 'women, who of course do not want any changes' in the organizational understanding. Also men in these stories may become tied up to one-sided, stereotyped masculine features, losing the nuances that come from their individuality. Newcomers to the organization face expectations about their behaviour and about their personality characteristics as well, according to their sex.

Gender, if not raised as a question as such, easily remains invisible in research settings, and because of that in their findings. Researchers may end up describing cultural core values as they are, without seeing their relationship to the vertical and horizontal issues of work segregation between men and women, and in that sense our knowledge easily becomes gender biased. Organizational language, organizational memory and, in general, collective ways of creating organizational understanding, are crucial in the production and maintenance of gender stereotypes in the organization, as well as in any attempt to change them.

Conclusions and discussion

The way questions of personality are dealt with in organization behaviour literature has developed towards the position where contextualism has assumed more importance. As stated earlier in this chapter, gender can be defined as a social relationship with a large variety of dimensions, a social construct without essential contents that can nevertheless dictate behaviour in a causal way, even if the biology is embedded in gender. Assumptions about gender and the meanings given to gender all change over time and over culture, and they inevitably influence the way we talk about and discuss gender. These factors also constrain the way we continuously reproduce, maintain and change ideas of gender through our behaviour and talk. We are continuously reproducing our ideas of gender, but also actively changing them. We hope that after reading this chapter that our readers too will look beyond the dichotomous male-female divisions and notice the deep cultural embeddedness of gender in society and in organizational lives.

We have argued in this chapter that it is still usual in mainstream OB theory to see the concept of gender as an issue without either practical consequences in organizational life, nor any theoretical importance either. These assumptions are, however, increasingly criticized, and thus although these ideas are still common, they do not maintain the same unassailable status. Organization behaviour theories receive impulses and influences from other social sciences, where the conceptual discussion on gender has already been adopted to a larger extent than in organizational and managerial theories (see e.g. Giddens, 1992).

Strict and rigid gender stereotypes may mask various capabilities of men and women. Internationalization of enterprises makes gender management even more complicated, because the images of men and women differ from each other cross-culturally as well as across generations. Within organizations we should ask what kind of changes are needed in order to facilitate a variety of gendered personalities who can exist and work within the workplace. There is a tendency in today's management to favour notions that equality between the two sexes is important, and many enterprises even compete with each other in order to show how modern their personnel policy is in this respect. Statistics are produced that compare enterprises in terms of female managers at the top, and firms do not want to be shown up as having none at all. As the proportion of women in lower management positions and in the workforce in general is growing, the number of capable women applicants with the potential for management positions in organizations is steadily growing.

Organizational management practices nurture the future images of gender within working life. During the 1990s growing critique has lead to discussion of the assumptions of individuality and personality in organizational settings. One crucial point has redirected organizational theoretical discussion, and that has been the move away from the idea of the essential individual that is normatively male. This approach has been influenced by feminist research, where the socio-biological theories have been strongly and solidly criticized. Thus we see that reinterpretations of the individual and individuality are apparent in organizational theory literature, and lead to considerations of social and relational contextuality. This does not mean, however, that individual or gender may lose their meaning in the organizational context. Instead they should be moving towards a more fluid notion of the gendered personality in the organizational behavioural context.

References

Aaltio-Marjosola, I. (1994) 'Gender stereotypes as cultural products of the organization', *Scandinavian Journal of Management Studies*, 10 (2): 147-62.

Aaltio-Marjosola, I. and Lehtinen, J. (1998) 'Male managers as fathers? Contrasting management, fatherhood, and masculinity', *Human Relations*, 51 (2): 121-36.

Acker, J. and van Houten, R. (1992) 'Different recruitment and control: the sex-structuring of organizations', in Mills A. and Tancred, P. (eds) *Gendering Organizational Analysis*. Newbury Park: Sage.

Arnold, J., Cooper, C. and Robertson, I. (1995) *Work Psychology. Understanding Human Behaviour in the Workplace*. London: Pitman Publishers.

Bion, S. (1959) *Experiences in Groups*. London: Tavistock.

Bryman, A. (1994) 'Introduction', in Bryman, A. and Burgess, R.G., *Analysing Qualitative Data*. London: Routledge.

Calas, M. and Smircich, L. (1992) 'Re-writing gender into organizational theorizing: directions from feminist perspectives', in Reed, M. and Hughes, M. (eds) *Rethinking Organization. New Directions in Organization Theory and Analysis*. London: Sage.

Calas, M. and Smircich, L. (1996) 'From the woman's point of view: feminist approaches to organization studies', in Clegg, S., Hardy, C. and Nord, W. (eds) *Handbook of Organization Studies*. London: Sage.

Chodorow, N. (1978) *The Reproduction of Mothering: Psychoanalysis and the Sociology of Gender*. Berkeley: University of California Press.

Clegg, S., Hardy, C. and Nord, W. (eds) (1996) *Handbook of Organization Studies*. London: Sage.

Connell, R.W. (1987) *Gender and Power: Society, the Person and Sexual Politics*. Oxford: Polity Press, Basil Blackwell.

Dakin, S., Nilakant, V. and Jensen, R. (1994) 'The role of personality testing in managerial selection', *Journal of Managerial Psychology*, 9 (5): 3-11.

Digman, J.M. (1990) 'Personality structure: emergence of the Five-Factor Model', *Annual Review of Psychology*, 41: 417-40.

Feldberg, R. and Glenn, E.N. (1979) 'Male and female: job versus gender models in the sociology of work', *Social Problems*, 26 (5): 524-38.

Garsombke, D. (1988) 'Organizational culture dons the mantle of militarism', *Organizational Dynamics*, Summer: 46-57.

Gerzon, M. (1992) *A Choice of Heroes. The Changing Face of American Manhood*. USA: Houghton Mifflin Company.

Gherardi, S. (1995) *Gender, Symbolism and Organizational Cultures*. London: Sage.

Giddens, A. (1992) *The Transformation of Intimacy: Sexuality, Love and Eroticism in Modern Societies*. Cambridge: Polity Press.

Gilligan, C. (1982) *In a Different Voice: Psychological Theory and Women's Development*. Cambridge: Harvard University Press.

Handy, C. (1993) *Understanding Organizations*. Oxford: Oxford University Press.

Hearn, J. (1993) 'Emotive subjects: organizational men, organizational masculinities and the (de)construction of "emotions"', in Fineman, S. (ed.) *Emotion in Organizations*. London: Sage. pp. 142-67.

Hennig M. and Jardim A. (1976) *The Managerial Woman*. New York: Doubleday & Co.

Hess, B.B. and Ferree, M.M. (1987) *Analyzing Gender*. Newsbury Park: Sage.

Hosking, D-M. and Morley, I.E. (1991) *A Social Psychology of Organizing*. London: Harvester Wheatsheaf.

Itzin, C. and Newman J. (1995) *Gender, Culture and Organizational Change: Putting Theory into Practice*. London: Routledge.

Jörstad, J. (1996) 'Narcissism and leadership: some differences in male and female leaders', *Leadership and Organization Development Journal*, 17 (6): 17-24.

Kets de Vries, M.F.R. (1995) *Organizational Paradoxes. Clinical Approaches to Management*. London: Routledge.

Kets de Vries, M.F.R. and Miller, D. (1984) *The Neurotic Organization*. San Francisco: Jossey-Bass Inc.

Knights, D. (1997) 'Organization theory in the age of deconstruction: dualism, gender and postmodernism revisited', *Organization Studies*, 18 (1): 1-19.

Korvajärvi, P. (1998) *Gendering Dynamics in White-Collar Work Organizations*. Series Acta Universitas Tamperensis 600, Tampere: University of Tampere.

Kovalainen, A. (1995) *At the Margins of the Economy: Women's Self-Employment in Finland, 1960-1990*. Aldershot: Avebury.

Kovalainen, A. (1999) 'The welfare state, gender system and public sector employment in Finland', in Christiansen, J., Koistinen, P. and Kovalainen, A. (eds) *Working Europe*. Aldershot: Ashgate. pp. 137-55.

Lewin K. (1951) 'Formalization and progress in psychology of personality', in Cartwright, D. (ed.) *Field Theory in Social Science*. New York: Harper.

Lorber, J. (1994) *Paradoxes of Gender*. New Haven: Yale University Press.

Marshall, J. (1989) 'Revisioning career concepts: a feminist invitation', in Arthur, D.J., Hall D.T. and Lawrence B.S. (eds) *Handbook of Career Theory*. Cambridge: Cambridge University Press. pp. 275-92.

Marshall, B.L. (1994) *Engendering Modernity: Feminism, Social Theory and Social Change*. Cambridge: Polity Press.

McFadden, M. and Sneddon, I. (1998) 'Sexuality', in Trew, K. and Kremer, J. (eds) *Gender and Psychology*. Great Britain: Arnold.

Mills, A.J. (1988) 'Organization, gender and culture', *Organization Studies*, 9: 351-69.

Mitchell, J. (1974) *Psychoanalysis and Feminism*. Harmondsworth: Penguin.

Pringle, R. (1989) 'Bureaucracy, rationality and sexuality: the case of secretaries', in Hearn, J. et al. (eds) *The Sexuality of Organization*. London: Sage. pp. 157-77.

Reskin, B.F. and Padavic, I. (1994) *Women and Men at Work*. London: Pine Forge Press.

Robbins, S.P. (1992) *Essentials of Organizational Behaviour*. New Jersey: Prentice-Hall International Inc.

Schein, E. (1985) *Organizational Culture and Leadership*. San-Francisco: Jossey-Bass.

Schein, V., Ruediger, M., Terri, L. and Jiang, L. (1994) 'Think manager - think male: a global phenomenon?', *Journal of Organizational Behaviour*, 17: 33-41.

Steyrer, J. (1998) 'Charisma and the archetypes of leadership', *Organization Studies*, 19 (5): 807-28.

Tyson, S. and Jackson, T. (1992) *The Essence of Organizational Behaviour*. London: Prentice Hall.

Weiss, J.W. (1996) *Organizational Behaviour and Change. Managing Diversity, Cross-Cultural Dynamics and Ethics*. New York: West Publishing Company.

Wilson, F. (1996) 'Research note: organizational theory: blind and deaf to gender?', *Organization Studies*, 17: 825-42.

Wilson, F. M. (1992) 'Language, technology, gender and power', *Human Relations*, 45: 883.

3   Perception and Stereotyping

Albert J. Mills and Elisabeth M. Wilson

Introduction

This chapter looks at perception, stereotyping, and attribution, first examining accounts of their functioning within organizational settings, then expanding the limited attention paid by conventional textbooks to their gendered aspects. A case study of the changing role of the flight attendant in British airlines follows.   This examines the influence of perception, stereotyping and attribution in the way that the profession was seen as a purely male job at one point in time, a purely female job at another point in time, and a mixed profession in the current era.   The persistent contemporary pervasiveness of gender stereotyping is noted.

Mainstream theory

In a popular introductory text on organizational behaviour (Buchanan and Huczynski, 1997), perception is described as 'the dynamic psychological process responsible for attending to, organizing and interpreting sensory data' (p. 46). Perception is not passive, but active (Mullins and Hicks, 1999), and Buchanan and Huczynski (1997) explain how this generally unconscious mechanism disregards information that is well known, safe and irrelevant to the task in hand. Buchanan and Huczynski (1997) assert that the classification systems that we customarily work with are not innate, but social constructs, and they acknowledge cultural differences.   In other words, when a person looks at something s/he does not have an inborn impression or idea about what it is, nor does s/he have a completely prefixed idea of that thing.   How an individual comes to see something will depend on a number of factors that are activated by the relationship between the person and the context in which s/he finds herself. What does appear to be more or less fixed is a predisposition to take short cuts in gathering information.   There is only so much that we can take in during a limited period of time so we tend to fill in the blanks by making assumptions about the missing information.   But what influences the active nature of perception and what are the implications of mental short cuts?

  Not merely societal culture, but also other factors influence the selectivity with which perceptions are organized.   Motivation, personality, past experiences and associated learning all contribute to expectation that mould the response to stimuli, and the amount and nature of the attention given, in addition to contextual factors (Buchanan and Huczynski, 1997). Language also shapes and guides thinking and in turn perception (Mullins and Hicks, 1999). Each individual's perceptual understanding of other people and their environment differs (Mullins and Hicks, 1999). Among the contextual factors that influence perception is group dynamics. A number of laboratory experiments, for example, have indicated that an individual's perception can be influenced by the opinions of others. In the Asch experiments (1952, 1956) an individual's perception of the comparative lengths of a set of lines was influenced to conform with a group of people who were secretly working with the experimenter: the experimenter's confederates all gave a uniform, but inaccurate, opinion on the length of each line to which 75 per cent of individual subjects conformed. Experiments by Moscovici and Mugny (1983), on the other hand, indicated that a majority of subjects could be influenced by minority opinion. In these experiments the researcher had secretly planted two confederates among a group of people. In this case the two confederates, by firmly holding to an agreed, but inaccurate, opinion of presented stimuli, managed to influence the perception of the majority of the others in the room.

What this tells us is that how we come to perceive something is arrived at through a process of interaction that is mediated by various factors. Some factors – such as a particular disposition to act in a certain way, and past experiences – contribute to a habitual predisposition to respond to events: we develop what is called a mental set, or perceptual expectations (Buchanan and Huczynski, 1997). Some factors are more immediately interactive in the way they influence what we are seeing; these include such things as group dynamics and social values. Yet other factors, such as an individual's motivation or how s/he is feeling at the time, are influenced by a combination of psychological and situational factors. All these factors are ultimately mediated by deep-rooted contextual factors, such as cultural norms, and language. That, perceptually, people approach situations in different ways suggests that 'external reality' is socially constructed and, thus, should be studied from a phenomenological perspective (Buchanan and Huczynski, 1997).

The process of perception is an invaluable aspect of decision making. On an ongoing basis we need to make a variety of decisions based on perception of something or someone. The problem is that how we perceive something is constrained by several factors, including time, information, and ability. We rarely have enough information and sometimes we have information overload. Often we are required to act within limited time periods. If we waited until we had the 'correct' amount of information or time available we would rarely make decisions. That is where perceptual short cuts prove invaluable. We use a combination of perceptual cues and mental set to fill in the information blanks. For example, to take a recent case from the headlines, just after midnight on February 4th, 1999, four New York police officers, looking for a rapist, saw a man 'peering up and down the block'. The man, who 'stepped backward, back into the vestibule . . . like he didn't want to be seen', turned, looked at the police men and removed 'a black object from his right side'. In a split second the police officers had to decide what they were seeing. Thinking that the man was drawing a gun the police opened fire, killing the man, Amadou Diallo. The time of night, the 'suspicious' actions of Diallo, the neighbourhood (the Bronx), the fact that a rapist was thought to be in the area, the sight of a black object, and recent experiences of gun violence all acted to cue the perception of a gun (Chua-Eoan, 2000). Of course, most perceptual decisions are far less dramatic but are, nonetheless, aided by short cuts. For example, when a company is hiring a new employee an interview may be an imperfect way of gaining information about applicants but it is a lot less quicker and cheaper than spending considerable time 'getting to know' each candidate.

On the other hand, perceptual short cuts can also lead to distortions, such as relying on first impressions (the primacy effect) or the most recent information (the recency effect), disregarding unwelcome information (Mullins and Hicks, 1999), or being influenced by deep-rooted biases and prejudices. Amadou Diallo, for example, was in fact an innocent man on his way home, who nervously reached for his (black) wallet.

Stereotyping is a particular form of perceptual short cut and involves making assumptions and judgements about other people on the basis of limited information. McShane (1999: 151) defines stereotyping as:

> The process of using a few observable characteristics to assign people to a preconceived social category, and then assigning less observable traits to those persons based on their membership in the group.

For example, if a person is dressed in a white lab coat and is wearing a stethoscope we may deduce that she is a doctor. We may then go on to assume that she is relatively wealthy. Arguably, stereotyping is convenient because it prevents us having to work out another person's attitudes and likely behaviour from first principles (Buchanan and Huczynski, 1997); enabling speedier situational scrutiny, short-term decision making and more manageable encounters with the world (Tobena et al., 1999). Indeed, Seligman (1997) suggests that stereotyping is a reasonable collection of social observations. On the other hand, this view of stereotyping ignores the fact that the process can lead to minor or gross inaccuracies, causing us to make judgements about others that are overly generous or prejudicial. It may come about because of convenience, laziness, or simply lack of additional information. Kobrynowicz (1998) reviews the fact that stereotypes sway opinions and decisions about others when there is little or rather ambiguous information about individuals, and further contends that traditional investigation of stereotyping may have underestimated its strength. Stereotyping is not however merely a subconscious activity. Kunda and Sinclair (1999) suggest that people can both activate and suppress stereotyping in relation to an individual, and even choose among available stereotypes. Incongruent information, for instance, may challenge some stereotypical views (Garcia Marques and Mackie, 1999). Thus police officers engage in broad stereotyping, but can voluntarily suspend this for individuals on whom they project some saving graces (Oberweis and Musheno, 1999). In the Diallo case, however, the fact that all four police officers were white and the victim was black has led some commentators to suggest that the shooting was motivated by racial stereotyping (Chua-Eoan, 2000).

Attribution is another aspect of the perceptual process, whereby notions of causality are assigned to perceptions (Buchanan and Huczynski, 1997). We attribute characteristics, intentions and motives to others on the basis of what we perceive and what we assume. Again, this can facilitate the speed by which we come to make necessary decisions about others. In seeking to explain the behaviour of others, causal theories may be either dispositional or situational, respectively construing behaviour as coming from the character or personality of the actor, or resulting from the situation (Ybarra and Stephan, 1999). When a person is perceiving him or herself as the actor, dispositional or situational explanations for events can be said to derive from internal or external loci of control (Mullins and Hicks, 1999). Persons tending to dispositional explanations are more likely to predict less positive and more negative behaviour from a subject (Ybarra and Stephan, 1999). To take the example of a company who, following the introduction of an employment equity policy, hires a well-known executive as its first woman Chief Executive Officer. Where people explain the situation in terms of the woman's track record they are taking a dispositional perspective. Where they explain the decision in terms of the equity policy they are taking a situational perspective.

Attribution is influenced by cultural factors but not in the tendency to infer people's dispositions from their behaviour (Krull et al., 1999). Research suggests that some cultures are more dispositional in orientation (e.g. East Asians), while others (e.g. North Americans) are more situational (Ybarra and Stephan, 1999; Choi et al., 1999); these differences seem to be in the extent to which individuals are seen as free agents (Menon et al., 1999). There are also differences between members of high and low status groups, with the former more likely to attribute career failure to discrimination rather than their own characteristics (Ruggiero and Marx, 1999). Attribution when evaluating cases of discrimination can vary with the extent to which an observer identifies with the victim, and whether the observer has perceived him or herself as having suffered from injustice (Davidson and Friedman, 1998). There are distinct differences in attributional style between those who make simple attributions, usually ascribing internal causes, and those who make more complex attributions, entailing both internal and external causes for behaviour (Pope and Meyer, 1999). Respondents have also varied their explanations according to the identified discipline of the researcher (Norenzayan and Schwarz, 1999). As pointed out by van Heerden (1999), researchers' findings of misattribution may themselves be subject to attributional error. All this indicates that attribution is a minefield, open to bias.

The interplay of perception, stereotyping and attribution can be seen in the oft-quoted example of identical behaviour that in a man is seen as justifiable anger, and in a woman as being emotional. Sex-role stereotyping means a different perception of similar behaviour, and a different attribution (judgement) as to its appropriateness. Biased perceptions, stereotyping and (mis)attributions are frequent in relation to all disadvantaged groups. The holding of stereotypes about other nationals is well documented and persistent (Cooper and Kirkcaldy, 1995; Soutar et al., 1999), as is that related to ethnic minorities within the same workforce (Myles, 1997). Stereotypes are one of a number of mechanisms affecting the treatment of persons with disabilities in the workplace (Stone and Colella, 1996). Perceptions about patients by nurses can vary according to their age and physical attractiveness (Hadjistavropoulos et al., 2000) and their sexuality (Guthrie, 1999). People who are different to the majority of the workforce in some way are more likely to report experiences that make them feel inferior, although contextual factors and attendant or absent cultural myths also contribute (Gomez and Trierweiler, 1999). Overweight men and women reported perceived mistreatment, and this was more likely the heavier they weighed (Falkner et al., 1999). Although there is some evidence that stereotypes can be modified by counter information (Guo et al., 1999), stereotyping seems to be a persistent mechanism, such as the current references to Generation X, composed of young people newly entering the labour market and workforce (Olesen, 1999).

In discussing perception, it was uncommon until recently for OB texts to acknowledge gender in regard to stereotyping, or any other aspect of organizational behaviour (Mills and Hatfield, 1999). Within more recent OB texts gender – along with race and ethnicity, nationality, age, disability, occupation, religious belief, sexual orientation, education, social class, and appearance – has been identified as a characteristic that tends toward stereotyping. Buchanan and Huczynski (1997), for example, summarize research that demonstrates the influence of sex and appearance on workplace success, measured in terms of recruitment and selection, remuneration, and promotion. In an implied criticism of gender stereotyping, they cite evidence (from Averett and Korenman, 1993) that overweight women earn less than those of average weight, although the reverse was true of men. However, Buchanan and Huczynski (1997) do not expand on their previous comments about social construction. In a similar vein, in relation to effective selection, Rosenfeld and Wilson (1999) acknowledge the deleterious effects of perceptual errors and stereotyping, which they ascribe to human failing. They go further than most accounts in suggesting ways in which the disadvantaged individual can counter this tendency, based on the strategies gay and lesbian employees may use to 'come out'. They also propose that contact with the unknown person/s may reduce unhelpful perceptions. Both strategies, however, are problematic. The first suggestion places responsibility on the victim rather than the perpetrator. The latter suggestion ignores the fact that sexual stereotyping is often played out in constant *interaction* between men and women.   Mullins and Hicks (1999) contend that the different types of stereotyping from which women can suffer, both inside and outside the organization, are often unconscious, and they suggest that managers should be aware of their own assumptions and hence tendencies to stereotype.

Many recently published OB textbooks argue that stereotyping is generally deleterious to some, clearly identifiable, groups. Yet none raise, let alone deal with, the question of 'to whom is this advantageous?' This point will be further explored later in this chapter.

Findings about perception, attribution and stereotyping in relation to gender

This section explores findings from the literature about perception, attribution and stereotyping and gender. It was noteworthy that most examples concerned women, and this is commented upon below. Some critiques start by suggesting that stereotyping processes commence in the way children are brought up. Case (1994) notes substantial differences between male and female communication styles, and states that this starts with the different games girls and boys are encouraged to play. This contributes to the social construction of notions of what it is to be a 'man' and a 'woman'. Women become associated with concern with establishing relationships, equality, focusing on feelings, conversational maintenance work, responsiveness, tentativeness, whereas men become associated with concern with exerting control, enhancing status, instrumentality, conversational dominance, being assertive, and absolute expressions; men are not highly responsive, speaking in general terms removed from concrete experience and feelings (Case, 1994). There were until recently widespread beliefs in society that academically successful women were not feminine, and girls who did well at school were not only disapproved of by boys but also suffered insults (Garrett, 1987). The continuing influence of childhood and early adulthood experiences is reported in a qualitative study of managers (Hale, 1999).

Studies from the UK and North America have identified persistent sex-role stereotyping not only in television commercials directed at children (Browne, 1998), but also in educational programmes made for children (Barner, 1999). This continues into adult programmes, for instance on radio in the UK (Karpf, 1994), and in the subtly different portrayal of men with children and women with children during daytime, sport and prime-time television (Kaufman, 1999). A review of studies in 12 countries spanning 6 continents indicated that this is a universal phenomenon (Furnham and Mak, 1999). Although not mentioned specifically in these studies, we can probably assume the men and women were usually portrayed as heterosexual. Sex-role stereotyping was identified as one of the big issues to be tackled by the UK Equal Opportunities Commission in 1999 (Rickford, 1999).

There are a number of societal inequalities that are bolstered by underlying assumptions (Schein, 1994) about the nature of women and men, career paths, assumptions about men's breadwinning and women's domestic roles, and prejudice about women's capability. Gendering of roles outside the workplace has a significant impact on gendering within the workplace. In a domestic setting role expectations for women centre around being a wife, partner, mother, housekeeper, and possibly daughter. Roles and stereotypes cause problems for women not apparent for men, because of the conflict inherent in being a partner and/or mother on the one hand, and an employee on the other, a conflict particularly acute in pregnancy (Sheppard, 1989). Role conflict and role overload are evident in the domestic demands of marriage and children, exemplified by research indicating that women managers compared with men are much less likely to be married or have children (Alban-Metcalfe, 1989). Women at work are likely to find themselves undertaking a 'double shift' of paid work and a disproportionate share of housework (Koncius, 1997), domestic burdens cast on women because of traditional role expectations, and the stereotyping of women as housewives and caregivers.

In a dual career partnership the impact on a woman's career is greater than the impact on a man's largely because of gendered role perceptions about domestic responsibility, providing, the spouse/support role and parenthood (Lewis, 1994). Because in many advanced economies the return to work after maternity leave is socially constructed as a choice, this puts pressure on the woman to manage and negotiate both roles (Lewis, 1994). The gradual lowering of the wife's occupational status can be attributed to the gendered distribution of domestic responsibilities (Gershuny, 1996), supported by stereotypical expectations. The counterpart of expectations about women's traditional roles is that women are assumed to have less commitment to the organization than men, that is, attributions are made about their motivation (Gale and Cartwright, 1995). Unhelpful stereotypes include the proposition that women are not motivated, and that women cannot cope with, or fear, success (Marshall, 1984). A belief that motherhood is the proper fulfilment for women is often used as a rationalization for the exclusion of women managers (Roper, 1994), even though the evidence suggests that having a family makes a woman less likely to change jobs (Brett and Stroh, 1994). Perception of gender difference appears to be firmly held (Bernstein, 1999).

Roles and stereotypes for men that impinge on working life are more likely to concern their breadwinner role (Collinson and Collinson, 1989; Aaltio-Marjosola and Lehtinen, 1998). Thus marriage for a young man is perceived as a stabilizing influence, but quite the opposite for a young woman from an employer's point of view. One recent construct is that of the 'new man' who supposedly embraces equality with his partner, sharing domestic and child care responsibilities, and thus encompassing some ostensibly feminine virtues of sensitivity and caring. This appears to be a class based construct, referring almost exclusively to middle-class men, some of whom might describe themselves as feminist sympathizers. Unfortunately this concept has been exposed as a cultural myth, with a gap between what men say they do and what they actually do in the home, largely because of the long hours worked by many young men with children (Saigol, 1996). Although 'helping' by men is socially constructed and perceived by many as a viable contribution to household and caring responsibilities, it is postulated that in their thirties most young men intent on establishing conventional middle-class careers are doing so at the expense of family life (Brindle, 1996). Aaltio-Marjosola and Lehtinen (1998) point out that fatherhood is an idealized part of masculinity, yet older managers advise younger ones not to take paternity leave.

Within the organization Mills and Murgatroyd (1991) suggest that different masculinities can be seen at different levels of the organization as responses to expectations of toughness: as aggression and competition for top managers, as coldness and lack of emotion for office workers, and as machismo among shop-floor workers. Jokes may be used to reinforce and maintain acceptable behaviour, which is assumed to be heterosexual (Mills and Murgatroyd, 1991). Collinson and Collinson (1989) found two discourses at shop-floor level, the first from younger men was overtly sexual and reduced women to objects; the second, associated with older men, was about their role as sire, breadwinner, and holder of domestic authority. In both cases it appeared that manual work was expressive of their power, masculine autonomy and independence, a discourse accepted by management (Collinson and Collinson, 1989). In many economically developed countries it appears that the societal culture is supportive of men in dominant positions (Sidney, 1994). Roper (1994) described a cult of toughness among managers which included coping successfully with manual workers, getting dirty hands and accepting and succeeding at difficult postings. Kerfoot and Knights (1993) and Collinson and Hearn (1994) identified a paternalistic masculinity which was nurturing and hierarchical, and exercised power by moral authority. In opposition they describe a competitive, rationalistic masculinity, more the province of younger managers, and associated with a highly competitive, highly demanding environment. Collinson and Hearn (1994) also identified authoritarianism, which was intolerant of any kind of difference or dissent, and achieved its ends by coercion, and informalism, composed of informal relationships that might cut across hierarchical levels, and based on shared interests in sport, cars, sex and drinking.

Thus masculinity may vary from being merely career enhancing to manifesting overt hostility to women (Collinson and Hearn, 1994), and as indicated in almost all cases it is strongly identified with heterosexuality (Mills and Murgatroyd, 1991). Roper (1994) asserts that there is no middle ground between masculinity and effeminacy, and Lorber and Farrell (1991) suggest that the social construction of masculinity in the US encourages homophobia. Thus the associated stereotyping of masculinity can be seen to limit men's choices and freedom of expression. Criticisms have been made of the fact that only one type of masculinity tends to be discussed in general terms (Cornwall and Lindisfarne, 1994a), and in relation to organizations (Alvesson and Due

Billing, 1992). This has been described as 'hegemonic masculinity', and predominates so that alternative ways of being a man are viewed as subordinate (Cornwall and Lindisfarne, 1994a: 3). As such it has a normative function (Cornwall and Lindisfarne, 1994b), that is, it provides a template or pattern for what 'proper' masculinity should be, a desirable stereotype. For instance stereotypical sex roles can make it difficult for men to expose anxieties to female colleagues (Hale, 1999).

There are more overt stereotypes in relation to women within the workplace. Kanter (1977) suggested that a women might take on the following stereotypical roles: the mother, who acts in a maternal fashion towards colleagues; the seductress, who uses her sexuality to her advantage; the pet, who is paraded as an example of the company's liberality; and last the iron maiden, who is feared. Women in authority are often stereotyped, for instance Hillary Clinton has been criticized as a 'careerist', and other stereotypes include dragon lady, and schoolmarm (Tannen, 1995). Roper (1994) remarked on the similarity between the role of the wife and the role of the secretary, the office wife. Both are perceived to provide emotional support and give emotional expression in lieu of the organization man, in a trade-off between vicarious status and vicarious emotional satisfaction. Helpmeet roles are taken for granted unless withdrawn, with ambivalence about the importance and skills of secretarial work (Roper, 1994). Although the social construction of secretarial roles is affected by societal and organizational variables, gender stereotypes are prevalent in many countries (Truss et al., 1995).

Gutek (1989: 59) writes about 'sexual role spillover', where there is a carry over of gender based expectations into the workplace. Thus attributes such as being sexy, affectionate, and attractive are associated with women, although there is no similar association for men. Whereas the stereotype for men is to be tough, competitive, assertive, and a leader, what is noticed and commented upon about women is if they are sexual or asexual, and there may be an unpredictable punitive use of sexuality as a way of devaluing and trivializing women (Gutek, 1989). In an experimental situation men observing male and female couples interacting attributed more sexuality and a greater wish for prospective contact than did women (Edmondson and Conger, 1995). The range of behaviour acceptable in general for women is very narrow, as they can be described as too severe, sexy, or feminine (Tannen, 1995), all descriptions assessing sexuality. Attributions of motivation for harassment have been found to vary according to whether women are employed in traditional or non-traditional occupations (Burgess and Borgida, 1997).

Men's sexuality is not noticed, or alternatively if noticed is excused (Gutek, 1989). A recent construct within the UK, acknowledging some aspects of male sexuality, is that of 'the lads', with the adjective 'laddish'. This refers to predominantly young men who indulge in exploits, horseplay and sex talk, and are in turn indulged for their behaviour, which is excused as letting off steam. This seems in some ways a re-working of older discourses about active sexuality (Collinson and Collinson, 1989), but is not restricted to manual workers, as young white-collar workers may similarly be described as lads. This can be seen in a middle-class interest in football, convivial drinking bouts, 'Loaded' magazine, and a general encouragement of hedonism.

One of the strongest areas for stereotyping and gendered perceptions is in relation to occupation. In almost any organization you enter, members can state which are men's and women's jobs (as well as acknowledging that some are in transition and some open to both). The gendered perception of jobs is all-pervasive. Gender roles lead to the sexual division of labour (Stanley and Wise, 1993) both in the home as indicated above, and also at work, leading to gender segregation, and a continued lower perceived value of women's jobs (Castro, 1997). Acker (1990) analyses the supposedly gender neutral process of job evaluation, which is linked to hierarchy, pointing out that positions are assumed to be occupied by a genderless, bodiless worker. Comparable worth arguments can be undermined because women's work is devalued relative to men and therefore perceived as unskilled, and women lack the power to define their work as skilled (Reskin, 1991). Subtle skills are perceived as innate rather than acquired (Reskin, 1991).

Reskin (1991) suggests that physical segregation on the basis of gender encourages unfair treatment and that men like this because of their desire to maintain differentiation and hence better pay (Reskin, 1991). She asserts that lower status groups are allocated lower status work and hence lower wages. Men therefore resist women's entry into traditional male work because it threatens differentiation (Reskin, 1991). In male dominated industries women tend to undertake peripheral jobs even when in core occupations, and in core jobs they tend to be in junior grades (Corcoran-Nantes and Roberts, 1995). In other occupations women gain entry only after substantial changes in the content of the work, where reduced rewards or autonomy or status make it less attractive (Reskin, 1991; Cockburn, 1991). 'Female' jobs are acceptable for women if they accord with conventional ideas of nurturing, such as a nurse; conversely gender stereotyping has acted to deter men from seeking careers in nursing (Squires, 1995).

One consequence of societal assumptions about roles and stereotypes is that there are still strong beliefs, held by men and women, that women are not capable of managing and leading. In this category come those explanations that postulate that women have insufficient intellect, physical and mental stamina, ambition or leadership skills. These locate deficiencies in the individual and genetic inheritance, and can thus allow for the exceptional woman. Although these opinions are not expressed overtly in academic literature, they surface in the press under the guise of stories about women 'wanting it all' and being stressed, creating a new stereotype of the selfish, stressed career woman (Faludi, 1992). Perceptions about the proper roles of men and women can be seen in subordinates' responses. Whereas men in authority are perceived as the boss, women in authority may be perceived as women. For instance, when a woman consults subordinates then male subordinates can think she is asking for advice (Tannen, 1995). Women are assumed to be emotional (Hale, 1999) or 'too emotional' for some managerial positions (Nation's Restaurant News, 1996) whereas men by contrast are perceived as under-emotional (Heesacker et al., 1999), but this is not a problem! Leadership is discussed more fully in Metcalfe and Altman (in this volume).

Perception, stereotyping and attribution have a part in gendered organizational processes. Despite evidence that the traditional interview is unreliable (Iles, 1992), it is still used as the preferred selection method for many jobs (Recruitment and Development Report, 1991), leaving scope for stereotyping, unfair discrimination and prejudice. In a discussion of assessment procedures, Alimo-Metcalfe (1993) links the defects in traditional interviewing to the pioneering research by Schein (1973, 1975) where male and female managers were asked to apply a number of descriptive terms to men and women in general, and to successful middle managers. Schein (1973, 1975) found that both men and women perceived successful middle managers possessing characteristics more usually associated with men. Repeated later (Brenner et al., 1989) the results were that women had changed their perceptions of successful middle managers, aligning them more closely with female characteristics, but men had not. Further cross-cultural studies reinforced these results (Schein, 1994; Norris and Wylie, 1995). This stereotyping persists alongside the growth of women managers in the US and UK (Schein, 1994), emphasizing its irrational basis. Alimo-Metcalfe (1993) points out that senior managers who are the gatekeepers for advancement are likely to be male, and hence likely to judge women against male stereotypes of successful managers. The enduring stereotype of management as a male preserve (Schein, 1973, 1975; Brenner et al., 1989) was encapsulated in the phrase: 'think manager, think male!'. Alimo-Metcalfe (1993) raises concerns about the use of assessment centres for managerial selection, particularly in relation to group tasks, citing studies that show women to be disadvantaged in mixed group situations. A woman's lesser contribution to a group discussion may thus be attributed to lack of knowledge or skills, rather than as the outcome of gendered group processes. Jackson and Hirsh (1991) voice concern about the possibility of subjective assessor bias, and sex-role stereotyping in assessment centres.

For those women who become managers, Kanter (1977) describes three perceptual tendencies by the dominant group in relation to tokens, members of the subordinate group. First there is visibility, where the tokens tend to receive an extra share of attention, and second, the contrast effect of polarization, where the dominant group see their own common characteristics and at the same time their differences from the tokens. Third, assimilation is where stereotypical generalizations are made about the token (Kanter, 1977). All these perceptual tendencies increase the emphasis of difference, at the expense of perceiving similarities between men and women.

Case study

Flight attending in Britain: from the white coated steward to the sexy girl in the paper dress. (This case was developed from a series of studies by Mills (1994, 1995, 1996a, 1996b, 1997a, 1997b, 1998.)

When you think of the word 'flight attendant' what image comes into your mind, what assumptions do you make about the type of person who does that kind of job? For many people an enduring image of the flight attendant is that of a female occupation that is typically done by a young, physically 'attractive', white, middle-class woman. If that is your perception then you are engaging in stereotyping. In most countries it is no longer legal to employ flight attendance on the basis of gender, assumptions of bodily attractiveness, racial/ethnic characteristics, or age. Today, a growing number of men and people of colour can be found among the ranks of flight attendants. However, while the stereotypical view of flight attending is deleterious to various groups of women it is not an entirely inaccurate perception, as white females still constitute the majority within the occupation.

The problem with stereotypes is that people often act on them and, in the process, bring their distorted perceptions to life. This was the case with the flight attending profession over the years.

The world's first flight attendant was hired by *The Daimler Airway*, in Britain, in 1922 but the seating capacity of the planes at that time (holding less than 14 passengers) did not make this a viable job. With the advent of larger planes in 1926 Daimler's successor, *Imperial Airways*, became the world's first commercial airline to hire flight attendants on a regular basis. As such flight attending was an entirely new job, with no pre-existing gendered perceptions. Nonetheless, the airline recruited male flight attendants and no woman was recruited until 1946.

Imperial Airways' decision to make flight attending a male only job is rooted in at least three main sets of assumptions. First, as a result of wartime associations with combat flying, piloting and other in-flight duties were seen as strictly male pursuits: past experiences strongly influenced perceptions of the suitability of female flight crew. In the mid-1920s respective meetings of the *International Commission for Air Navigation* (ICAN) and the *International Civil Aviation Organization* (ICAO) explicitly banned the employment of women as flight crew members: in a classic example of stereotyping, it was argued that a woman's menstruation cycle would incapacitate her during flight and be a danger to herself and others. This attitude was reinforced by a second set of assumptions, drawing broadly on the social attitudes of the day, that a woman's place was in the home. In Britain in the 1920s and 1930s, despite the fact that ships and airlines carried numerous female passengers, travel and adventure were almost exclusively associated with men. Third, taking their cues from existing examples, Imperial Airways mimicked existing practices in other forms of luxury travel (i.e. rail, ocean-going vessels) where white-coated male stewards served the passengers; the airline replicated the dress, the name, and the male-only hiring practices. In short, in the absence of existing examples, the perception of flight attending was influenced by societal culture (notions about 'women's place'), past experiences (wartime associations), dominant practices in associated contexts (ocean-going liners), and relevant symbolism (white coats) and language (stewards, stewarding).

In short order, other international airlines followed Imperial Airways' lead and the new job of 'in-flight steward' became a male-only profession. Before long male stewarding was not only an established practice but a mental set or strongly held perceptual expectation. Managers and passengers alike expected to be served in flight by a white-coated steward.

In 1930 a US airline – *Boeing Air Transport* (BAT) – was asked to consider 'experimenting' with the use of female flight attendants. So strong was the mental set of senior management that they initially rejected the idea out of hand. While they were drawn to the psychological advantages, they feared public reaction to the hiring of young female stewards. On the one hand, BAT could see the advantage of playing on the stereotype of young women as weak to shame male passengers into flying: it was still difficult at that time to convince sufficient numbers of people to fly. On the other hand, the stereotype could be counter-productive if people perceived the female attendants as 'cheap', perhaps promiscuous women – a popular notion was that 'good girls' would not be found engaging in travel. In the end an ingenious compromise was arrived at that was to influence flight attendant recruitment in North America for two decades. It was decided to hire only young women with nursing qualifications and to advertise them as some kind of flying nurse. The women, who would perform the normal duties of the steward, gave every appearance of being there to deal with a number of in-flight ailments, that were frequent in the early days of flying. Termed 'sky girls', they wore a modified form of nurses uniform while in flight and a green two piece uniform while on the ground. The compromise worked and over the next two decades airlines in the US and Europe switched from male stewards to female flight attendants. British airlines were among the very last to adopt this practice.

Imperial Airways and its successors, the British Overseas Airways Corporation (BOAC) and British European Airways (BEA) steadfastly resisted hiring female flight attendants until 1946. Before World War II, the airline bosses remained firmly convinced that women had no place among air crews. If anything airline experiences in North America had reinforced that viewpoint. Once female flight attending had become established as 'normal' practice, airlines began to experiment with the way that they 'sold' the idea to the public. While airlines continued to require nursing credentials some companies began to sell the idea of the flight attendant as a kind of 'in-flight hostess', dressing her in the fashion of a middle-class debutante and calling her an 'air hostess'. It was this latter image that troubled the senior management of BOAC and BEA. In an atmosphere of post-war austerity,

Britain's airline chiefs feared a public backlash if there was any hint that they were hiring 'flying hostesses'. After much soul searching, and not without some commercial pressure from US competitors who carried female flight attendants, BOAC and BEA both hired an 'experimental' group of female 'stewards'.

The publicity surrounding the new female stewards provides an insight to existing stereotyping and how the airlines attempted to deal with it. Under the incongruous title, 'We Had To Kill the Stewardess', the *BEA* Magazine (September, 1947) justified the hiring of female flight attendants thus:

> We launched the slogan 'Glamour is Out'; we even de-sexed her by knocking the -ess off her title. Picture Post did us proud over the whole thing, showing the intelligence and hard work that goes into making a good stewardess: foreign languages and training in first aid and navigation, apart from the expected ability to serve hot coffee and administer air-sickness pills. We thought of substituting the steward, boy instead of girl, but somehow it hasn't worked out. The steward is another hard worker, with lots of training and experience, as well, usually, as an RAF background, but there's no doubt that his lady companion has stolen the market for the time being. So we're keeping him in cold storage.

Over the next 15 years the intended equity image, whereby male and female flight attendants wore similar uniforms and operated under the single title of 'steward', gave way to a new, eroticized image of the female flight attendant.

From the beginning of the 1960s to the middle of the 1970s airlines in North America and Europe, in fierce competition to fill seats on the new jumbo jets, developed marketing strategies around overtly sexualized forms of female sexuality. In this era, across the airline industry, the symbolism of sexuality was often crude: uniforms ranged from Continental Airways' Playboy Bunny outfits, to TWA's series of paper dresses in the style of serving wench, Roman toga, gold lamé cocktail dress, and Manhattan lounging pyjamas. Even the usually staid British Airways introduced a 'sexy style' paper dress on some of its routes. Advertisements utilized implicit and not so implicit sexualized slogans, such as Continental Airline's, 'We really move our tail for you'.

The new sexualized marketing built on existing recruitment practices where only women of a certain age and weight/height ratio were hired; most airlines did not recruit women less than 19 years old and required them to leave the company before they reached 30 years old, or if they married in the meantime; flight attendants were expected to be between 5'2" and 5'7" 'with weight proportionate to height' (i.e., slender); women were often fired if they exceeded expected weights by more than four pounds.

These marketing and recruitment strategies indelibly marked the public perception of the flight attendant through much of the remainder of the Twentieth Century and became part of popular culture, as seen in such films and books as *Coffee, Tea, or Me: The Uninhibited Memoirs of Two Airline Stewardesses* (Baker and Jones, 1967).

It took the advent of the new women's liberation movement, airline deregulation, employment equity legislation, and industry speed-up, to challenge the narrow eroticized image of female flight attendants. In the UK and most North American airlines today you will find a range of flight attendants including a number of men, various people of colour, and a range of age groups. Glamour is still a pervasive element of the image of the female flight attendant, as recent advertising attests, and one ironic twist of the changing image of the job is that many of the men who have entered a supposedly female occupation may find themselves perceived as gay, irrespective of their sexual orientation.

Discussion

We can learn several things from the case. First, stereotyping is a continual, pervasive aspect of social life, whether it is the conjuring up of images of male stewards in the 1920s or female air hostesses in the 1970s. Second, perception is often gendered, creating specific images of men and women. Third, the processes of stereotyping and attribution contribute to the social construction of masculinity and femininity. The role of the 'sexy flight attendant', for example, did not simply provide certain types of work for women but helped to define the character of womanhood in the public mind. Third, gendered stereotyping can result in a range of images, from the deleterious to the potentially positive. The equity imaging of BOAC and BEA in 1946 was just as much an attempt to create a gendered ('desexed') perception of the role of the steward, as were the eroticized images of the air hostess two decades later. Four, gendered stereotyping operates at several different levels. At one level stereotypes can be seen influencing the actions of airline managers as they attempt to gauge public reaction to the introduction of female flight attendants. At another level the stereotyping forms part of deliberate strategies to either sell or de-emphasize sexuality. Fifth, gendered perceptions have implications and outcomes for women *and* men. Gendered stereotypes help to define expected masculine and feminine behaviour. More often than not this privileges masculinity over femininity but it also privileges some forms of masculinity over others. The attribution of gayness to men in female-typed professions is but one example of how men's sexuality can be called into question where their work does not follow stereotypical masculine pursuits. In such cases the attribution of 'gay' is usually framed within a narrow heterosexist viewpoint. Finally, gendered perceptions change over time and are influenced by a number of factors. Sometimes change is reactive as people adjust to changing styles (e.g. the introduction of flying nurses, the air hostess, equity stewarding, sexy fly girls). Sometimes change is engineered by those who stand to gain (e.g. the creation of the flying nurse image). And sometimes change comes about through protest and negotiation, as in the case of the female flight attendants of TWA whose protests against sexist practices was part of the early wave of the new women's liberation movement in the late 1960s/early 1970s.

Critique

It is noteworthy that in conducting a search of the literature for this chapter, considerably more papers were found, for instance investigating gender stereotyping, in relation to women than in relation to men (e.g. Heilman, 1997), and the balance in the chapter reflects this. In other words, women were problematized. Only rarely was no adverse effect found (e.g. Hull and Umansky, 1997). Stereotyping was generally assumed to be detrimental to women, as discussed above (Buchanan and Huczynski, 1997; Mullins and Hicks, 1999).

If these processes are so well documented, why has nothing changed? There was much less discussion of the implications for men, and the implications for relations between women and men in the workplace, let alone including discussion of those whose sexual preferences do not accord with the norm for their sex. In some books there is an almost value-free discussion. Wilson's (1995) account of the perception of women in organizations follows this trend of concentrating on women's detriment, although with more critique, pointing out for example that the tendency to think in bipolar constructs reinforces perceptual bias. If stereotyping, perception and attribution are generally unhelpful for women, the converse must be that they are generally helpful for men, in keeping women in their place actually and metaphorically. Marshall (1984: 36) sees change as a joint project:

> Stereotypes trap women and men. But we create them so we can also change them. If attitudes to women changed, their views of themselves, and their behaviour, would change too.

However generally stereotyping tends to be described as an individual process, even when accumulated results of research are described. However on an individual level it is not an occasional quirk, but habitual, and on an organizational level not an accidental aberration, but systemic and structural.

There are other ways of framing the processes described. Mills and Murgatroyd (1991) for instance propose that there are gender rules: first about a man's world to prevent women entering the work domain at all; and second about a man's work to limit women to certain jobs and positions within the organization. Development studies as a discipline has long since abandoned conceptualizing gender roles, and attendant stereotyping, in favour of acknowledging gendered power relations. Wilson (in this volume) discusses the concept of 'doing gender', a continual process of creation and recreation. All of these approaches make a clearer statement about exactly who benefits, and who suffers. By contrast the limp explanations offered by conventional textbooks in relation to the gendered effects of perception, stereotyping, and attribution appear limited to say the least. The hope that was raised at the beginning of this chapter for elucidation of gendered processes has therefore been only partially fulfilled. Readers must look elsewhere in this volume for further explanation.

Post script

Whilst reviewing this chapter one of the co-authors (Elisabeth) stopped in a workmen's cafe. As male banter arose, the perpetrators were chided by the female assistant: 'Language ... ladies present'. Neatly stereotyped by class and gender, I smiled and enjoyed my egg sandwich.

References

Aaltio-Marjosola, Iiris and Lehtinen, Jyri (1998) 'Male managers as fathers? Contrasting management, fatherhood and masculinity', *Human Relations*, 51 (2): 121-36.

Acker, Joan (1990) 'Hierarchies, jobs, bodies: a theory of gendered organizations', *Gender and Society*, 4 (2): 139-58.

Alban-Metcalfe, Beverly (1989) 'What motivates managers: an investigation by gender and sector of employment', *Public Administration*, 67 (Spring): 95-108.

Alimo-Metcalfe, Beverly (1993) 'Women in management: organizational socialization and assessment practices that prevent career advancement', *International Journal of Selection and* Assessment, 1 (2): 68-82.

Alvesson, Mats and Due Billing, Yvonne (1992) 'Gender and organization: towards a differentiated understanding', *Organization Studies*, 13 (12): 73-103.

Asch, Soloman E. (1952) *Social Psychology*. Englewood Cliffs, NJ: Prentice Hall.

Asch, Soloman E. (1956) 'Studies of independence and conformity: 1. A minority of one against a unanimous majority', *Psychological Monographs. General and Applied*, 70 (9): whole no. 416.

Averett, S. and Korenman, S. (1993), 'The economic reality of the beauty myth', NBER Working Paper No. 4521, cited in Buchanan, D. and Huczynski, A. (eds) (1997) *Organizational Behaviour: An Introductory Text*. 3rd Edition. London, New York Toronto: Prentice Hall.

Baker, T. and Jones, R. (1967) *Coffee, Tea or Me? The Uninhibited Memoirs of Two Airline Stewardesses*. London: Bartholomew House.

Barner, M.R. (1999) 'Sex-role stereotyping in FCC-mandated children's educational television', *Journal of Broadcasting and Electronic Media*, 43 (4): 551-64.

Bernstein, D. (ed.) (1999) *Gender and Motivation*. Lincoln, NE: University of Nebraska Press.

Brenner, O., Tomkiewicz, J. and Schein, V.E. (1989) 'The relationship between sex role stereotypes and requisite managerial characteristics revisited', *Academy of Management Journal*, 32 (3): 662-9.

Brett, Jeanne and Stroh, Linda K. (1994): 'Turnover of female managers', in Davidson, Marilyn J. and Burke, Ronald J. (eds) *Women In Management: Current Research Issues*. London: Paul Chapman. pp. 55-64.

Brindle, David (1996) 'Mythical "new man" hard at work', *Guardian*, 4 (Nov): 2.

Browne, B.A. (1998) 'Gender stereotypes in advertising on children's television in the 1990s: a cross-national analysis', *Journal of Advertising*, 27 (1): 83-97.

Buchanan, D. and Huczynski, A. (1997) *Organizational Behaviour: An Introductory Text*. 3rd Edition. London, New York, Toronto: Prentice Hall.

Burgess, D. and Borgida, E. (1997) 'Refining sex-role spillover theory: the role of gender subtypes and harasser attributions', *Social Cognition*, 15 (4): 291-311.

Case, Susan Schick (1994) 'Gender differences in communication and behaviour in organizations', in Davidson, Marilyn and Burke, Ronald (eds) *Women in Management, Current Research Issues*. London: Paul Chapman Publishing. pp. 148-60.

Castro, Ida L. (1997) 'Worth more than we earn: fair pay as a step toward gender equity', *National Forum*, 77 (2): 17-22.

Choi, I., Nisbett, R.E. and Norenzayan, A. (1999) 'Causal attribution across cultures: variation and universality', *Psychological Bulletin,* 125 (1): 47-63.

Chua-Eoan, Howard (2000) 'Black and blue', *Time*, March 6, Canadian Edition. pp. 22-26.

Cockburn, Cynthia (1991) *In the Way of Women: Men's Resistance to Sex Equality in Organizations.* Basingstoke and London: Macmillan.

Collinson, David and Collinson, Margaret (1989) 'The domination of men's sexuality', in Hearn, Jeff, Sheppard, Deborah, Tancred-Sheriff, Peta and Burrell, Gibson (eds) *The Sexuality of Organization.* London: Sage. pp. 91-109.

Collinson, David and Hearn, Jeff (1994) 'Naming men as men: implications for work, organization and management', *Gender, Work and Organization*, 1 (1): 2-22.

Cooper, C.L. and Kirkcaldy, B.D. (1995): 'Executive stereotyping between culture: the British vs German manager', *Journal of Managerial Psychology*, 10 (1): 3-6.

Corcoran-Nantes, Yvonne and Roberts, Ken (1995) '"We've got one of those": the peripheral status of women in male dominated industries', *Gender, Work and Organization*, 2 (1): 21-33.

Cornwall, Andrea and Lindisfarne, Nancy (1994a) 'Introduction to *Dislocating Masculinity: Comparative Ethnographies.* London: Routledge. pp. 1-10.

Cornwall, Andrea and Lindisfarne, Nancy (1994b) 'Dislocating masculinity: gender, power and anthropology', in Cornwall, Andrea and Lindisfarne, Nancy (eds) *Dislocating Masculinity: Comparative Ethnographies.* London: Routledge. pp. 11-47.

Davidson, M. and Friedman, R.A. (1998) 'When excuses don't work: the persistent injustice effect among Black managers', *Administrative Science Quarterly*, 43 (1): 154-83.

Edmondson, C.B. and Conger, J.C. (1995) 'The impact of mode of presentation on gender differences in social perception', *Sex Roles*, 32 (3-4): 169-83.

Falkner, N.H., French, S.A., Jeffery, R.W., NeumarkSztainer, D., Sherwood, N.E. and Morton, N. (1999) 'Mistreatment due to weight: prevalence and sources of perceived mistreatment in women and men', *Obesity* Research, 7 (6): 572-76.

Faludi, Susan (1992) *Backlash: The Undeclared War Against Women.* London: Vintage.

Furnham, A. and Mak, T. (1999) 'Sex-role stereotyping in television commercials: a review and comparison of fourteen studies done on five continents over 25 years', *Sex Roles*, 41 (5-6): 413-37.

Gale, A. and Cartwright, S. (1995) 'Women in project management: entry into a male domain?: a discussion on gender and organizational culture – part 1', *Leadership and Organization Development Journal*, 16 (2): 3-8.

Garcia Marques, L. and Mackie, D.M. (1999) 'The impact of stereotype-incongruent information on perceived group variability and stereotype change', *Journal of Personality and Social Psychology*, 77 (5): 979-90.

Garrett, Stephanie (1987) *Gender.* London: Routledge.

Gershuny, Jonathan (1996) 'From gemstone to millstone', *Times Higher Education Supplement*, 2 August, No. 1239: 16-17.

Gomez, J.P. and Trierweiler, S.J. (1999) 'Exploring cross-group discrimination: measuring the dimensions of inferiorization', *Journal of Applied Social Psychology*, 29 (9): 1900-26.

Guo, X.H., Erber, J.T. and Szuchman, L.T. (1999) 'Age and forgetfulness: can stereotypes be modified?', *Educational Gerontology*, 25 (5): 457-66.

Gutek, Barbara (1989) 'Sexuality in the workplace: key issues in social research and organizational practice', in Hearn, Jeff, Sheppard, Deborah, Tancred-Sheriff, Peta and

Burrell, Gibson (eds) *The Sexuality of Organization.* London, Newbury Park, New Delhi: Sage. pp. 56-70.

Guthrie, C. (1999) 'Nurses perceptions of sexuality relating to patient care', *Journal of Clinical Nursing*, 8 (3): 313-21.

Hadjistavropoulos, T., LaChapelle, D., Hale, C. and MacLeod, F.K. (2000) 'Age- and appearance-related stereotypes about patients undergoing a painful medical procedure', *Pain Clinic*, 12 (1): 25-33.

Hale, Mary (1999) 'He says, she says: gender and worklife', *Public Administration Review*, 59 (I5): 410.

Heesacker, M., Webster, S.R., Vogel, D.L., Wentzel, J.T., MejiaMillan, C.M. and Goodholm, C.R. (1999) 'Gender-based emotional stereotyping', *Journal of Counseling Psychology*, 46 (4): 483-95.

Heilman, M.E. (1997) 'Sex discrimination and the affirmative action remedy: the role of sex stereotypes', *Journal of Business Ethics*, 16 (9): 877-89.

Hull, R.P. and Umansky, P.H. (1997) 'An examination of gender stereotyping in public accounting', *Accounting, Organizations and Society*, 22 (6): 7-28.

Iles, Paul (1992) *Managing Assessment and Selection Processes,* Unit 8 of B884 Human Resource Strategies, Block 4, Personnel Strategies, Open University, Milton Keynes.

Jackson, Charles and Hirsh, Wendy (1991) 'Women managers and career progression: the British experience', *Women in Management Review and Abstracts*, 6 (2): 10-16.

Kanter, R.M. (1977) *Men and Women of the Corporation.* USA: Basic Books.

Karpf, A. (1994) 'Making airwaves', *The Guardian*, 17 October. p. 2.13.

Kaufman, G. (1999) 'The portrayal of men's family roles in television commercials', *Sex Roles*, 41 (5-6): 439-58.

Kerfoot, Deborah and Knights, David (1993) 'Management, masculinity and manipulation: from paternalism to corporate strategy in financial services in Britain', *Journal of Management Studies*, 30 (4): 659-77.

Kobrynowicz, D. (1998) 'Stealthy stereotypes: revealing the ubiquitous but hidden effects of gender stereotypes on judgments of individuals', *Dissertation Abstracts International: Section B: The Sciences and Engineering*, 58 (10-B): 5699.

Koncius, Jura (1997) 'A man's place is in the home - but only if chores are mechanised', *Guardian*, 18 February. p. 13.

Krull, D.S., Loy, M.H.M., Lin, J., Wang, C.F., Chen, S.H. and Zhao, X.D. (1999) 'The fundamental attribution error: correspondence bias in individualist and collectivist cultures', *Personality and Social Psychology Bulletin*, 25 (10): 1208-19.

Kunda, Z. and Sinclair, L. (1999) 'Motivated reasoning with stereotypes: activation, application, and inhibition', *Psychological Inquiry*, 10 (1): 12-22.

Lewis, Suzan (1994) 'Role tensions and dual career couples', in Davidson, Marilyn J. and Burke, Ronald J. (eds) *Women In Management: Current Research Issues.* London: Paul Chapman. pp. 230-41.

Lorber, Judith and Farrell, Susan A. (1991) *The Social Construction of Gender.* London: Sage.

Marshall, Judi (1984) *Women Managers: Travellers in a Male World.* Wiley: Chichester.

McShane, Steven L. (1999) *Canadian Organizational Behaviour.* 3rd Edition. Toronto: McGraw-Hill Ryerson.

Menon, T., Morris, M.W., Chiu, C.Y. and Hong, Y.Y. (1999) 'Culture and the construal of agency: attribution to individual versus group dispositions', *Journal of Personality and Social Psychology*, 76 (5): 701-17.

Mills, A.J. (1994) 'The gendering of organizational culture: social and organizational discourses in the making of British Airways', in DesRosiers, M. (ed.) *Administrative Sciences Association of Canada, Women in Management Division*, 15, Halifax, Nova Scotia: ASAC. pp. 11-20.

Mills, A.J. (1995a) 'Managing subjectivity, silencing diversity: organizational imagery in the airline industry – the case of British Airways', *Organization*, 2 (2): 243-69.

Mills, A.J. (1995b) 'Practice makes perfect: corporate practices, bureaucratization and the idealized gendered self'. Paper presented at the 13th annual Standing Conference on Organizational Symbolism (SCOS), in Turku, Finland.

Mills, A.J. (1996a) 'Corporate image, gendered subjects and the company newsletter – the changing faces of British Airways', in Palmer, G. and Clegg, S. (eds), *Constituting Management: Markets, Meanings And Identities*. Berlin: de Gruyter. pp. 191-211.

Mills, A.J. (1996b) 'Strategy, sexuality and the stratosphere: airlines and the gendering of organization', in Lyon, E.S. and Morris, L. (eds), *Gender Relations In Public and Private: New Research Perspectives*. London: Macmillan. pp. 77-94.

Mills, A.J. (1997a) 'Duelling discourses – desexulization versus eroticism in the corporate framing of female sexuality in the British airline industry, 1945-60', in Prasad, P., Mills, A.J., Elmes, M. and Prasad, A. (eds), *Managing The Organizational Melting Pot: Dilemmas of Workplace Diversity*. Newbury Park, CA: Sage.

Mills, A.J. (1997b) 'Practice makes perfect: corporate practices, bureaucratization and the idealized gendered self', *Hallinnon Tutkimus (Finnish Journal of Administrative Studies*, (4): 272-88.

Mills, A.J. (1998) 'Cockpits, hangars, boys and galleys: corporate masculinities and the development of British Airways', *Gender, Work and Organization*, 5 (3): 172-88.

Mills, A. and Hatfield, J. (1999) 'From Imperialism to Globalization: Internationalization and the Management Text', in Clegg, S.R., Ibarra, E. and Bueno, L. (eds) *Global Management: Universal Theories and Local Realities*, London: Sage, pp. 37-67.

Mills, Albert J. and Murgatroyd, Stephen, J. (1991*) Organizational Rules: A Framework for Understanding Organizational Action*. Milton Keynes: Open University Press.

Moscovici, S. and Mugny, G. (1983) 'Minority influence', in Paulus, P. B. (ed.) *Basic Group Processes*. New York: Springer Verlag.

Mullins, Laurie J. and Hicks, Linda (1999) 'The process of perception', in Mullins, Laurie J. (ed.) *Management and Organizational Behaviour*. 5th Edition. London, San Francisco: Financial Times/Pitman Publishing. pp. 376-448.

Myles, C. (1997) 'Fording the mainstream: moving out of niche marketing isn't always easy for minority professionals', *Washington Business Journal*, 16 (14): 19-21.

Nation's Restaurant News (1996) 'When it comes to women execs, industry has a long way to go, baby', (restaurant industry), (editorial), 30 (10): 27.

Norenzayan, A. and Schwarz, N. (1999) 'Telling what they want to know: participants tailor causal attributions to researchers' interests', *European Journal of Social Psychology*, 29 (8): 1011-20.

Norris, J.M. and Wylie, A.M. (1995) 'Gender stereotyping of the managerial role among students in Canada and the United States', *Group and Organization Management*, 20 (2): 167-82.

Oberweis, T. and Musheno, M. (1999) 'Policing identities: cop decision making and the constitution of citizens', *Law and Social Inquiry – Journal of the American Bar Foundation*, 24 (4): 897-923.

Olesen, M. (1999): 'What makes employees stay', *Training and Development*, 53 (10): 48-53.

Pope, J. and Meyer, R. (1999) 'An attributional analysis of jurors' judgments in a criminal case: a preliminary investigation', *Social Behaviour and Personality*, 27 (6): 563-74.

Recruitment and Development Report (1991) 'The state of selection - 1. Current practice and main results', *Industrial Relations Review and Report* 16, 26 April: 2-5.

Reskin, Barbara F.(1991) 'Bringing the men back in: sex differentiation and the devaluation of women's work', in Lorber, Judith and Farrell, Susan (eds) *The Social Construction of Gender.* London: Sage. pp. 141-61.

Rickford, F. (1999) 'Women's work', *The Guardian*, 11 August, p. S9.

Roper, Michael (1994) *Masculinity and the British Organization Man since 1945.* Oxford: Oxford University Press.

Rosenfeld, Robert H. and Wilson, David C. (1999) *Managing Organizations: Text, Readings and Cases.* London, New York: McGrawHill.

Ruggiero, K.M. and Marx, D.M. (1999) 'Less pain and more to gain: why high-status group members blame their failure on discrimination', *Journal of Personality and Social Psychology*, 77 (4): 774-84.

Saigol, Lina (1996) 'Myth of "new man" hides blight on families', *Guardian Jobs and Money*, 9 November. p. 18.

Schein, Virginia (1973) 'The relationship between sex-role stereotypes and requisite management characteristics', *Journal of Applied Psychology*, 57 (2): 95-100.

Schein, Virginia (1975) 'Relationships between sex-role stereotypes and requisite management characteristics among female managers', *Journal of Applied Psychology*, 60 (3): 330-44.

Schein, Virginia (1994) 'Managerial sex typing: a persistent and pervasive barrier to women's opportunities', in Davidson, Marilyn J. and Burke, Ronald J. (eds) *Women In Management: Current Research Issues.* London: Paul Chapman. pp. 41-54.

Seligman, D. (1997) 'In defense of stereotypes', *Forbes*, 160 (12): 112-113.

Sheppard, Deborah L. (1989) 'Organizations, power and sexuality: the image and self-image of women managers', in Hearn, Jeff, Sheppard, Deborah, Tancred-Sheriff, Peta and Burrell, Gibson (eds) *The Sexuality of Organization.* London, Newbury Park, New Delhi: Sage. pp. 139-57.

Sidney, Elizabeth (1994) 'Dragging a ball and chain: moving to equal opportunity in the NHS', *International Journal of Selection and* Assessment, 2 (3) July: 176-85.

Soutar, G.N., Grainger, R. and Hedges, P. (1999) 'Australian and Japanese value stereotypes: a two country study', *Journal of International Business Studies*, 30 (1): 203-16.

Squires, T.E. (1995) 'Men in nursing', *RN*, 58 (7): 26-28.

Stanley, Liz and Wise, Sue (1993) *Breaking Out Again: Feminist Ontology and Epistemology.* 2nd Edition. London: Routledge.

Stone, D.L. and Colella, A. (1996) 'A model of factors affecting the treatment of disabled individuals in organizations', *Academy of Management Review*, 21 (2): 352-401. Special Topic Forum on Diversity within and Among Organizations.

Tannen, Deborah (1995) *Talking From 9 to 5: How Women's and Men's Conversational Styles Affects Who Gets Heard, Who Gets Credit, and What Gets Done at Work.* London: Virago.

Tobena, A., Marks, I. and Dar, R. (1999) 'Advantage of bias and prejudice: an exploration of their neurocognitive templates', *Neuroscience and Biobehavioural Reviews*, November, 23 (7): 1047-58.

Truss, C., Goffee, R. and Jones, G. (1995) 'Segregated occupations and gender stereotyping: a study of secretarial work in Europe', *Human Relations*, 48 (11): 1331-54.

van Heerden, J. (1999) 'Explaining misattribution', *New Ideas in Psychology*, 17 (1): 67-70.

Wilson, Fiona (1995) *Organizational Behaviour and Gender.* London, New York: McGraw Hill.

Ybarra, O. and Stephan, W.G. (1999) 'Attributional orientations and the prediction of behaviour: the attribution-prediction bias', *Journal of Personality and Social Psychology*, 76 (5): 718-27.

4   Communication

Sue Newell

Introduction

Communication, by definition implies a relationship – we communicate with others. Communication is central to the existence of organizations, even in animal communities, although it is often not until there has been some breakdown in communication that its centrality becomes apparent. For example, losing a vital employee because no one communicated to her how important she was to the organization, either in words ('well done, you are doing a great job') or deeds (pay increase).

This chapter will begin by considering the concept of communication itself and will review models and metaphors that help us to explore communication and its influence in organizational settings. The next section in the chapter will look at how traditional OB textbooks present the topic of communication. It will be shown that some of the important communication issues which explain women's relative lack of power and influence within organizations have been ignored by this mainstream body of literature, despite considerable research and theory from a feminist perspective which demonstrates the link. Finally, the chapter will turn to those issues, which become fundamental to understanding communication from a gendered perspective, that is the issue of language and the relationship between gender, communication and power.

A review of mainstream theories

Definition: models

Communication is derived from the Latin work 'communis', which means common. To communicate means literally for two or more people to come to a common understanding, that is to derive shared meaning about something, be it a person, an object, or an event. Common understanding comes from common experiences and reflection about those experiences, which leads to a shared understanding of reality. For example, a friend recently related a story to me concerning her daughter's confusion over the title 'Ms'. My friend, who is divorced and using her maiden name was recently having to sign lots of documents in relation to a new mortgage. Her eight-year-old daughter finally burst out, very upset, demanding to know why her mother was letting everyone know that she was divorced. She had come to understand that 'Ms' was the term used to describe a woman following a divorce – with 'Mrs.' confined to women who were married and 'Miss' to unmarried women. The confusion in this example was only possible because the meaning of 'Ms' had never been fully discussed with the child, although she clearly believed she 'knew' what it meant. What this example demonstrates is the importance of meaning in communication. Meaning is created between people over time through interaction. However, this example also provides an insight into the gendered nature of much of our language. There are no labels that 'give away' the marital status of men, only of women. As Spender (1985) notes, labelling women as married or single serves sexist aims because it indicates who is likely to be 'fair game'. In turn, this perpetuates the propensity of men to make the 'first move' in a relationship, reinforcing the stereotype of the dominant male and submissive female.

Early models of communication totally failed to capture the importance of meaning. They were linear models, depicting a sender and a receiver. For example, the Shannon and Weaver (1949) model, while it replaced earlier structural approaches by recognizing the importance of process, still depicted communication as a linear flow of information and was very mechanistic and overly rationalistic.

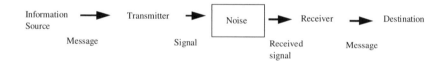

Figure 4.1 Model of the communication process from C.E. Shannon and W. Weaver (1949) *The Mathematical Theory of Communication.* Copyright 1949 by the Board of Trustees of the University of Illinois. Used with permission of the University of Illinois Press.

In this model there is some active source who is seeking to affect a passive receiver. Research thus concentrates on studying the effects of communication on the receiver's knowledge, attitudes or behaviour (the dependent variable). The source, message, channel and/or receiver variables are manipulated as independent variables to see what effect this has on the dependent variable. The problem with this model is that sending and receiving information is not communication. It is a necessary but insufficient condition for communication to take place.

Later models developed from this, recognizing the ongoing, dynamic and continuous nature of communication. A good example of this is the model developed by Berlo (1960).

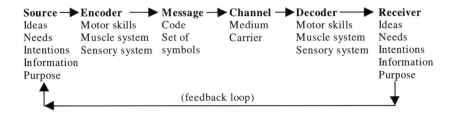

Figure 4.2 Model of the communication process, adapted from D. Berlo (1960) *The Process of Communication*, New York, Holt. Used with the permission of Harcourt Brace and Company.

While this model does capture more adequately the processual nature of communication, it still stresses a source and a receiver, and depicts communication as a process that occurs between two or more people. It still fails to capture the negotiation process whereby shared meaning is established. It continues to distinguish between a sender and a receiver. On the other hand, the convergence model of Rogers and Kincaid (1981) sees communication as a continuous process, with people engaged simultaneously in sharing information with one another in order to achieve some common purpose such as mutual understanding or collective action. Each person is thus reciprocally affecting the other in a process of mutual causation leading to understanding, consensus and collective action. For example, I might be communicating to a group of students via a lecture but they are simultaneously communicating back to me, (e.g. their level of interest in the subject by their non-verbal (and at times verbal!) communication behaviour). This captures much better the essence of communication. When we communicate with someone we are trying to establish a 'commonness' with him/her: 'Effective communication is about agreements, unities, common goods and common concerns' (Reilly and DiAngelo, 1990: 139). The goal is understanding such that the meaning of the message is exactly what it was intended to be. This does not imply that X (person one) has to agree with Y (person two) but that X understands Y's point of view. Understanding and agreement are not necessarily related.

The convergence model of communication stresses that the major barrier to effective communication is the tendency to evaluate and judge. Effective communication is achieved through active listening (Rogers and Rothlisberger, 1952). Without this positive orientation on each side of the message process, the ability to perceive value in the other and understand that person's significance and meaning, there is no hope for mutual understanding. Yet the reality in most organizations is that of separation and competition which denies the integrating and contributing contexts of the communication process. So every message is filtered by self-interest. Thus, for example, functional organizational structures promote communication barriers between departments, which encourage individuals within a particular department to view people in other departments as potential competitors, rather than as allies within the larger organization.

What we could say is that the Shannon and Weaver model above (Figure 4.1) depicts the process of information exchange: one person exchanges information with another. Whether or not this will achieve communication, that is a common understanding, depends on how far those involved in the exchange confer the same meaning on the words or symbols used. Where two people will, without discussion, read the same meaning into a set of words, information exchange is sufficient to establish communication. Where two people come from very different backgrounds there will need to be a process of mutual interaction in order to come to that common understanding. This is especially relevant since the feminist literature has tended to stress that males and females come from different backgrounds (see below) such that they actually speak different languages. So, given that those in positions of power are more likely to be men from similar backgrounds, communication can be achieved by relatively straightforward information flows, at least within this group. Women will find it difficult to break into this group, because of the communication barriers that exist between men and women. Kanter (1989) confirmed this in her study of Indsco. Given the time pressures, which the managers (all men) in her study faced, communication often had to be rapid as well as reach many different people within the management hierarchy. Acceptance and ease of communication was ensured by limiting managerial jobs to those who were homogenous, both in terms of social background and gender. This made it possible to avoid communication with people where it was likely to be difficult or problematic. The male managers in her study decidedly placed communication with women in the category of 'difficult' (Kanter, 1989).

Definition: metaphors

Although models, as used in traditional science, may be helpful in developing our understanding of a phenomenon, more recently methods borrowed from arts and humanities have also been adopted by those seeking to understand organizational behaviour. In particular metaphors have been found to be useful as a way of recognizing the essence of a given phenomenon (Hatch, 1997). Metaphor allows us to understand one kind of experience in terms of another by suggesting an identity between the two things, which would not normally be considered as equivalent. Using metaphors allows us to understand something abstract (communication) in terms of something which is more concrete (glue and water, see below). Because the properties of the concrete are more familiar we can learn something about the abstract. There are two metaphors that may be helpful in trying to understand communication within organizations. One metaphor, which has been used in the past, is to depict communication as 'glue'. Katz and Kahn (1978) originally used this metaphor back in the 1970s.

Glue suggests something planned and structured – gluing bits together in order to make or create some intended object. If the created form does not work effectively you can try another approach and glue the bits together in different ways or even glue on new bits.

The glue metaphor, however, suggested a very structural understanding of communication. An alternative, more processual metaphor could be to see communication as 'water'. The known properties of water provide us with some interesting insights. Water flows naturally, finding its own course across the land, unless channelled artificially (e.g. through a canal). Water is life-giving, a basic life requirement. Communication is essentially the creation of meaning, produced through language and interaction. We can attempt to control water and water availability (e.g. through building damns and reservoirs) but this will always be only partial as evidenced by recurrent droughts and floods. So, communication is all pervasive, it cannot be controlled as it penetrates the very meaning of life.

An illustration of these two different metaphors 'in action' can be seen in the comparison of two opposing views of the selection interview (Newell and Rice, 1999). An interview clearly involves communication between a candidate and an interviewer, but there are different ways of characterizing this communication. The traditional view of the interview is as a structured interrogation to assess which of a set of candidates has the required attributes for a particular job. This assumes that there is a particular 'type' of person needed to do a particular job. What the candidate says in the interview situation is used to infer whether they are indeed this 'type'. The key to a successful interview is then to ensure that the interviewer structures the communication so that each candidate is exposed to identical questions. In this way, fair and reliable comparisons can be made between the various candidates. The alternative, negotiation view (Herriot, 1984), assumes that there are multiple ways to carry out a particular job and that individuals are shaped by the situations in which they find themselves, rather than having fixed attributes. From this perspective, the interview is an opportunity for exchange and negotiation between the candidate and the interviewer to see whether there is any possibility for a 'fit', which will be satisfying to both sides. The interview is then understood as a relationship in which both parties are attempting to make sense of the other through communication.

The two metaphors thus present very different images of communication. One (glue) suggests planning and control, epitomized in the traditional view of communication within a selection interview, while the other (water) suggests something natural, life-giving and ultimately uncontrollable, epitomized in the negotiation view of the interview. It is useful to keep these two images in mind as we look at how academics have researched and written about organizational communication. Traditional writers in the OB area have tended to treat communication as 'glue', thus focusing on structure rather than meaning.

Communication in conventional OB textbooks

As a starting point for this chapter I went to look at what was covered in the wide array of organizational behaviour/organizational psychology textbooks I have collected on my shelves over the years (e.g. Arnold et al., 1991; Hellriegel et al., 1989; Huczynski and Buchanan, 1991; Luthans, 1992; Martin, 1998; McKenna, 1994; Moorhead and Griffin, 1998; Mullins, 1993; Wilson and Rosenfeld, 1990). Interestingly, while virtually all of these included somewhere within the text the idea that communication was crucial for organizations, many did not have a chapter dedicated to the topic. However, there was, in most, considerable space devoted to the topic. Chester Barnard (1938) was the first management writer to meaningfully develop communication as a vital dynamic of organizational behaviour. He was convinced that communication was the major shaping force in the organization:

> In an exhaustive theory of organization, communication would occupy a central place, because the structure, extensiveness and scope of organization are almost entirely determined by communication techniques (1938: 91).

We can consider the main areas of communication research by looking at four distinct themes, which are commonly covered: content, direction, network, noise and barriers.

Communication content

Communication between two or more people is usually about something, so there needs to be a consideration of the reasons for communicating. Thus, communication takes place in organizations for example, to reduce uncertainty, solve problems, confirm beliefs, control the situation or to provide feedback. There is an acknowledgement in many of the OB textbooks cited above that the choice of words and the accompanying non-verbal gestures are important, such that the content of the message conveys much more information than just the textbook definition of the words. However, there is rarely consideration of the more general issue of language and in particular the gendered nature of communication content. Yet, in the feminist literature, differences in communication content and style between men and women have been a dominant interest: 'Not only do men and women communicate differently but they think, feel, perceive, react, respond, love, need, and appreciate differently. They almost seem to be on different planets' (Gray, 1992: 5).

Initial interest in this theme of gendered language began in the 1970s when substantial research was undertaken to identify linguistic and stylistic differences between men and women. Differences in pronunciation, grammar, vocabulary, syntax, hesitancy, non-assertion and so on were studied in order to uncover differences between male and female speakers (West and Zimmerman,

1985). The most prominent writer from this era was Robin Lakoff who first talked about 'women's language' in an article in *Language in Society* in 1973. She went on to develop her ideas which culminated in her influential book *Language and Women's Place* (1975). In this book Lakoff suggests that there are a distinct group of features which distinguish the speech of women from the speech of men. These include:

1. Specialized vocabulary. Men and women, Lakoff argues, have traditionally specialized in different areas and within these specialisms each have developed their own more precise and richer vocabulary which is not used nor accessible to the other sex.
2. Expletives. Women are characterized as using milder forms of expletives ('Oh, dear!'), men stronger ones ('Oh, shit!').
3. Empty adjectives. This refers to adjectives that convey an emotional reaction ('cute cat') rather than any information ('black cat'). Lakoff argues that only women use many of these 'empty' adjectives.
4. Tag questions. A tag question refers to the use of a question tag at the end of a statement: 'It's very expensive, *isn't it?*' Lakoff concluded that women tend to use more tag questions at the end of statements expressing their own opinions, conveying the impression of uncertainty and lack of conviction. On the other hand, men, by avoiding the use of such 'tags' convey the impression of certainty, confidence and dictatorial tendencies.
5. Intonation. Women use a wider range of pitch and intonation and are more likely to exaggerate their expressions. Again, the effect of this, Lakoff argued, was to convey indecision and uncertainty.
6. 'Superpolite' forms. Women's speech was said to demonstrate much more polite ways of making requests than men's: 'I wonder if you would mind passing me the sugar, please'.

Lakoff concluded that these distinguishing speech features amounted to a recognizable style of speaking, that is a woman's language. More importantly, she argued that the effect of this woman's speech style was largely negative. It was a style that tended to imply powerlessness on the part of the users (i.e. women), since it portrayed confusion, deference and uncertainty. She further argued that women use this style, despite changes in the position of women in society. This is because their early socialization instills in them a sense of incompetence and 'learned helplessness' (Seligman, 1975). Women's language, Lakoff claimed, allows them to maintain non-responsibility for their actions, which is the product of such learned helplessness. By implication, Lakoff is arguing that this woman's language is inferior to its opposite, man's language. Men use a language style that implies powerfulness, since it portrays certainty and authority.

Lakoff's work was based on her own intuition rather than empirical data collection. Her work, however, stimulated considerable interest and many studies were undertaken to find systematic evidence for her claims. Despite this effort, results have been inconclusive and as Crawford (1995) points out it is possible to find support for either the claim that the differences are reliable and important (Mulac et al., 1988) or minimal (Graddol and Swann, 1989).

Despite this lack of empirical evidence, the accepted wisdom of Lakoff's (1975) conclusions led to a concentration on training women to overcome this suggested negative style. The assertiveness bandwagon was thus begun. Ruben (1985) estimated that between 1973 and 1983 there were 892 journal articles, 664 dissertations, 34 educational films and 82 books, totalling 1672 publications devoted to encouraging women (since the majority of these publications were specifically aimed at women) to become more assertive and so adopt a more effective communication style. That is, the aim of this assertiveness training was to encourage women to stop using inferior 'woman's language' and start to use the superior 'man's language' instead. The general theme of this work was that, through socialization women have learnt to be helpless, and this is reflected in their generally negative speech style which results in a lack of assertiveness in their communication behaviour. So, through assertiveness training, the idea was that women could learn to take back personal control and behave responsibly and act decisively.

A criticism of this assertiveness movement was that it considered only one side of the problem. Women might need assertiveness training to counter socialized passivity, but equally men may need training to counter socialized insensitivity and aggression. The assertiveness movement ignored this, putting the onus squarely on women to 'improve' their communication style because it was women's style that was seen to be inadequate, not men's. However, the acknowledgement of this one-sided approach led to the development of what was called the 'two-cultures' approach (Maltz and Borker, 1982), which proposed that men and women find it difficult to communicate with each other because they come from very different cultural backgrounds. The 'fault' was on neither side, but rather on both. Communication between men and women was seen to have the same potential for misunderstanding as communication between people from different ethnic groups. As seen, communication must rely on shared assumptions. Where these assumptions are not shared, miscommunication will occur (Maltz and Borker, 1982).

The two-cultures approach considers that women have problems in communicating 'in a man's world', not because of deficiencies in women's speech, but as a result of deeply ingrained cultural differences between males and females. These differences are the result of very different socialization experiences. In particular the differences are seen to be the outcome of the 'voluntary' choices made by boys and girls to play in single-sex groups. For example, Maltz and Borker (1982) argue that girls and boys learn to do different things during play. Girls learn to create and maintain relationships with others on an equal basis, to avoid direct criticism of others, and to be sensitive to their playmates. On the other hand, boys in play learn to be dominant and assert themselves, to try and get others to listen to them rather than listen sensitively to others, and to interrupt others when they are talking

(Maltz and Borker, 1982). Indeed, recent research by Skuse (1997) suggests that these differences between the play behaviour of boys and girls are the result of genetic differences. Skuse argues that women have a particular gene, which makes them responsive to others and able to recognize social norms without prompting. Men can learn these skills but they do not come naturally.

The most popular rendition of this two-cultures approach was written by Gray (1992), in his book titled *Men are from Mars, Women are from Venus*. In this book, every aspect of male and female behaviour is polarized. Women and men are seen as so fundamentally different that they need a translator to enable them to communicate with each other. Similarly, Deborah Tannen's book *You Just Don't Understand: Women and Men in Conversation* (1990), presents a view of men and women living in different worlds, and, in consequence using different speech styles; men use 'report talk' and women 'rapport talk'. In both texts, the writers make clear that while miscommunication between men and women is inevitable, no one is to blame for this. The solution is for men and women to learn to understand each other, rather than change to accommodate the other's style. This is because the differences in communication style are seen to be the result of deeply ingrained attitudes and beliefs instilled over a long period, which would be almost impossible to change.

This two-cultures approach is thus a step beyond the original gender difference approach because it examines the behaviour of men as well as women. Women are no longer simply compared to men and found wanting. Aspects of women's speech can be re-evaluated positively and aspects of men's speech re-evaluated negatively. For example, using tag questions may not be a sign of insecurity on the part of the speaker (as Lakoff (1975) would suggest), but a positive attempt to involve the listener in the discussion. Likewise, men's propensity to interrupt during conversation may be seen as a sign of a closed mind (unable to be open to other points of view), rather than as a sign of assertiveness. From the two-cultures approach, both speech styles are said to occur naturally as a result of different socialization experiences which themselves are the inevitable outcome of natural tendencies to choose to play with members of the same sex. The different communication styles are simply a reflection of the different identities assumed by men and women; women as nurturing and caring and men as dominant and assertive.

While this two-cultures approach is potentially empowering for women, since it values women's way of communicating as valuable in its own right, it can also be criticized for being overly-reductionist. It creates a simple dichotomy between men and women. Such a dualism between men and women neglects the complexities within each gender, ignoring differences based on age, class, ethnicity, religion, nationality and so on. As such, it solidifies stereotypes about male and female differences, which is not helpful (Nichols, 1993). Moreover, what this two-cultures approach continues to ignore is issues of power and status. Thus, it fails to explain why girls should choose to assume a gendered identity that is associated with powerlessness and devaluation (Unger and Crawford, 1992). As Crawford writes: 'It does not take into account the coercion, persuasion, and closing of options that underlie girls' acceptance of their subordinate status' (1995: 95). That is, to accept that communication differences are the result of different socialization experiences fails to consider the processes through which gender identities are interactively produced through day-to-day relationships. It is the existence of gendered relations of power that are continuously reproduced through interactions that is the key to understanding. To focus on the differences between boys and girls in play per se, ignores the embedded power relations within society, which infuse our interactions and create the conditions through which these differences are reproduced (see below).

To summarize, many traditional OB textbooks do acknowledge that the content of communication is important, and make the distinction between the surface and deep levels of meaning. However, they fail to take this further and consider how gender relations influence this process of 'making meaning'. Feminists on the other hand, have expended considerable effort trying to establish how the content and style of male and female communication is very different. Until recently, however, this work has treated these communication differences as the result of 'natural' differences in the socialization experiences of boys and girls. These different socialization experiences lead to the formation of gender specific identities, which in turn lead to differences in style of communication. The problem with this approach is that it ignores the relationship between these observed communication differences and structural and institutional power and status realities. McConnell-Ginet (1980) and Nichols (1980), for example, both argue that women draw upon different communication strategies and use different linguistic resources *because* of their relatively powerless social situations and social relations. This implies that we need to treat gender as an effect rather than as a cause of communication. Gender differences are not the cause of communication differences between men and women, rather communication is the medium through which gendered relations of power are reproduced (Mumby, 1996). This will be dealt with more fully in the final section of this chapter.

Communication direction

Communication is involved in basic organizational co-ordination. The two primary characteristics of organizations are differentiation and integration. That is, tasks within organizations are divided up (differentiation), so even in relatively small organizations there is some element of job specialization; one person makes the product while another person sells it and another keeps the books. As organizations grow, so this specialization increases. But, with different people doing different things, there is a clear need to co-ordinate efforts (integration). It is no good the sales specialist selling 100 'widgets' a week if the production specialist is making only 50. The question considered is how this co-ordination is achieved and the focus is on the direction of communication (vertical and/or lateral).

In terms of formal communication, the point is that organizations are designed in ways that specify who may and may not communicate with whom. The organization chart (the organigram) depicts the formally prescribed pattern of inter-relationships existing between the various units of an organization. The lines of authority depicted on the chart show the pathways through which messages are supposed to flow within the organization. In terms of vertical communication, instructions or directions are passed down the organizational hierarchy and information on the impact of implementing these instructions then comes back up the chain at some later point in time. This communication is therefore one-way communication (i.e. information transfer). Being one-way there is no assurance that the 'commonness' has been achieved. While this is acknowledged as a problem for organizational communication it is also recognized that formal communication in organizations is supplemented by informal communication, which is much more likely to be two-way and interactive.

Informal communication within organizations depends on the network of relationships between people that arises spontaneously. Informal communication between members of this network can then supplement the formal communication. This informal communication is commonly referred to as 'the grapevine' and tends to be word of mouth. The grapevine can transmit rumour and gossip, as well as authentic information (McKenna, 1994), but is typically seen as having beneficial effects (Zaremba, 1988). However, given that the grapevine tends to be strong among those who work together and given that men and women have traditionally worked in ways which are both horizontally and vertically segregated (Newell, 1995), grapevines are likely to be highly gendered. That is, grapevines are likely to be either all men or all women but rarely a mix. Such informal communication can, therefore, perpetuate the status and power inequalities within organizations (Coe, 1992).

More importantly, taking a gendered perspective, what many of the traditional OB textbooks do not consider are any alternative ways of organizing. There is an implicit acceptance that hierarchical power structures are a necessary condition for achieving co-ordination in work organizations. The feminist literature, on the other hand, has been more involved in a) examining the processes through which women workers attempt to develop autonomous spheres of culture and identity within existing organizational settings and b) considering the development of alternative organizational forms devoted specifically to women's issues. In relation to the first of these issues, for example, Gottfried and Weiss (1994) looked at how a women's faculty at a university created their own collective, non-hierarchical, decision-making system, very different to the traditional hierarchical decision-making systems in existence within the larger bureaucratic organization. They devised the term feminist 'compound' organization as a metaphor to depict multiplicity, allowing women with different perspectives to work together. In relation to the second issue, Marshall (1989) describes organizational heterarchy: 'A heterarchy has no one person or principle in command. Rather, temporary pyramids of authority form as and when appropriate in a system of mutual constraints and influences' (p. 289). Such feminist structures are based on the recognition that mainstream bureaucratic structures are an important locus of male domination and control which must be replaced with participative and egalitarian structures in order to alleviate women's oppression. Both of these approaches thus demonstrate alternatives to the traditional linear and hierarchical communication structure, which is not gender-neutral, and which are rarely discussed in the traditional OB literature. These feminist alternatives to organizing highlight the possibilities for resisting and overcoming patriarchal institutional forms (Mumby, 1996). Organizational design is discussed more fully in Dale (in this volume).

Communication networks

Communication networks are a structural aspect of a group. They tell us how the group is hung together. Networks are considered to establish which 'shape' is most effective for solving problems and generally facilitate group performance. Research here has focused on how different communication patterns influence group performance in solving a problem. For example, Shaw (1978) conducted a laboratory experiment in which 5-person groups were arranged in one of 4 different ways (see Figure 4.3).

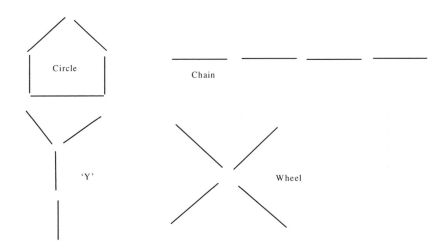

Figure 4.3 Communication networks used in research, taken from M.E. Shaw (1978), 'Communication networks fourteen years later'. Used with permission of Academic Press, USA.

Each person in the group had some information which was needed for the group to be able to solve the problem. The information had to be shared with the rest of the group. He found that the centralized networks (wheel and 'Y'), where group members were forced to go through the central person in order to communicate with others, were quicker at solving the problem but periphery members were less satisfied. The more decentralized networks (circle and chain) were slower at solving the problem but members were more satisfied. Subsequent research has found that centralized networks are only quicker for simple tasks. Where the task becomes more complex, the centralized network is slower as the central person becomes overloaded and unable to cope with all the information which is being channelled his/her way. Decentralized networks can cope better with this complexity as members can share the information load (Baron and Greenberg, 1990: 348).

What is not covered in many of the traditional OB textbooks is any discussion about how these communication networks have a differential impact on the experience of men and women in the organization. Belonging to networks has long been recognized as important for organizational success. The saying 'it is not what you know, but who you know' clearly has some basis in reality. Initially, the key will be belonging to informal networks where key organizational members belong, for example the golf club. Belonging to such informal networks allows people to develop an 'intelligence or communication base' (Coe, 1992), which might help them to penetrate the formal positions. Indeed, in the research by Coe (1992), which included data from a large sample of female managers in the UK, the old boys network was identified as the single biggest barrier to their career progression, ahead of domestic juggling and stereotypes. Ibarra (1993) describes a slightly different picture in the advertising agency, which she was studying. Females had been successful in moving into senior positions within the company and so were involved in the formal networks. However, what she observed was that these senior women did not find these formal networks very supportive interpersonally and so these women got involved in a second informal, all-women network, where relationships were important. For the men in senior positions in the organization the formal and informal network was one and the same. The problem for the women was not access to the male network but having to divide time between two networks while for their male counterparts the formal and informal were self-reinforcing.

Communication barriers

Communication barriers occur where individual, group and organizational level variables are linked to breakdowns in communication. Two types of barriers can be identified: interpersonal and structural barriers. Interpersonal barriers relate to perceptual problems, which limit the extent to which the message has the same meaning for the sender and the receiver. So barriers here relate to trust between those engaged in communication, perceptions of influence and power and so on. Structural barriers include hierarchy, which restricts the free flow of communication, specialization which reduces communication between sub-units, and centralization which means that decision makers are too far removed from reality to function effectively.

So if communication is about coming to or creating shared meaning the most crucial communication skill is active listening, that is concentrating on what is being said with empathy and acceptance. McKenna (1994) lists a number of criteria to assess active listening including: establishing eye contact, showing interest in the speaker, e.g. by nodding; avoiding distracting actions or gestures; asking questions; paraphrasing what has been said by others; avoiding interruptions; not talking too much so that the other does not get a chance to speak; and facilitating a smooth transition between the speaker and the listener. There is certainly considerable empirical evidence to support the claim that women are better on virtually all these criteria of active listening than are men. For example, Howard and Bray (1988), found women to be superior to men on a variety of measures related to communication during a selection process: on an oral presentation exercise; on a test of verbal ability; and on a written communication assessment. Similarly, in research which has considered male and female leadership styles, women are said to adopt a much more open style than men (Rosener, 1990; Bass, 1990; Eagly et al., 1992). Gilligan (1982) argues that women managers use a 'different voice' compared to their male counterparts, developing a communication style that encourages participation, shares information and power, and enhances the self-worth of subordinates. That is, they adopt a style based on supportiveness, empathy, sharing and listening that is more conducive to creating effective communication (Gilligan, 1982).

Research such as this emphasizes 'differences' between men and women and uses these differences to explain behaviour. The main problem with such a 'difference' approach, as already discussed, is that it under-theorizes issues of communication, power, and identity (Fairhurst, 1993; Mumby, 1996). While these studies typically view gender as being constructed through socialization processes, they do not consider

> (how) such social constructions occur through gendered relations of power that are communicatively produced, resisted, and potentially transformed; as such gender is taken as a given and non-problematic (Mumby, 1996: 273).

Thus, considering communication barriers from a gendered perspective, we need to understand that

> The critical heartland for the understanding of communication is not what is visible but rather what is invisible and hidden. Forms and messages are secondary to pre-defined meanings within the organization (Reilly and DiAngelo, 1990: 129).

Reilly and DiAngelo are here suggesting that it is the organization's culture, the deep structure of meaning, involving values, beliefs and critical symbols, which tells people what is important, who is important, and therefore the 'significance' of the communication elements:

> Culture is not an individual event but a historical reality with symbols, myths, and meanings. These become embedded in the organizational reality and are the medium through which messages are filtered (p. 130).

When people first enter a work organization they learn, through a process of socialization, the organizational language that provides the context of meaning. But organizational culture is not neutral. Rather it represents relations of power and control, thus pre-defining who and what is important and significant. These cultural realities will filter messages within the organization, thus establishing barriers to communication. This issue of culture is discussed more fully by Wilson (Chapter 9 in this volume).

Alternative approaches: adopting a gendered perspective

We finish this analysis of communication by considering the crucial relationship between gender and power, hinted at throughout this chapter. In understanding the relationship between communication, gender, and power we need to be clear about the underlying position we are adopting. In other words, we need to consider our underlying assumptions about ontology and the associated epistemological perspective we are favouring. Ontology refers to our understanding of 'the nature of being', while epistemology refers to our understanding of how we 'can know the world'. Objectivist epistemology rests on the idea that we can know something through independent observation, because it assumes that the world exists independently of our knowledge of it. For the subjectivist, on the other hand, all knowledge is filtered through the knower, whose 'knowing' depends on social and cultural forces which shape the process of interpretation.

The objectivist assumes that there is a specific reality 'out there', so we need to develop theories and test these objectively against that reality. So, there are distinguishable trait differences between men and women, which determine how they behave. In the past the nature-nurture debate focused on how far these differences were biologically determined, that is sex differences, or the result of socialization experiences, that is gender differences. However, today it is commonly accepted that such a dichotomy is false and that most differences will be a reflection of the interaction between biology and socialization. But the key issue from this objectivist perspective is that gender is considered to be a fundamental attribute of an individual, particularly important in determining behaviour. The focus of communication research from this perspective is then to understand differences in communication, which are viewed as a reflection of these underlying differences between men and women. We are explicitly rejecting this biological (sex) and/or social (gender) determinism in this chapter in favour of a subjectivist or social constructionist perspective.

The subjectivist makes no claims about whether a specific reality exists because it assumes that this can never be known since all knowledge is mediated by experience, that is, knowledge is socially constructed. So biological sex is a given, but the translation of that in to specific gender understandings is a result of interactions over time. So, communication is the fundamental process whereby meaning is created, it is a process of sense-making. Here we are adopting an interpretative paradigm (Burrell and Morgan, 1979) where the social world is created through the relationships of the individuals involved. Reality is thus created through communication. Gender is then a social construction, which implies that it can have multiple meanings, way beyond the male-female dichotomy favoured by the objectivists. The reality of a black, working-class woman is likely to be very different to that of a white, middle-class woman. We now adopt this subjectivist perspective in considering the role of communication in maintaining the gendered system of inequality.

Discourse and knowledge

Communication helps to determine how we think and what we see. Foucault (1980) goes further, arguing that experience and knowledge do not exist outside the language in which they are talked about; discourse creates the experience. To 'know' something is to give that something meaning through language. While we may say that we know something intuitively, we have to verbalize that intuition, even if only to ourselves. In the same way processes of organizational construction can only occur through language: 'Talk and text produce and reproduce organizations' (Hatch, 1997). There is no meaning in a message except what people put into it. Thus, to understand the communication process it is necessary to understand how people relate to each other.

In Foucault's analysis, discourse is the key concept (Foucault, 1972). Discourse refers to the underlying rules, which determine what is taken as known and how this is established. Foucault does not assume that knowledge is neutral or that it progresses naturally. Rather he looks at how knowledge is constructed by discourse, which determines what can be seen or said. Discourse then, refers to the way in which things become spoken about in a certain way. What counts as 'truth' depends on this system of underlying rules, rather than on some objective given. Central to the establishment of a particular discourse are mechanisms of power, since these mechanisms are used to both formulate and accumulate knowledge. But power is not something that an individual or a group has. Power belongs to relationships, rather than to individuals, and is always present in relationships. And it is power that produces reality, which can be both repressive and creative, repressive in that power enacted within relationships seeks to maintain the dominance relationship, but creative in that relations of power are always contestable (Foucault, 1991). The reality created through relations of power extends to the individual's own reality: individuals' identities are not considered to be fixed and given but are rather constructed and known through being made an 'object' of knowledge and a target of power (Townley, 1994). Identities themselves are therefore always relational – I am only thin in comparison with another. Thus, in understanding gendered relations we need to focus on the discursive practices, which create the subordinate status for women in relation to the superior status of males; the discourse of patriarchy. Language and communication are central to these discursive practices.

Language

Language is a system of spoken or written symbols that can be used to communicate ideas, emotions and experiences. Obviously one of the central features of the English language is the sexism inherent in the vocabulary and structure of the language itself. For example, the generic use of male nouns (he, mankind, men) to refer to everyone, both males and females. Sexist language in any form emphasizes the appropriateness of one gender and the inappropriateness of the other (Daily and Finch, 1993). Empirical studies indicate that the use of traditional generic pronouns ('he', 'his') encourages a male bias (Pearson et al., 1991). Moreover, in terms of generic words to describe women, there is a much stronger tendency for these words to have developed a sexual connotation for the female form, for example, madam, lady, queen, mistress. Indeed, Spender (1985) found 220 words in the English language to describe sexually promiscuous women but only 20 words for men. In this way language embodies sexual inequality. Similarly, Schulz (1975) noted a process of semantic derogation when a word becomes associated with women, for example secretary.

  Spender (1985) concludes that men are able to exercise power through their means of defining reality, that is through language. Men have been able to structure and name a world that is amenable to their experiences and at the same time negates and devalues women's experiences. So language is the medium through which power is enacted. As Morris wrote, back in 1949: 'Sharing a language with other persons provides the subtlest and most powerful of all tools for controlling the behaviour of these other persons to one's advantage' (p. 214). Controlling meaning is the key, not the language per se. The words, or the lexicon, is not what is important, but the meaning attached to the words. The same words can mean different things, and language can be shared by sharing experiences and talking about them; using words and so establishing a shared meaning (Wittgenstein, 1974). It is not sufficient to enact a shared environment; it has to be talked about. Wittgenstein goes on to describe the 'language game' which is essentially the ability to play games to ensure that one particular meaning becomes dominant. But these language games, if carried out effectively by those in powerful positions, leave the control structure invisible, achieving compliance with the particular version of reality accepted on the basis of value premises rather than coercion (Smircich, 1983). As Pfeffer (1981) also argues, the distribution of power is perpetuated because people believe that this is 'how things always were, always will be and always should be' (p. 299).

The gender system

From this perspective issues of differences between men and women in communication content or style are trivial compared to the more fundamental issue of the role of communication in the construction and accomplishment of a gender system (Rakow, 1986). Communication implies an interaction. In any interaction, issues of power and status will affect the exchange. People who possess more real or perceived power or authority use language differently than do people who lack power. Gender differences in language use are simply a reflection of gender differences in power. In other words, the gender differences that have been observed in research are an artefact of the confounding of gender and status. The finding that certain language features are used more frequently by women is best explained by women's subordinate and relatively powerless place in society (West and Zimmerman, 1985).

This is summed up very succinctly by Troemel-Ploetz (1991):

> If you leave out power, you do not understand any talk, be it the discussion after your speech, the conversation at your own dinner-table, in a doctor's office, in the back yards of West Philadelphia, in an Italian village, on a street in Turkey, in an court room or in a day-care centre, in a women's group or at a UN conference. It is like saying Black English and Oxford English are just two different varieties of English, each valid on its own; it just so happens that the speakers of one variety find themselves in high-paying positions with a lot of prestige and power of decision-making, and the others are found more in low-paying jobs, or on the streets and in prisons (pp. 497-8).

Here Troemel-Ploetz is reviewing the book by Tannen (1990) *You Just Don't Understand*, and disagreeing with the analysis that it is simply a case that men and women need to accommodate to each other's different language style. Troemel-Ploetz argues that the majority of relationships between men and women in our society are asymmetrical, to the clear advantage of men. Therefore, to argue that men and women simply need to understand each other better for the miscommunication problems to be resolved, greatly underestimates the ways in which structural and institutional forces continuously bolster and support these status differences, thereby defining gender differences. Moreover, power is not an individual attribute, but an attribute of the situational relationship. As Crawford (1995) writes:

> In a social context of unequal structural and social power, differences become deficiencies of women, possibilities for social change are dissipated into limited efforts on the part of individual women, and women are encouraged to believe that in recreating themselves they can resolve problems of inequality (p. 21).

From this perspective, gender is a social construct.

Gender as a social construct

Understanding gender as a social construct (as discussed in Wilson, Chapter 1, in this volume) rather than as an individual attribute focuses our attention not on gender differences in language and communication style, rather it draws us towards understanding the processes by which differences are created and power is allocated. This helps us to understand why the earlier attempts to 'solve the problem' through assertiveness training were bound to fail. At the individual level, the individual will be placed in a 'double-bind' situation. That is, if a woman adopts the traditional women's style of deference, she will be considered as weak and ineffectual. But if she is direct and forthright, she is not a woman any more, 'certainly not a lady', and is dismissed for this as well.

Moreover, the idea that interactional problems within relationships can be resolved by changing individual communication skills is an example of the fundamental attribution error (Kelley, 1971). In attributional terms, when we look at the outcome of some action we make attributions about what caused that outcome. These attributions can either be internal (the individual(s) involved caused the outcome) or external (aspects of the situation caused the outcome). The fundamental attribution error refers to the tendency to over-emphasise internal causes and under-emphasize external causes. Thus, we tend to hold individuals responsible for the outcomes of their actions and neglect the way in which the situation influenced the outcome. For example, if an individual has not been able to influence others to accept her ideas, it is because she has not been persuasive enough, rather than because the situation did not allow her to exert interpersonal influence. This led Foder (1985: 258) to raise the question

> Is assertiveness training yet another 'treatment' that is directed at the victim of social injustice, placing the burden for social change on the backs of individual women?

At the societal level, it stops short of the kind of social critique, which might open up the possibility of change. While society is blamed for women's problems in that the socialization process is seen to be the cause of language deficiencies or differences, the burden of change remains with the individual, either to overcome her deficiencies or put effort into understanding communication from 'the other sex'. By focusing on individual strategies of change it draws attention away from the processes through which gender inequity is constituted and continually reproduced. Even the two-cultures approach, with its explicit assertion that neither male nor female speech patterns are superior (just different), fails to theorize how power relations at the structural level are recreated and maintained at the interactional level (Crawford, 1995). As such, the differences examined have very different consequences for males and females.

The problem from the two-cultures perspective is then that the term gender becomes synonymous with difference. Yet as Barrett (1988) points out:

> It is vital for our purposes to establish its (gender) meaning in contemporary capitalism as not simply 'difference', but as division, oppression, inequality, internalised inferiority for women (p. 112).

The issue is not whether males and females communicate differently, but the role of discourse in the construction of gendered relations of power. Gender is not possessed but interactively produced (Mumby, 1996):

> Gender has meaning, is organized and structured, and takes place as interaction and social practice, all of which are communication processes. That is, communication creates genders who create communication (Rakow, 1986: 23).

A good example of the role of communication in the creation of gender was provided by Finder (1987) in his recollection of his personal experiences as a male secretary. He told how his male boss refused to treat him as a secretary, making sure that he was given different work to the 'real' secretaries (the women!) and treating him as 'one of the boys' by telling dirty jokes and talking about sports. The female secretaries were definitely excluded from any of this 'boys talk'. Even the other secretaries questioned his secretarial role, claiming that 'guys aren't secretaries'. This helps us to understand how different, gendered positions are constructed within institutionalized relations of meaning and power.

Case study

Information Systems/Information Technology (IS/IT) is a relatively new profession that focuses on the relationships between organizations, technology, and information. It is interesting to consider the ways in which the profession is developing as a highly gendered profession and relate this back to some of the issues raised in this chapter. That the profession is dominated by males is very clear and indeed the proportion of males is increasing rather than decreasing (Booth, 1999). For example, in the UK IS/IT is dominated by males at all levels – students (Sian, 1997), academics (Wilson, 1997) and practitioners (Panteli et al., 1999) are predominantly men. While part of the reason for this may be overt discrimination (DiDo, 1997), there are other more subtle processes at work which illustrate some of the communication issues highlighted in the last section of this chapter:

1. Discourse and knowledge: While women are under-represented in IS/IT generally, even more important is the segregation that exists within the profession. In the UK in 1996, women constituted only 12 per cent of managerial jobs in IT (Panteli et al., 1999). This is a reflection of the way in which the 'hard' technical aspects of the profession, where men dominate, have been defined as more important (therefore warranting promotion) compared to the 'soft' more people oriented aspects, where women are more likely to be found. For example, men dominate in areas such as analyst and programmer while 62 per cent of help desk assistants are women.

2. Language: in terms of the domain of computing, while the computer itself displays no gender bias computer culture and the language used in relation to computing is heavily masculine (Turkle, 1988). For example, workbenches, tool kits, drives etc. are part of the computing jargon. As Booth (1999) notes the outcome is that few women yet see IT as a desirable profession, which is a reflection of its techie image.

3. The gender system: it is clear that there are gender differences in power within the profession. For example, in the Society for Information Management, a US organization of senior IT executives, only 195 of its 2,700 members were women (Candee, 1997). Similarly, in the academic area, the important professional networks where decisions are made have very few female representatives. For example, the European Conference on Information Systems (ECIS) is the key European conference for academics involved in the area. For the year 2000 conference, 12 of the 13 conference officers were men. The 'token' woman phenomenon is clearly evident here. These informal networks that control editorial boards, conference programmes, and appointment boards are very powerful. They influence the general image of IS as a profession and, more importantly can also influence the career progression of individuals.

4. Gender as a social construct: Several attempts have been made to increase the numbers of women studying IS/IT but this has had relatively little impact. For example, Salminen-Karlsson (1997) looked at attempts by three of Sweden's five technical universities to reform their computing engineering courses in order to attract more women. While they did manage to achieve some slight increase in the numbers of women students, Salminen-Karlsson argues that the underlying masculine culture and normativity of the male at the institutional level did not really change. Indeed, those involved in the change process did not really understand or

give due regard to gender issues, focusing the reform process instead on pedagogical issues. This corroborates the point made by Crawford (1995), discussed above, and illustrates how power relations at the structural level are recreated and maintained at the interactional level.

This example of the developing profession of IS/IT demonstrates clearly how gendered relations of power within organizations and academic disciplines are interactively reproduced through communication. It exposes the systems of domination that women experience in their everyday lives. The masculine discourse creates and perpetuates the gender segregation within the profession and explains why women are actually turning away from IS/IT either as students, academics or practitioners.

Summary

Adopting a critical feminist perspective changes the focus of our analysis from communication structure to an emphasis on language and meaning; communication as water rather than communication as glue. Gender is not possessed but interactively produced through communication (Mumby, 1996). It is in this sense that organizations are gendered. The research agenda must be to examine organizations empirically as structured sites of power, domination, and resistance. Communication needs to be analysed as the medium through which these gendered relations of power are produced. Only recently have communication scholars acknowledged this agenda. Exploring the connections between everyday communicative practices and the underlying power structures of institutional life will expose the systems of domination which women experience in their everyday lives. Gender is not a property or an attribute of an individual, but an integral dynamic of organizations. As such the key questions are not those which have dominated research to date, such as 'What are the differences in the communication styles of men and women?' and 'How can organizations reduce discrimination or manage diversity?'. Rather, the key question becomes, 'How do communication processes contribute to the maintenance of systems of domination?'. Communication research will then not concern itself with examining arbitrary communication differences between men and women which are explained by benign socialization practices traced back to childhood, but will ask fundamental questions about how gender is daily constructed and reconstructed through discourse to create a gendered rationality.

References

Arnold, J., Robertson, I. and Cooper, C. (1991) *Work Psychology: Understanding Human Behaviour in the Workplace.* London: Pitman.
Barnard, C. (1938) *The Functions of the Executive.* Oxford: Oxford University Press.
Baron, R.A. and Greenberg, J. (1990) *Behaviour in Organizations.* 3rd Edition. London: Allyn and Bacon.
Barrett, M. (1988) *Women's Oppression Today: the Marxist/Feminist Encounter.* London: Verso.
Bass, B.M. (1990) *Handbook of Leadership: Theory, Research, and Managerial Applications.* 3rd Edition. New York: Free Press.
Berlo, D. (1960) *The Process of Communication.* New York: Holt.
Booth, N. (1999) 'Gender offender', *Business and Technology*, 47-50.
Burrell, G. and Morgan, G. (1979) *Sociological Paradigms and Organizational Analysis.* London: Heinemann.
Candee, W. (1997) 'Women cut through IT's glass ceiling', *Information Week*, 614: 83-6.
Coe, T. (1992) *The Key to the Men's Club: Opening the Doors to Women in Management.* Corby: IM Foundation.
Crawford, M. (1995) *Talking Difference: on Gender and Language.* London: Sage.
Daily, B. and Finch, M. (1993) 'Benefiting from nonsexist language in the workplace', *Business Horizons*, March-April: 30-4.
DiDo, L. (1997) 'Look out for techno-hazing', *Computerworld*, 31 (39): 72-3.
Eagly, A.H., Makhijani, M.G. and Klonsky, B.G. (1992) 'Gender and the evaluation of leaders: a meta-analysis', *Psychological Bulletin*, 111 (1): 3-22.
Fairhurst, G. (1993) 'The leader-member exchange patterns of women leaders in industry: a discourse analysis', *Communication Monographs*, 60, 321-51.
Finder, J. (1987) 'A male secretary', *New York Times Magazine*, 68 (February).
Foder, I.G. (1985) 'Assertiveness training for the eighties: moving beyond the personal', in Rosewater, L.B. and Walker, L.E. (eds) *Handbook of Feminist Therapy.* New York: Springer. pp. 257-65.
Foucault, M. (1972) *The Archaeology of Knowledge.* London: Routledge.
Foucault, M. (1980) *The History of Sexuality: an Introduction.* (R. Hurley, Trans.). New York: Vintage.
Foucault, M. (1991) 'The ethic of care for the self as a practice of freedom', in Bernauer, J. and Ramussen, D. (eds) *The Final Foucault.* Cambridge, MA: MIT Press.
Gilligan, C. (1982) *In a Different Voice: Psychological Theory and Women's Development.* Cambridge, MA: Harvard University Press.
Gottfried, H. and Weiss, P. (1994) 'A compound feminist organization: Purdue University's Council on the status of women', *Women and Politics*, 14, 23-44.
Graddol, D. and Swann, J. (1989) *Gender Voices.* Oxford: Basil Blackwell.
Gray, J. (1992) *Men are from Mars, Women are from Venus.* New York: Harper Collins.
Hatch, M.J. (1997) *Organization Theory: Modern Symbolic and Postmodern Perspectives.* Oxford: Oxford University Press.
Hellriegel, D., Slocum, J. and Woodman, R. (1989) *Organizational Behaviour.* 5th Edition. New York: West Publishing Company.
Herriot, P. (1984) *Down from the Ivory Tower.* Chichester: John Wiley and Sons Ltd.

Howard, A. and Bray, D.W. (1988) *Managerial Lives in Transition: Advancement in Age and Changing Times*. New York: Guildford Press.

Huczynski, A. and Buchanan, D. (1991) *Organizational Behaviour: An Introductory Text*. 2nd Edition. London: Prentice Hall.

Ibarra, H. (1993) 'Network centrality, power, and innovation involvement: determinants of technical and administrative roles', *Academy of Management Journal*, 36 (3): 471-501.

Kanter, R.M. (1989) *Men and Women of the Corporation*. New York: Basic Books.

Katz, D. and Kahn, R.L. (1978) *The Social Psychology of Organizations*. 2nd Edition. New York: John Wiley.

Kelley, H.H. (1971) *Attribution in Social Interaction*. Morristown, Tn: General Learning Press.

Lakoff, R. (1975) *Language and Women's Place*. New York: Harper and Row.

Luthans, F. (1992) *Organizational Behaviour*. 6th Edition. New York: McGraw Hill.

Maltz, D.N. and Borker, R.A. (1982) 'A cultural approach to male-female miscommunication', in Gumperz, J. (ed.) *Language and Social Identity*. Cambridge: Cambridge University Press. pp. 195-216.

Marshall, J. (1989) 'Re-visioning career concepts: a feminist invitation', in Arthur, M.B., Hall, D. and Lawrence, B. (eds) *Handbook of Career Theory*. Cambridge: Cambridge University Press. pp. 275-91.

Martin, J. (1998) *Organizational Behaviour*. London: International Thomson Business Press.

McConnell-Ginet, S. (1980) 'Linguistics and the feminist challenge', in McConnell-Ginet, S., Borker, R. and Furman, N. (eds) *Women and Language in Literature and Society*. New York: Praeger. pp. 3-25.

McKenna, E. (1994) *Business Psychology and Organizational Behaviour*. Hove: Lawrence Erlbaum Associates Ltd.

Moorhead, G. and Griffin, R. (1998) *Organizational Behaviour: Managing People and Organizations*. New York: Houghton Mifflin Co.

Mulac, A., Wiemann, J.M., Widenmann, S.J. and Gibson, T.W. (1988) 'Male/female language differences and effects in same-sex dyads: the gender-linked language effect', *Communication Monographs*, 55 (4): 215-335.

Mullins, L. (1993) *Management and Organizational Behaviour*. 3rd Edition. London: Pitman Publishing.

Mumby, D. (1996) 'Feminism, postmodernism, and organizational communication studies: a critical reading', *Management Communication Quarterly*, 9 (3): 259-95.

Newell, S. (1995) *The Healthy Organization: Fairness, Ethics and Effective Management*. London: Routledge.

Newell, S. and Rice, C. (1999) 'Assessment, selection and evaluation', in Leopold, J., Harris, L. and Watson, J. (eds) *Strategic Human Resourcing*. London: FT Pitman Publishing. pp. 129-65.

Nichols, P.C. (1980) 'Women in their speech communities', in McConnell-Ginet, S., Borker, R. and Furman, N. (eds) *Women and Language in Literature and Society*. New York: Praeger. pp. 140-49.

Nichols, N.A. (1993) 'Whatever happened to Rosie the riveter?', *Harvard Business Review*, 71 (4): 57-60.

Panteli, A., Stack, J., Atkinson, M. and Ramsay, H. (1999) 'The status of women in the UK IT industry: an empirical study', *European Journal of Information Systems*, 8 (3): 170-82.

Pearson, J.C., Turner, L.H. and Todd-Mancillas, W. (1991) *Gender and Communication*. 2nd Edition. Dubuque: Wm. C. Brown.

Pfeffer, J. (1981) *Power in Organizations*. Marshfield, MA: Pitman Publishing.

Rakow, L.F. (1986) 'Rethinking gender research in communication', *Journal of Communication*, 36 (4): 11-26.

Reilly, B.J. and DiAngelo, J.A. (1990) 'Communication: a cultural system of meaning and value', *Human Relations*, 43 (2): 129-40.

Rogers, E.M. and Kincaid, D.L. (1981) *Communication Networks: Towards a New Paradigm for Research*. New York: Free Press.

Rogers, C. and Rothlisberger, F. (1952) 'Barriers and gateways to communication', *Harvard Business Review*, 30 (4): 46-52.

Rosener, J.B. (1990) 'Ways women lead', *Harvard Business Review*, 68 (6): 119-25.

Ruben, D. (1985) *Progress in Assertiveness, 1973-1983: An Analytical Bibliography*. Metuchen, NJ: Scarecrow Press.

Salminen-Karlsson, M. (1997) 'Why do they never talk about girls?', in Lander, R. and Adams, A. (eds) *Women in Computing*. Exeter: Intellect publishing. pp. 160-72.

Schulz, M.R. (1975) 'The semantic derogation of women', in Thorne, B. and Henley, N. (eds) *Language and Sex: Difference and Dominance*. Rowley, Mass: Newbury House. pp. 64-73.

Seligman, M. (1975) *Helplessness: On Depression, Development and Death*. San Francisco: Freeman.

Shannon, C.E. and Weaver, W. (1949) *The Mathematical Theory of Communication*. Urbana: University of Illinois Press.

Shaw, M.E. (1978) 'Communication networks fourteen years later', in Berkowitz, L. (ed.) *Group Processes*. New York: Academic Press. pp. 351-61.

Siann, G. (1997) 'We can, we don't want to: factors influencing women's participation in computing', in Lander, R. and Adams, A. (eds) *Women in Computing*. Exeter: Intellect publishing. pp. 113-21.

Skuse (1997)

Smircich, L. (1983) 'Concepts of culture in organizational analysis', *Administrative Science Quarterly*, 28, 339-58.

Spender, D. (1985) *Man Made Language*, 2nd Edition. London: Routledge and Kegan Paul.

Tannen, D. (1990) *You Just Don't Understand: Women and Men in Conversation*. New York: Ballantine.

Townley, B. (1994) *Reframing Human Resource Management*. London: Sage.

Troemel-Ploetz, S. (1991) 'Review essays: selling the apolitical', *Discourse and Society*, 2, 489-502.

Turkle, S. (1988) 'Computational reticence: why women fear the intimate machine', in Kramarea, C. (ed.) *Technology and Women's Voices: Keeping in Touch*. New York: Routledge.

Unger, R. and Crawford, M. (1992) *Women and Gender: A Feminist Psychology*. New York: McGraw-Hill.

West, C. and Zimmerman, D.H. (1985) 'Gender, language, and discourse', in van Dijk, T. A. (ed.) *Handbook of Discourse Analysis*, 4. Orlando, FL: Academic. pp. 103-24.

Wilson, F. (1997) 'Computing, computer science and computer scientists: how they are perceived', in Lander, R. and Adams, A. (eds) *Women in Computing*. Exeter: Intellect publishing. pp. 122-33.

Wilson, D. and Rosenfeld, R. (1990) *Managing Organizations: Texts, Readings and Cases*. Berkshire: McGraw-Hill.

Wittgenstein, L. (1974) *Philosophical Investigations*. (G. Anscombe, Trans.). Oxford: Basil Blackwell.

Zaremba, A. (1988) 'Working with the Organizational Grapevine', *Personnel Journal*, 67 (7) July: 38-42.

5 Motivation

Heather Höpfl

Introduction

The chapter examines gender differences in relation to organizational commitment and motivation. It considers the ways in which organizations seek to secure commitment via consensual values and common behaviours and actions. The differences between men and women's capacity for enticement into this construction of meaning are examined. As such the chapter makes a gross distinction between men and women in order to make a case for the gendered discussion of theories of work motivation. However, it should be obvious that this is not a distinction between men and women per se but between linear and rational conceptions of the organization and embodied, experiential approaches, between instrumental behaviour and a sense of community. In this sense, women are used in the text as a cipher for a range of experiences which are subordinated by the logical trajectory of the organization. Of course, this is not to say that the argument is purely about abstractions. The subordination of women in organizations is observably commonplace. However, the satisfactions which men derive from work appear to make them more susceptible to the construction of particular frames of organizational behaviour. In this sense, motivation can be viewed as rooted in a consensually agreed interpretation of appropriate organizational action. Women, it might be argued, have more ambiguous and conflictual encultured imagery, more complex material from which to construct the notion of self, and this is not easily reconciled with male reality definitions (Eagleton, 1990; Höpfl, 1992). Hence, women introduce ambivalence into the workplace. This inevitably constitutes a threat to male consensus and to the framing of male action. Women's action lacks propriety within male frames because women embody ambivalence. Therefore, by virtue of their mere presence, women threaten the deconstruction/destabilization of male motivation. Women are excluded from male action unless a common, that is, male motivation can be demonstrated. However, the argument runs, it is men who have most to lose from the instrumental motivation which companies require and which requires that the individual tie personal destiny with corporate destiny. Men diminish women's motivation in order to protect themselves from the threat of ambivalence.

Context and caveats

It is an interesting feature of the work on motivational psychology which is detailed in virtually every undergraduate textbook on organizational behaviour that not only does it deal in gross simplifications and an absurdly tightly bounded notion of organizational context but, significantly for the argument presented here, most of the theoretical work on motivation in such texts pretends to be gender neutral. In practice, this means that most theories of motivation are implicitly male. A mere cursory examination of the works of Maslow (1987), Herzberg (1968), Vroom and Yetton (1973), McClelland (1967) or Alderfer (1972), reveals the extent to which this is the case (Cullen, 1994). In other words, most theorists of motivation presuppose that the theoretical positions they describe apply equally to men and to women. In other words, women are subsumed with male categories of reasoning. This is not to say that theoretical work is not being undertaken into differences in motivation. Goffee and Nicholson (1994), for example, provide an illuminating study of the relationship between gender and the psychological contract of work and specifically advocate that researchers should give attention to differences in the career experiences of male and female managers rather than concentrate on similarities. Hearn (1994) refers to Maccoby and Jacklin's (1974) examination of 1,400 studies of sex-role differences which suggested that assumptions of difference in motivation, achievement and intelligence were rare (Hearn, 1994). Marshall (1984) in her tentative move towards constructing a female paradigm of employment suggests that women managers are motivated by the job itself rather than by instrumental motives. At the same time, Davidson and Cooper (1992) in their influential study of limitations to women's career development discuss the extent to which successful female managers tend to be Type A personalities, that is to say, competitive, achievement motivated, frenetic, impatient and so on. Czarniawska (1997) comments how, in her study of collected stories from various countries which were supposed to deal with organizational power, she was intrigued to discover the extent to which these stories were devoid of reference to gender, 'the non-issue of gender' as she puts it (Czarniawska, 1997: 2). Indeed, little of the emergent body of literature on gender finds its way into the standard texts. Even Hatch's (1997) otherwise excellent introductory text, *Organizational Theory*, gives a mere two sides to issues of gender construction and gender politics. Rollinson et al. (1998) refer to neither gender, feminism, nor women, apart from a brief reference to exclusion which argues that 'most of the arguments that have been put forward to exclude women, for example, that they lack the necessary personal and psychological characteristics, or that they lack loyalty to an employer because they will always put their family before their career, *have now been demolished*. However', they continue, '*no matter how hard they try*, very few women seem to be able to reach a senior level' (italics added), (Rollinson et al., 1998: 46). Likewise, *Human Resource Management, The New Agenda*

(Sparrow and Marchington, 1998) appears to offer a new agenda which is devoid of any recognition of gender issues and, indeed, the only acknowledgement of the issue is reported to be the fact that racial and sexual discrimination might result from flexible working (Sparrow and Marchington, 1998). Leopold et al. (1999), to their credit, do include a chapter on equality of opportunity but even this succumbs to the rhetoric of 'managing diversity' which, it might be claimed, actually obscures issues of difference of contribution and diffuses political impact (Czarniawska and Höpfl, 2000). It seems that the arguments have not so much been demolished as side stepped. There are real issues here which have been distorted by the recent rhetoric of diversity management which still presupposes a male construction of work and working lives.

To be fair, the absence of writing on gender and organizations is not surprising. The territory is a minefield and feminist writing is by no means representative of anything like a unified standpoint. Attempts by some feminist writers to produce a coherent paradigm from which to define the field have tended to be undermined by the fact that they employ the same devices to achieve a position of dominance as those which they seek to criticize as being primarily male. Consequently, it is necessary to preface this paper with some indication of the standpoint from which it has been written. On the one hand, it has to be accepted that to a great extent gender is largely socially constructed with all the baggage that this implies for the construction of women's work. At the same time, it could be argued that it is precisely from this gendered construction and its consequences for women's experience of work that the potential for a change can occur. In this respect, it is important to examine the meaning and political basis of work motivation. In other words, the very reasons why gendered experiences of work are asymmetrical can provide insights into the nature of the psychological contract of work and the politics of commitment and motivation. Thirty years after the concept of equality in the workplace was given legal impetus the reality of inequality is very much a feature of day-to-day working life. The current feminist preoccupation with the similarity between men and women as 'prisoners of gender' (Flax, 1990: 139; Hatch, 1997: 294) is appealing but is an inevitable outcome of the previous neglect of difference for understanding commitment and motivation. Unfortunately, by reducing the position of women to issues about inequities of social ordering, priority is given to an economic and social rationality which might argue that change could be achieved by social education, social engineering or social adjustment. Such simplifications are often bought at the cost of richer interpretations which offer the opportunity for a radical challenge to social values of commitment and work motivation.

The position adopted here is clearly contentious. To differentiate between male and female motivation might be considered by some to be essentialist. However, taking this into account, as Eagleton comments, 'The historical evidence would seem to suggest that women are on the whole less likely than men to come under the thrall of transcendent signifiers ... to be less easily duped by the arrogance of power' (Eagleton, 1990: 280). Building on this observation, the argument takes its standpoint from the supposition that whatever the basis of such differences, it is possible to adopt a radical structuralist position, that is to say, to concentrate on structural relations with a realist social world (Burrell and Morgan, 1979: 33-34) in an attempt to pursue changes in working practices which rely on gendered assumptions about the nature of work. Therefore, it is important to consider whether or not women, in part as a result of conflicting cultural imagery of home and work life, might be regarded as the possessors of an understanding of work and working arrangements which is of value in the pursuit of social change. If this were to be the case, despite the fact that women are disadvantaged by working arrangements, women might be in a position to throw light on the substitutions and delusions which appear to give work meaning for men and which lay them open to the confusion of work role with identity. It is precisely such knowledge which poses a threat to the ordered regularity of the organization by implicitly challenging rationality, linearity of direction and purpose, and instrumental motivation. If there is a difference in emphasis which women by virtue of their lack of singular commitment contribute to organizations, it is this difference which is regulated by the social construction of gender. If women by their mere presence threaten to deconstruct the univocal language of organizational rhetoric, it is this threat which is conciliated by patriarchal language. Perhaps more disturbingly, it is this difference which is denied by those feminist positions which, oblivious to their capture by patriarchal reasoning, prefer to argue for absence of difference. In short, the argument put forward here is that men and women have different motivations to work and, moreover, that it is important for women to rediscover and regain the awareness of such difference since, ironically, this difference is capable of leading to a fundamental shift in the psychological contract of work in the next decade. With this awareness, an acknowledgement of gender differences might be able to exert some influence on changing working arrangements to the benefit of both men and women.

Commitment and motivation

Before developing these ideas further it is necessary to give some thought to the ways in which men and women 'make sense of' their day-to-day experience of work and, in particular, to consider what these experiences might mean for the ways in which individuals come to experience a sense of attachment to the organization and define what they expect in return.

Organizational commitment is a term that has received a considerable amount of attention in management literature in recent years. The main focus of much of this research has been on the ways in which commitment can be used in relation to theories of motivation and job satisfaction as an indicator or predictor of operational variables such as labour turnover (Mowday, Porter and

Steers, 1982; Reichers, 1985). Barling et al. (1990) argue that job satisfaction, organizational climate and job involvement are significant predictors of company commitment. Oliver (1990) offers empirical evidence to suggest that 'primary commitment targets are not ... organizations per se, but rather the goals and values that they embody'. There have been empirical studies which attempt to identify the determinants of organizational commitment and its consequences (Griffin and Bateman, 1986). Allen and Meyer (1990) concern themselves with the measurement of normative commitment to the organization in order to argue that future research may be able to identify commitment profiles that differentiate employees on the basis of the effectiveness of their commitment to the organization. The difficulty with much of this research is that it treats the notion of commitment uncritically, as unproblematic. The term commitment tends to be used to describe very different constructs, experiences, degrees of involvement and motivations. Moreover, despite the obvious affective dimensions of commitment, there is little or no attention to its emotional aspects as Hosking and Fineman (1990) point out.

In broad terms, the literature on commitment has considered calculative involvement with organization and moral or attitudinal approaches (Amernic and Aranya, 1983; Ferris and Aranya, 1983). Most of this material takes a rather simplistic view of the ways in which individuals engage with the organization and of what people are prepared to do to comply with the demands an organization might make of them. This chapter, in contrast, relates commitment to the definition of the situation and to the ways in which that definition is maintained in emergent processes, that is to say, in the ways in which situations are constructed, maintained and regulated. It is in this sense that commitment and motivation can be considered in relation to gender differences. This seems an entirely appropriate way to approach differences in commitment and motivation as they are perceived within organizations since clearly gender roles themselves form part of the process in emergence. Day-to-day experiences would suggest that men regard women as being deficient in commitment and that this deficiency must be understood in negative terms. It is this superficial equation of difference with deficiency that is challenged by the argument presented here. More, it is a difference which provides a potentially liberating challenge to traditional ways of engaging with work relations and modes of organizing.

Women and propriety

Marshall (1984) says that

> Women are traditionally excluded from management jobs because they are
> judged less serious, less highly motivated than male employees ... they are
> supposed to demonstrate low organizational commitment because they do not

assign their jobs precedence over all other life areas, may leave to have children, and demonstrate less company loyalty than do male colleagues.

and continues

the woman manager may be seen as a threat to organizational stability because of her apparent independence and lack of commitment ... women create uncertainty (Marshall, 1984: 21-22).

As an illustration of this point, an MBA student who was a Clinical Nurse Manager told me that when she went to discuss temporary problems of family commitments with her Senior Manager, a man, she was asked if she should consider reverting to being a Health Visitor which would, in effect, have been a demotion. In contrast, male staff experiencing domestic problems such as a sick partner or child were treated sympathetically and offered support. *Her* request was regarded as indicative of a lack of commitment. She was seen to be putting the needs of her family over and above what was perceived to be her primary commitment, her work. Commitment, seen in this way, seems to have a good deal to do with the acceptance of a consensual frame of action and with an appropriate performance: a performance with propriety or 'fit'. The primacy of the world of work as a male domain means that, for men, commitment is largely taken as read. Hence, men were treated sympathetically because their problems were not seen as an absence of commitment but rather as situations which were unfortunate and temporary distractions from an already established commitment. Women, as in the case of the Clinical Nurse Manager, merely reveal their ambivalences when they seek respite from the demands of work.

As such, commitment is concerned with the management of appearances. It is important to be seen to behave in a way that demonstrates commitment to the organization and young members of staff may be exhorted to behave explicitly with this in mind. Middle managers in British Airways, both male and female, explained their tactics for demonstrating their commitment via physical presence by extending their working day. Some members of staff explained how they arrived early in the morning and left late at night in order to demonstrate their commitment. Jackets were commonly left on the backs of chairs to suggest that staff were still in the building: a gesture that implicitly casts doubt of the sincerity of their apparent visible commitment. Commitment is affirmed and hence defined by what the organization privileges and rewards for the appearance of commitment. When employees demonstrate that they can perform what commitment is supposed to entail, they are rewarded accordingly. To the extent that women cannot, will not, or do not, demonstrate a complete commitment to their work to the exclusion of all other areas of their lives, this means that their motivation is suspect and their lack of career progression justified by appeal to this dubious logic. Significantly, such explanations of the relationship between motivation and commitment, and commitment and career, insofar as they purport to offer explanations of women's lack of progression, can only be understood from the point of view of defensive male behaviour and the appeal to a logic rooted in economic rationality. However, at root is an anxiety and the fear of the absence of meaning in work being revealed.

A female Locality Nurse Manager aged around 50 with responsibility for 70 staff told me, 'I am the wife of a man whose job has caused us to move house several times. On at least three occasions, I have been in a job that I have enjoyed immensely, had a career progression which I could have mapped out and yet it was automatically assumed that I would give up my job to follow my husband to his new promotion. I felt resentful and angry and yet faced with the choice gave up my job and moved house rather than live apart from my husband ... Had I decided my job and career were more important I would then have had the dilemma of sorting out child-minding facilities for my family, coping alone, apart from weekends and at a cost that would have made my working life a nonsense'. The social construction of the respective gender roles and responsibilities determined her opportunities, social obligations and demonstrable commitment.

Another woman, a Benefits Team Leader with a staff of seven in a local authority housing department said, 'I often wonder if you are not the major bread winner therefore your job is not that important. Is it more logical that I pick Katie up from school or is it because my job isn't as important'. Another woman, whom I taught on a DMS course explained, 'I have great difficulties with conflict between home and the residential course on the DMS (one overnight stay in a hotel). My husband feels that at the weekend I should be a wife and mother and should not be away from my family on courses that are often no more than excuses for boozing sessions!', she added, 'my husband has very strong views on women in management', as if it required no further explanation to indicate what they were.

There is clearly a great deal that is taken-for-granted in these statements. The point is, that women are often unable or unwilling to effect the subordination of one life-world to another in any sustainable way, and so have to 'manage' their own embodiment of difference – as experience, as dilemma, as dissociation. However, once the suspension of disbelief required to sustain the performance of corporate commitment is breached, the management of the performance is in jeopardy and the usual range of corporate inducements by way of office furniture, car, bonuses and privileges of one sort or another are deprived of their capacity to exercise power over organization members. In other words, in dramaturgical terms the organization plays out the performance of purposive behaviour as if working to an agreed script and along a given trajectory. When this movement and direction is interrupted, the play may collapse to reveal itself to be mere acting; representation which draws on but is not synonymous with lived experience.

Seductions in the form of organization rewards and instrumentalism go hand in hand. Hence, commitment and single-minded dedication to work involve a mutuality of ends. If women cannot demonstrate their submission or enthralment, that is to say, if their commitment is only partial, it seems that the reciprocity they receive from the organization will also be partial. However, when individuals experience some disjuncture of expectation in their relationship with the organization, for example, when rewards are not forthcoming or when contracts are terminated, they can usually see the performance for what it is. People say they are 'disenchanted', 'betrayed', 'let down', 'screwed', 'used', 'cut up', 'choked': words which are commonly used to describe the end of a relationship and which suggest that something which once gave meaning has been withdrawn. Experience and the sense of a coherent self are broken down.

In terms of the social regulation of organization (Clegg, 1981), women constitute a considerable threat precisely because their commitment is problematic: they have difficulty presenting themselves 'as a full organizational member, as someone who 'fits in' as a committed person' (Hearn et al., 1989) because they are perceived as having an ambivalent commitment to the organization as a consequence of their primary commitment to domestic life. What this means is that the partial commitment of women members of organizations disconcerts male organizational members by reminding them implicitly that work is not an end in itself, of the transitory nature of the relationship, and of the threat of incoherence which is concealed by the apparent meaning offered by the experience of work.

Competing demands

The world of the subject is made up of multiple interpretations and 'realities'. This is an everyday experience and yet one which has important implications for understanding the disjunctions and conjunctions which occur between different life worlds. In particular, it leads to an understanding of some of the commitment issues which differentiate men and women. Because of the ambivalent demands of distinct life worlds, women are unable to achieve or sustain the suspension of disbelief that is required for organizational commitment unless they operate as quasi men or become the vestal virgins of the corporation.

Long-term prisoners will often initiate a break with their families and refuse letters or visits because they cannot cope with two separate realities (Höpfl, 1982). Women with domestic responsibilities cannot renounce or subordinate life worlds that are incompatible with corporate commitment. One woman, a partner in a family electrical goods business and Company Secretary told me, 'When my son was ill he was unable to go to the childminder and both my mother-in-law and mother were ill and unable to look after him. In this position, I had no other option but to take my son to work with me. I was unable to concentrate and work even though he was very well behaved and didn't interrupt. I felt extremely guilty and unprofessional taking a child in with me even though I own part of the company and I had every right to do as

I please'. Her brother and partner said, '... you made the rod for your own back and so you'll just have to deal with it. Why should you expect special consideration because of your circumstances, it's what you chose to do'. She added, 'Male colleagues do not have to deal with these types of situation ... they have wives at home who deal with these types of problem'. She could not compartmentalize her experiences and responsibilities – her male colleagues could.

Anyone who has interviewed working women will confirm that a recurrent theme is guilt: guilt about not giving a hundred percent to work or non-work life. Compare the statements from the woman above, 'I have to leave meetings early and I feel I am undermining my position with colleagues and missing out on all the after meeting socializing and manoeuvring that occurs so putting myself at a disadvantage' ... and her son 'often says that he would like me to be a "mum" ... he doesn't see me as a "mum" as portrayed by the media and so feels cheated'. My own children are respectful of their father's need for space to work in the evenings but invade my work space on any pretext and, of course, like other working women, I feel guilty when I send them away.

Women and authority

The ways in which symbols function to construct and order experience means that women are confronted by a multiplicity of complementary and contradictory images and symbols of selfhood. This is no less so for men. However, men have more opportunities to assemble a unitary notion of self. That is to say, men are frequently able to construct a notion of self that denies differences, pluralities, contradictions and ambivalence by centring their constructions of the idea of a work-self, a professional identity or an occupational notion of selfhood. Such an approach allows contradictions and ambiguities to be ignored, subsumed or denied. Women's opportunity to assemble a construction of self is more difficult because of a fundamental ambivalence in the imagery. So, whereas the encultured images of what might be termed 'manhood' offer opportunities to combine aspects of self in such a way that a man may assume authorship for a relatively coherent self, this is not the case for women. This is what Marshall refers to as 'the double bind' (1984: 21). The irreconcilable images of the symbolic order which are available to construct a woman's notion of self means that women's authorship, in both the sense of authoritative control and *mastery* of the text, becomes problematic. It is the authorship of experience which gives coherence to the standpoint and hence confers authority on a particular view of the world. To exercise such authority is *implicitly* to perform with propriety, that is, to behave appropriately for the circumstances. In other words to be 'fit' for the performance and to fit in. Women are subject to competing demands, must adopt competing standpoints and move between them as circumstances require playing a range of roles. This is particularly true where women have domestic or other social responsibilities but the social construction of gendered situations means that even for women who are exclusively committed to their careers there is a disjunction between imagery and expectations. Given this, it is extremely difficult for women to *exercise* authority. Of course, here the notion of authority is used in a very specific sense to refer to the command of a situation, to authorship of one's own experience, to the kind of certainty in the articulation of a position which is predominantly male, that is to say, unambivalent, commitment which is single minded and without hesitation. Inevitably, this lack of authority as defined by patriarchal reasoning produces an ontological insecurity and, more powerfully, it is an insecurity that threatens the coherence of the male self. The self as an artefact, that is to say, as a thing assembled, is incoherent. The authority of the constructed notion of what it is to be male, 'manhood', made as an artefact and unitary in character is thus contravened and controverted by the absence of a singular authority in the artefact of what it is to be a woman, 'womanhood'.

Collinson and Collinson (1989) have undertaken empirical work to examine how men's sexuality is routinely privileged and embedded within particular organizational practices and they provide examples of male power, dignity and sexual identity and comment that male dominated labour organizations can be characterized by assumptions and practices which seek both to discredit and to exclude women. Men rehearse and reinforce the corporate rhetoric and appear to have strong needs for the informal network of the organization. Women for various reasons are often excluded or exclude themselves from such activities. After all, many of these activities are to do with reinforcing male worldviews and sexual identity. Women are excluded because they hold in tension fragments of disjunct encultured imagery which relate to their sexuality and reproductive powers. This is a threat to male inclusivity. Sexually mature women are considered to constitute the greatest threat. Women in their reproductive years receive most attention in symbol, myth and ritual where their reproductive capacity is seen to be in need of control. Women as 'untainted symbolic vessels' and women as witch and prostitute provide complex positive and negative metaphors of 'womanhood' (Hoch-Smith and Spring, 1978). Role performance requires that the rhetorical acts required by organizational life be executed with authority and must 'fit' in with the demands of organizational life. If for women there is no single authority, the propriety or suitability of women's corporate behaviour will fail. It will not be 'fit' as performance, and as performance-in-context. Once again, women come to be defined by their lack, only this time it is not Freud's assertions about the lack of a penis which defines woman as incomplete and inadequate but the lack of an authoritative standpoint. What Kristeva (1983 in Moi, 1986) states is that women must either live as male constructions or *be found wanting*. In this sense, to lack a penis is a very serious deficiency from a male point of view and one that renders women lacking in every respect, in this case, in terms of an appropriate degree of commitment.

The authoritative self

Therefore, the female self, lacking in authority, will not sustain the illusion of the performance-as-action. What this means is that, if in order to take part in the playing out of the corporate drama there must be a 'suspension of disbelief', women are considered to be unable to sustain a coherent, enduring and (in this sense) authoritative self within the work role. The implicit incoherence of the demands of multiple life-worlds, types of performance, types of act and, by implication, ability to enter the vocational world of corporate commitment, all pose a threat to the coherence of male authority (Höpfl, 1991). What is at issue here is the extent to which the illusion of control or of authorship within an organization can be sustained. It is important to make a distinction between those experiences over which the actor believes he/she can exercise authority and those which he/she cannot. Inevitably work imposes a distinction between experiences which the subject construes as being under the control of the self and those which must be 'performed' or 'managed' to meet the demands of the action, the drama itself – corporate objectives. Experiences, which are perceived as not being within the authority of the actor, constitute a threat. It is the threat of what is being suppressed by the demands of the action being revealed. The contradiction is denied. Daudi (1983) expresses this as follows, 'Each culture has its particular acts, forms, gestures, in order to reject and exclude, to control and keep in place, its ways of shutting its eyes to what it does not want to see. The liberating, challenging knowledge of ourselves does not come through our knowledge of what we do not want to know.' Women, therefore, are regulated in the workplace in order to enable men to avoid having to come to terms with the terror of the abyss of meaning which ambivalent commitment threatens to reveal. Not least, women are regulated to prevent men from coming to terms with their own finitude and the recognition that their frenetic commitment to work is, at heart, a denial of death (Sievers, 1986).

Partial commitment

The ways in which an organization plays out its corporate script, its corporate performance, is rooted in the creation and re-creation of appearance, that is to say, in the creation of a dramaturgical production, which functions to suppress difference, reduce ambiguity and sustain a world of 'make believe' in the way it is acted out. Threat is conciliated by a commitment to a common world-view, the world-view of the organization. The organization imposes its own specific and internally consistent demands of the corporate actors. Anyone who works in a job that requires a 'public face' must prepare, exactly as a stage actor does, to perform the role, to create the character and apply the make-up –

these aspects of work intrude far into non-work life. The enclaves of time left may thus appear so insignificant that it is easier to marginalize them in order to avoid the threat of acknowledging them. Men are encultured in such a way as to enable them to make work a vocation. The seductions of corporate culture gloss the significance of the deprivations. This is not to say that the lack is not felt in experience but rather to say that the pastiche of 'selfhood' over which men feel that they can exercise control is more easily reconciled. Women may attempt the same conciliation but it is not sustainable. Fundamentally, this is what poses the threat to the male world-view. Women, therefore, must either conform to the male world-view, accept their role or be excluded because they introduce ambivalence into the taken-for-granted ordering of the male definition of the frame of action.

There is a specific tension of consciousness that binds the employee to the life-world of their work. To increase organizational commitment involves creating a greater tension and, by implication, places a strain on the other life-worlds in which there is partial inclusion. It gives emphasis to the precariousness of the notion of a unitary self. For women managers the exhortation to greater commitment forms part of the way in which male managers and, for different and similar reasons some female managers, come to terms with the threatened incoherence of the powerfully conflictual notion of 'selfhood' in those women. The self as artefact, imbued with contradiction and remembered parts, cannot sustain its role in the corporate drama. It threatens to expose the illusion for what it is, to subvert the action by its ability to offer only partial commitment. Partial inclusion in multiple life-worlds does not necessarily mean that each imposes partial demands (Luckmann, 1970). There are conflicts of obligation and as the demands of the organization increase, the amount of time required to service and maintain oneself for work – resting, sleeping, washing and chores – means that increasing amounts of time become centred on the world of work (de Grazia, 1962).

The Company Secretary quoted earlier told me: 'I feel I must do everything correctly and repeatedly show colleagues that being a woman and mother does not affect my capabilities at work'. In contrast, the Benefits Team Leader commented that men can be seen to take a much more phlegmatic attitude to work, 'I am usually there when they arrive and still there when they go home. In general, my male peers are the ones who seem to spend less time doing their job, "just got to go and pick the wife up", "just got to go to the doctors, dentists etc" ... attitudes which in women would be commented on as absence of commitment. Women are expected to demonstrate by their physical presence that they have made up the time'. In other words, women have to demonstrate their commitment more convincingly than men do. However, the very fact of multiple demands and commitments mean that women reject-in-being male reality definitions. Therefore women's ambivalence must be contained and, moreover, ambivalence must be regarded as a negative quality in order to preserve male order, an ordering based on the promises of future coherence via rewards and seductions in the present.

Case study

I remember when I was pregnant I worked until about two months before the baby was born and although no one said so directly I felt that my colleagues regarded me as indecent or contaminated in some way. Of course, they were kind and affectionate but they felt that I shouldn't be there. My physical presence seemed to violate their sense of purpose. It was as if I had stepped into a parallel universe and should know that I belonged there at least until I had given birth. My very physical presence seemed to be a renunciation of my commitment to my work. I could hardly avoid my awareness of my own physicality as I became more obviously large and ponderous in my movements. I began to get the feeling that I smelt differently. Perhaps, in fact, I did. I was aware that people regarded me differently. I found it strange that sex was still a big part of work and the way that colleagues talked about other colleagues, about who was going after whom, about physical attributes of other members of staff. Yet, I thought that this very real process of becoming a mother was something different and defining. It separated me from them because my life was functioning on a physical plane and they were caught up in the abstractions of corporate life. It did seem to me that they had completely lost the plot. That they could no longer remember what it is to be human. Organizations encourage that detachment. For my part, I felt that I might smell of breast milk, or menstrual blood. I felt that I might, by simply being there, remind them of what it is to live in the present and to have contact with your physical being. It made me feel that organizations don't really want real people, only abstract aspects of them. You are paid for being less than human. They really want you away from the place. You might remember you have a life and expect something more of the organization than the promise that tomorrow will be a better day. Everyone was really nice when I left and gave me presents for the baby. I felt amongst my own kind with the bloated women at the antenatal clinic. I started working again on a part-time contract about six weeks after the baby was born but I didn't take him into work and I didn't mix work and my private life for some months. It was as if I had to find a sense of my singular commitment again before I could rejoin the club.

Researcher aged 40, IT Design Team, three year contract.

Calculative involvement

Implicitly, a calculative involvement with work is related to future expectations and their realization and so involves an instrumental view of the present. The apparently purposive nature of organizations reinforces this directional activity. Yet, planning and decision making are a kind of 'make believe' (Cooper and Fox, 1990: 597) which arise from the indeterminate nature of the world. Organizations may confer power, status, and wealth; may meet needs for affiliation and belonging; may bolster self-esteem – yet, at a fundamental level, the issue of choice and control is not resolved. The play of power is intrinsic to this process of order and giving orders. Hence, what traditional theories of motivation seek to offer in terms of the rewards a company can offer, whilst they undoubtedly attach meaning to behaviour and experience, are in themselves insufficient to sustain the deferred absence of meaning. As Sievers (1986) consistently argues, motivation is a surrogate for meaning and a means of avoiding the inevitably of mortality. In other words, motivation and the idea of progression and purposive futurity obscure the very real fact that we all die. By becoming preoccupied with the future, with success and career planning we lose sight of the present moment and of our inevitable death. Women's ambivalence stands as a cipher for this mortality by subverting the logic of calculative engagement. The necessary ambivalence of performance, the immediate and the prospective playing out of roles, acknowledges the disjunction that is, in the day-to-day, concealed by appearance. Such performance requires exceptional powers of invention and make-believe in order to permit the organization, in its actors, to create and re-create each successive moment, to achieve a presentation and re-presentation of appearance. The meaning that is offered as part of the corporate definition of reality, located as it is in an instrumental approach to the present, is both conflictual and powerfully seductive. The problem is that it cannot be exposed or seen for what it is until some dislocation of expectation occurs. This can happen, for example, when someone is made redundant, becomes ill and has to take time off work, sees some injustice perpetrated on a colleague or fails to gain an expected promotion.

The paradox of power

The presence of women in management poses the threat of disjunction and threatens to expose the underlying ambivalence. In part, corporate inducements frustrate any immediate disjunction of meaning by 'making sense of' behaviour and experience via the promise of future rewards and coherence. The difficulty here is the strength and coherence of the apparent meaning of attachment to a corporate philosophy and the range of inducements that reinforce it. However, such commitment leads to a level of engagement where the need for reflexive action is minimized. The necessary conciliation between the world of the corporate culture and the other multiple life-worlds, which the individual inhabits, is achieved by an act of self-deception. In order to minimize the ambivalence, contradictions are ignored or denied. While the corporate and, as has been argued here, male definition of the situation remains the mediator of meaning, its rewards have considerable power. Disillusionment occurs when issues of choice, personal responsibilities and personal meaning are thrown into focus as in the examples given above. If in corporate life the irresolvable conflicts of authority which confront women who work, thrust into the corporate arena those aspects of life which male managers would prefer to keep off-stage it is inevitable that women will only be given minor roles – if they are to be given roles at all. Women need to be kept to well-scripted roles with limited opportunities for improvisation if the threat they bring to the organization performance is to be conciliated.

Marshall (1989) provides an account of a UK conference entitled 'Asserting the Female Perspective' at which the view was expressed that it was important to 'stay marginal' and to retain a 'suspicion of organizations and the values they embody'. Marshall comments that this could be viewed as 'negative ambivalence and lack of commitment' but could also provide the challenge to develop organizational practices which permit 'healthy scepticism and do not call it organizational disloyalty' (1989: 283). This is the liberating challenge of 'those things which we do not want to know' (Daudi, 1983). The argument presented here makes the case for a greater understanding of the way in which men's fear of women's powerful reality definitions and perceptions operates in organizational dynamics. That women are not so easily seduced into the illusions of future satisfactions causes a number of tensions and oscillations. These occur between the purposive nature of organizational trajectory and progress into the future and the ambivalence of women as corporate actors. The paradox at the root of this argument is one of power. Women have a powerfully realistic perception of their own experiences and cannot easily be seduced by corporate promises. Men find personal satisfaction and rewards in work and need to reinforce the supporting rhetoric even if only in paying lip service to organizational values. Women threaten these reality definitions and therefore men seek to control the extent of their participation. These positions cannot easily be reconciled. Women should trust their own experiences and understandings and regard them as a positive indication of their relationship with the organization and personal equilibrium. Commitment and motivation are not simply about theorizing behaviour or about the manipulation of organizational members. Women's ambivalence, albeit the product of gendered constructions, is a powerful political knowledge with significant import for changing the nature of the psychological contract of work.

Note: Some of the ideas presented in this chapter had their origins in a paper entitled (1992) 'Corporate Seduction and Ambivalence in Women Managers', *Women in Management Review and Abstracts*, 7(1): 9-17.

References

Alderfer, C. (1972) *Existence, Relatedness and Growth.* New York: Free Press.

Allen, N.J. and Meyer, J.P. (1990) 'The measurement and antecedents of affective, continuance and normative commitment to the organization', *Journal of Occupational Psychology*, 63: 1-18.

Armernic, J.H. and Aranya, N. (1983) 'Organizational commitment: testing two theories', *Relations Industrielles*, 38: 319-41.

Barling, J., Wade, B. and Fullanger, C. (1990) 'Predicting employee commitment to company and union: divergent models', *Journal of Occupational Psychology*, 63: 49-61.

Burrell, G. and Morgan, G. (1979) *Sociological Paradigms and Organizational Analysis.* London: Heinemann.

Clegg, A. (1981) 'Organization and control', *Administrative Science Quarterly*, 26: 545-62.

Collinson, D.L. and Collinson, M. (1989) 'Sexuality in the workplace: the domination of men's sexuality', in Hearn, J. Sheppard, D.L., Tancred-Sheriff, P. and Burrell, G. (eds) *The Sexuality of Organizations.* London: Sage. pp. 91-109.

Cooper, R. and Fox, S. (1990) 'The texture of organizing', *Journal of Management Studies*, 27 (6): 575-82.

Cullen, D. (1994) 'Feminism, management and self-actualization', *Gender, Work and Organization*, 1 (3): 127-37.

Czarniawska, B. (1997) 'On the imperative and the impossibility of polyphony in organization studies', a Keynote Address to the Organizing in a Multi-Voiced World Conference, Leuven, Belgium, June.

Czarniawska, B. and Höpfl, H. (2000) 'Casting the other, the production and maintenance of inequality', a stream convened at the EGOS Conference on Organizational Praxis, Helsinki.

Daudi, P. (1983) 'The discourse of power or the power of discourse', *Alternatives*, IX: 317-25.

Davidson, M.J. and Cooper, C.L. (1992) *Shattering the Glass Ceiling.* London: Paul Chapman Publishing Ltd.

de Grazia, S. (1962) *Of Time, Work and Leisure.* New York: Twentieth Century Fund.

Eagleton, T. (1990) *The Ideology of the Aesthetic.* Oxford: Blackwell.

Ferris, K.R. and Aranya, N. (1983) 'A comparison of two organizational commitment scales', *Personnel Psychology*, 36: 87-89.

Flax, J. (1990) *Thinking Fragments: Psychoanalysis, Feminism and Postmodernism in the Contemporary West.* Berkeley: University of California Press.

Goffee, R. and Nicholson, N. (1994) 'Career development in male and female managers - convergence or collapse', in Davidson, M.J. and Burke, R.J. (eds) *Women in Management, Current Issues in Research.* London: Paul Chapman Publishing Ltd. pp. 80-92.

Griffin, R.W. and Bateman, T.S. (1986) 'Job satisfaction and organizational commitment', in Cooper, C.L. and Robertson, I. (eds) *International Review of Industrial and Organizational Psychology.* New York: John Wiley and Sons. pp. 157-88.

Hatch, M.J. (1997) *Organizational Theory, Modern, Symbolic and Postmodern Perspectives.* Oxford: Oxford University Press.

Hearn, J. (1994) 'Changing men and changing managements: social change, social research and social action', in Davidson, M.J. and Burke, R.J. (eds) *Women in Management, Current Issues in Research*. London: Paul Chapman Publishing Ltd. pp. 192-212.

Hearn, J., Sheppard, D.L., Tancred-Sheriff, P. and Burrell, G. (eds) (1989) *The Sexuality of Organizations*. London: Sage.

Herzberg, (1968) *Work and the Nature of Man*. London: Crosby Lockwood Staples.

Herzberg, F., Mausner, B. and Synderman, B.B. (1959) *The Motivation to Work*. New York: John Wiley and Sons.

Hoch-Smith, J. and Spring, A. (1978) *Women in Ritual and Symbolic Roles*. New York: Plenum.

Höpfl, H. (Hopkins, H.J.) (1982) 'The subjective experience of time in time bounded institutions', unpublished PhD thesis, University of Lancaster.

Höpfl, H. (1991) 'The corpse in the deconstruction of culture', a paper presented to the 8th International SCOS Conference, Copenhagen, June.

Höpfl, H. (1992) 'Corporate seduction and ambivalence in women managers', *Women in Management Review and Abstracts*, 7 (1): 9-17.

Hosking, D.W. and Fineman, S. (1990) 'Organizing processes', *Journal of Management Studies*, 27 (6): 583-604.

Kristeva, J. (1983) 'Stabat Mater' in Moi, T. *The Kristeva Reader*. Oxford: Blackwell (1986), (for Leon Roudiez' translation of Kristeva's Stabat Mater).

Leopold, J., Harris, L. and Watson, T. (1999) *Strategic Human Resourcing, Principles, Perspectives and Practices*. London: Financial Times Management.

Luckmann, B. (1970) 'The small life-worlds of modern man', *Social Research*, 37: 580-96. (Reprinted in Brown, H. and Stevens, R. (eds) (1975) *Social Behaviour and Experience*. London: Hodder and Stoughton. pp. 311-23.)

Maccoby, E.E. and Jacklin, C.N. (1974) *The Psychology of Sex Differences*. Stanford, CA: Stanford University Press.

Marshall, J. (1984) *Women Managers, Travellers in a Male World*. Chichester: Wiley.

Marshall, J. (1989) 'Re-visioning career concepts: a feminist perspective', in Arthur, M.B., Hall, D.T. and Lawrence, B.S. (eds) *Handbook of Career Theory*. Cambridge: Cambridge University Press.

Maslow, A.H. (1987) *Motivation and Personality*. 3rd Edition (1st Edition, 1954). New York: Harper and Row.

McClelland, D.C. (1961) *The Achieving Society*. Princton: Van Nostrand.

Mowday, R.T., Porter, L.W. and Steers, R.M. (1982) *Employee-Organization Linkages: The Psychology of Commitment, Absenteeism, and Turnover*. New York: Academic Press.

Oliver, N. (1990) 'Rewards, investments, alternatives and organizational commitment: empirical evidence and theoretical development', *Journal of Occupational Psychology*, 63: 19-31.

Reichers, A.E. (1985) 'A review and reconceptualisation of organizational commitment', *Academy of Management Journal*, 10: 465-576.

Rollinson, D., Broadfield, A. and Edwards, D. (1998) *Organizational Behaviour and Analysis*. Harrow: Addison-Wesley.

Sievers, B. (1986) 'Beyond the surrogate of meaning', *Organization Studies*, 7 (4): 335-51.

Sparrow, P. and Marchington, M. (eds) (1998) *Human Resource Management, The New Agenda*. London: Financial Times Management.

Vroom, V.H. and Yetton, P.W. (1973) *Leadership and Decision Making*. Pittsburg, PA: University of Pittsburg Press.

6   Leadership

Beverly Metcalfe and Yochanan Altman

Introduction

Leadership is an attribute that is highly prized in most organizations and this has resulted in the topic becoming one of the most extensively researched and debated in organizational behaviour (Bass and Avolio, 1997). Yet studies rarely analyse sex or sex roles. We read as if leaders have no sex. However, on close reading of these texts it is quite apparent that when we read about leadership theory we are identifying with forms and realizations of 'idealized masculinity' (Oseen, 1997: 170). Very little research has examined the relationship between masculinity and femininity and leadership. The chapter begins by presenting the organization and managerial contexts within which the interest in gender and leadership theorizing has developed. We then provide an overview of trait, behavioural and contingency leadership studies and highlight their gendered perspectives. The discussion in particular draws attention to the differences and complementary qualities of men and women leaders. Recent developments in gender and management theorizing are then addressed. The analysis of 'masculinity and management' questions the ways in which gender relations and management practices sustain the power of men in organizational hierarchies. The section on the 'feminization of management' debates the changing cultural and organizational preferences for female qualities. The chapter concludes by reviewing the first ever recorded story of a woman assigned a leadership role. The biblical tale of *Deborah and Barak* represents a creative and dynamic way to explore how women have, historically and socially, been assigned roles that emphasize their reproductive and sexual attributes. Many would argue this is still the case today.

The context of women and leadership

The literature on management has failed to acknowledge that historically, and in different societies, leaders generally, and managers more specifically, have been predominantly men (Collinson and Hearn, 1994). Management is perceived as a male function. As Oseen highlights it is the 'sexually indifferent which obscures the sexually specific' (1997: 170). This is a major oversight because as workplace structures are changing, and as traditional hierarchical and command and control arrangements are disintegrating, working women are predicted to outnumber men by the beginning of the twenty-first century, as well as continuing to make headway in many management occupations (see Table 6.1).

Table 6.1 *Female executives by responsibility level*

Responsibility Level	1995	1996	1997	1998
Director	3.0	3.3	4.5	4.6
Function Head	5.8	6.8	8.3	10.7
Department Head	9.7	12.2	14.0	16.2
Section Leader	14.3	14.4	18.2	21.9

Source: 'The National Management Salary Survey', published by Remuneration Economics in association with Institute of Management, *National Salary Survey*, 1998: 3

The growing number of females in the workforce 'present a challenge to who we are as men and how we relate to men both to ourselves and to others' (Siedler, 1994: 215). Yet while women have increasingly become economically independent as they enter the workplace in a world that has been dominated by men, they have to fight and struggle with 'conditions of worklife that have been created by men, for men, with no consideration given to the women's attitude or point of view' (Damatteo, 1994: 21). It is disappointing that although women are playing a more active role in the labour market the majority are subjugated to lower level positions than service men. It is also significant that women are still often seen as commodities to be 'dehumanised, objectified, sold to and purchased by men' (Burrell, 1986: 89), and often represent sexual symbols or adornments supporting male leadership power and status. The aesthetics associated with women and professional managerial competence (Kanter, 1977) are clear signifiers of the roles they can expect to perform, usually reporting to and under a man.

If we examine any major text on leadership it will reveal a similar phenomenon: that gender is totally ignored as a pertinent issue. It does not constitute a relevant variable in the theory itself; it does not feature in the empirical validation of that theory and one will not find it referenced in the indices. That statement holds true to any theory on leadership, whether trait, situational, contingency, decision making or impact; whether formulated in the first part of this century, with the emergence of the Ohio and Michigan studies, or as late as the 1980s with the focus on transformational leadership. When one says 'ignored', that is not quite true. The implicit reading of any such text is that leadership equates with man-leadership. Up to the 1970s that would have been no more than a reflection of reality. There were no women in top positions to be found at the helm of public and corporate life in the Western world. (In the now defunct communist system, women held prominent positions in a wide range of social, communal and industrial roles, though that did not materially change their position in society.) Classical texts such as Whyte's *The Organization Man* (1957) and Dalton's *Men who Manage* (1959) cannot be accused of chauvinism; they are representing the reality and prevailing values of their day. Dalton, in a thorough investigation of three enterprises, refers to women only in a footnote which provides a glimpse into the normative perception of the times: 'several female secretaries and clerks were helpful in this research. The potential contributions of persons in these roles are usually unappreciated. For where female secretaries are treated as intellectual menials, they are disposed to be communicative with those who show awareness of their insights' (1959: 275-6). Women, quite simply, were not seen to be relevant to a managerial/leadership context, except as in Whyte's encompassing social analysis, in the role of partners to men in such positions, thereby helping to sustain and perpetuate the paradigm of middle-class organizational (male) careers.

More surprising perhaps is that as late as the 1980s and beyond – well after the establishment of the feminist movement and the inroads women made into boardrooms, gender does not feature in the texts on leadership. Bennis and Nanus' *Leaders* (1985), possibly the best selling book on the topic (200,000 copies sold by 1990: Bennis, 1990), lists the following as influential figures in informing a theory of leadership: Moses; Pericles; Julius Caesar; Jesus Christ; Martin Luther; Niccolo Machiavelli; James Madison. They add the following as contemporary 'sources of wisdom': Gandhi; Lenin; Churchill; De Gaulle; Dean Acheson; Mao Tse-Tung; Chester Bernard; Martin Luther King Jr.; John Gardner and Henry Kissinger (1985: 3-4). While the American bias may be excused in a popular book aimed at the American market, the lack of any woman figure in these lists is puzzling. What about Helen of Troy, Cleopatra, Elizabeth I, Isabella of Spain, Yakhaterina the Great, Madame Pompadour and among our contemporaries: Margaret Thatcher, Indira Gandhi, Eleanore Roosevelt, as examples of prominent female leaders who stirred the world. Bennis and Nanus (1985) are typical in overlooking women's contributions to business organization and business success as relevant sources of leadership theory formulation. Figures like Mary Kay Ash, Steve Shirley and Anita Roddick have been pioneers in creating new businesses, in advancing new organizational forms and contributing to business thinking. The bias in management literature towards 'big' business (e.g. Drucker's (1973) standard text) withholds recognition from those who are leaders of middle-sized enterprises, among them prominent women who are well in the public limelight.

One way of interpreting all that is, quite rightly, as an unwritten agenda of male domination to exclude women from discourses on power, related to their exclusion from positions of power. Yet, the 'fault' in the neglect of gender as a relevant factor in the study of leadership may well lie in the general and historical approach to the subject. Leadership, as an empirical genre of study, has focused on the task of leading and managing resources, even when consideration was given to the mobilization of people as 'people' not just as resources. That is, the leader him/her self was neglected as an issue. Emphases changed over the past sixty years and have been variably placed on the *situation* (Hersey and Blanchard, 1994) the *interaction* (Fiedler, 1967; Blake and Mouton, 1964), and the *influence process* (Yukl, 1994). Or, in other words, what Zuboff labelled, 'the pre-eminence of action centred skills' (1989: 102), which is the name of one theory, emanating from the armed forces and rather popular in the United Kingdom (Adair, 1973). Even in the treatment of charismatic and transformative leadership the onus is not on the person of the leader, rather the relations with followers. From an agency perspective, the person of the leader has been, by and large, treated as a void. The person as an agent of signification (Silverman, 1970) has taken on selected meanings in the study of leadership. Gender is not one of them.

Trait, behavioural and contingency theories of leadership

Trait theories

Most of the early leadership in the 1930s and 1940s used a trait theory approach based on the premise that successful leaders would possess distinguishable characteristics not found in their followers. Stodgill (1948 in Tosi et al., 1990) for example argued that leaders were more likely to display *intelligence, superior judgement, decisiveness* and have a high need for *achievement.* Trait approaches also linked physical characteristics such as weight, height, physique and energy to effective leadership. The emphasis on physical stature and body strength is not surprising given the minimum requirements for law enforcement and military occupations. These results signify why the majority of leaders are men and there has been little research on the relationship between masculinity or femininity and leadership. Women are generally afforded a lower status in the public sphere and are seen to occupy the domestic sphere by virtue of their reproductive capacities. Overall women are perceived (stereotypically) as less intelligent, emotional and therefore irrational. Physically they do not have the same presence or strength and power of men.

The traits of female leaders have been overlooked as it has generally been the case that for women to succeed they should conform to the cultural practices and behavioural characteristics prevalent in masculine dominated organizations (see White et al., 1997). Maddock and Parkin's (1993) research on gendered organization cultures highlighted how contextual and social differences in male management behaviour resulted in women struggling to convey both appropriate female behaviours and also valued management competence. In particular, Maddock and Parkin refer to the pre-eminence of a *gentlemen's* culture which acknowledges the special skills and abilities of women in a deferential way. Women are perceived very much as 'ladies' and play a key role in 'supporting' male management decision making. In *locker room* cultures the emphasis on 'male bonding and sporting relationships between men serves to exclude women from the men's club. Inclusion may mean women are expected to attend football matches, play golf and cricket and partake in male sexual banter and joking that often undermines women, and treats them nothing less than as a sexual object. Women are thus forced to 'play the game' and compromise their feminine identity. Where the emphasis is on leadership traits representing different representations of 'idealised masculinity' (the gentlemen or lad) it is problematic for women who have to juggle being a woman as well as a competent management professional.

Behavioural theories

An alternative approach would be to focus on the behavioural styles of leaders. Behavioural models suggest that effective leaders help their subordinates achieve goals in two ways: first by having task centred relations that focus on the quantity and quality of work; and second by being considerate and supportive of subordinates' needs and personal ambitions. The Ohio studies led to the classification of leadership styles in terms of initiating structure and consideration (Stodgill and Caan, 1957 in Tosi et al., 1990). Initiating structure focuses on the degree to which the leader assigns tasks, schedules work, and specifies procedures for the group members (task orientation). Consideration is defined as the degree to which the leader facilitates support, warmth and trust amongst his/her followers. Along similar lines a two dimensional classification was developed in the Michigan studies. Research by Likert (1961 in Grint, 1997) explained leadership in terms of leaders who were employee centred or production centred. The production centred leaders were those who defined precise work tasks and specified exact work standards. The employee centred leaders involved the subordinates in goal setting and decision making. Despite the differences in terminology the concept of autocratic and democratic leadership styles is clearly evident in behavioural theories. Eagly and Johnson (1990) and Eagly et al. (1992) recently pointed out that skill in interpersonal interaction may naturally lead to a management style that is democratic and participative, whereas those leaders lacking interpersonal skills would be more likely to be autocratic in their style. Given this it is surprising that little research on leadership styles and the dichotomy between autocratic and democratic has not considered gender as a relevant variable in shaping leadership behaviour.

A recent study by Luthar (1996) considered the gender differences in the evaluation of performance and leadership ability utilizing the autocratic – democratic manager framework. Luthar (1996) found that identical leadership style may be seen differently depending on the gender of the manager exhibiting that style (see Eagly et al., 1992). Indeed the view that female leaders are reacted to both in terms of their sex and their managerial position in the organization is consistent with the idea of 'sex-role spillover' discussed by Gutek and Marsh (1982 in Luthar, 1996). Sex-role spillover refers to the gender based expectations for behaviour that are irrelevant or inappropriate to work. In this sense women are more likely to suffer the consequences of the effects of sex-role spillover because male managers do not often experience incompatible role expectations.

Luthar's (1996) research found that in general democratic managers are rated higher performers than autocratic managers and this is consistent with earlier studies (Eagly et al., 1992). Interestingly, autocratic female managers were rated higher than autocratic male managers. This evaluation was greater among the female subjects. In contrast female subjects gave autocratic male managers low evaluations and judged them to be inferior leaders. Luthar (1996) suggests that perceptions of appropriate gender roles may be changing to the extent that females feel comfortable negatively evaluating an autocratic male leader and positively supporting a female autocratic leader. Theoretically the study is interesting as autocratic behaviour may not always put a female leader at a disadvantage. However, an earlier study by Eagly et al. (1992) found that autocratic female leaders will be devalued compared to autocratic male leaders.

While behavioural theories have provided an insight into the relationships between employees and leader their principal limitation is that they have paid little attention to the situation in which the relationships occurred and its effects on leadership style. Do different situations/contexts account for the success of the different leadership styles? The importance of the situation formed the basis of contingency models of leadership.

Contingency theories

Contingency theorists evaluate the variables that make certain leadership characteristics and behaviours effective in a specific organization context (Hellriegal et al., 1995; Hersey and Blanchard, 1994; Tosi et al., 1990). The contingency variables most often used are: first, a leader's personal characteristics; second, employees' personal characteristics; third, the group's characteristics; and fourth, the structure of the organization. Fiedler's (1967) contingency model specifies that performance is contingent on the leader's motivational system and the extent to which the leader controls the situation. The principal effect on group performance is the leader's Least Preferred Co-worker Score, but this can be mediated by contingent variables of group atmosphere, task structure and position power (Hellriegal et al., 1995).

Fiedler (1967) developed the Least Preferred Co-Worker (LPC) Scale to measure leadership style. Ratings are obtained by asking them to think about all the people they have worked with and then describe the person with whom they worked least well. Scales cover characteristics such as pleasant-unpleasant; accepting-rejecting; relaxed-tense; close-distant and so on. Low

LPC leaders tend to describe their colleagues in negative terms, and are primarily motivated by the achievement of the task. High LPC leaders describe their colleagues in a more positive way. They are motivated by establishing and maintaining close interpersonal relationships with subordinates. So which style is more effective? Fiedler's (1967) answer is that it all depends on the situation factors; and the degree to which the situation is favourable to the leader.

Given the emphasis on the 'situation' it is surprising that gender as a variable has not been considered. The working environment (group atmosphere) is undoubtedly affected by all female/all male/mixed sexed groups as indeed are dominant organization cultures (see Maddock and Parkin, 1993). Rosener (1997) for example refers to the concept of 'sexual static' which encompasses an array of misunderstandings in the workplace which cause frustration for women and discomfort for men. In essence men and women work differently and deal with work problems in different ways. She cites role confusion; garbled communication and culture clashes to articulate the differences in men and women's work experiences. Role confusion refers to the tensions that both men and women feel as their workplace and societal roles are changing. Communication stresses the differences in male and female communication patterns. Women communicate in a way that exchanges feelings and creates personal relationships. Men communicate to establish their status and show independence. Culture clash conveys the difference between male and female cultural values.

Individually and collectively the above generate 'sexual static' and unquestionably impact work attitudes/working relationships and the overall organizational climate.

When we talk of position power it is easy to conceptualize the phrase exclusively as something belonging to men. Men are socialized to believe that they have the right to influence and this is supported by the historical dominance of men in organizations. Within the discourses of contemporary organization analysis men are associated as '...in power, with power, and of power' (Kimmel, 1994 in Telford, 1996). Kanter (1977) argues women are more likely than men to be in lower level positions, are often outside the malestream work networks and relationships, and therefore have minimal power and influence. Attempts then to articulate women, leadership and power are problematic as it is assumed that women are more likely to exhibit powerlessness.

Whichever contingency model we analyse there is no consideration given to gender as a pertinent variable, and this is a key oversight given that women are increasingly taking on leadership roles. It could be argued that gender by itself has nothing to do with leadership theory per se. There are of course gender related attributes to leadership behaviour: strengths, preferences and tendencies that are gender based; and these will be elaborated later in this chapter. However, gender as a key variable does not necessarily inform a theory of leadership more than, say, personality or social class. We have neither personality nor class based leadership theories. Why should we expect to have a gender based leadership theory? Because, ignoring the gender based nature of leadership discourse would be a major omission for it is underwritten by a male perspective (Burke and McKeen, 1996).

Gender differences and managerial leadership: 'plus ça change, plus c'est la même chose'

One attempt to overcome this inadequate treatment of gender in leadership theorizing can be found in the women in management literature. However the approach has tended to concentrate on the under-utilization of women's skills by emphasizing their personal 'nurturing' qualities and to advocate the need for advancing the number of women managers and 'feminine leadership styles' (Rosener, 1990; Alimo-Metcalfe, 1994a, 1994b). Consultants and management trainers thus work on developing women's competencies so that they can more easily fit into the existing managerial structure or on highlighting the positive contributions and special feminine qualities of female managers. Yet this prescriptive analysis clearly can be seen as either 'blaming' women for not being like 'men' or for essentializing women's difference (Calas and Smircich, 1993). There is a persistent and frequently taken for granted assumption about the relationships between gender hierarchy and power in contemporary organizations (Collinson and Hearn, 1994; 1996). Theorizing in leadership has tended to link biological essentialism to leadership behaviour and represent idealized masculinity as the basis for, and the content of, the leader and leadership knowledge (Oseen, 1997). This weakness has been highlighted by many organizational theorists who treat the categories of sex and gender as distinct concepts, as discussed by Wilson (Chapter 1 in this volume).

This is a critical point when reviewing studies of gender and leadership for research clearly indicates that *gender* and not sex accounts for the socially learned traits and behaviours associated with, and, expected of men and women. Korabik (1990) argues that:

> Leadership is a function of sex role orientation rather than biological sex. The demonstration that socialisation rather than biology is responsible for leadership style means that females should not be excluded from positions which require instrumental ability merely on the basis of their sex (283).

This does not mean the study of men and women and management and leadership is not problematic as we struggle to conceptualize notions of gender, sexuality and organization representation. Occupations are clearly sex-typed, since the characteristics required for professional advancement are those seen as more commonly held by the majority sex occupant (Schein et al., 1996; Burke and McKeen, 1996).

This was demonstrated by the early work of Schein (1973, 1975) who sought to examine the relationship between sex-role stereotypes and the perceived personal characteristics of successful middle managers. Schein specifically tested the proposition that middle management effectiveness was correlated to the characteristics and attitudes associated with men rather than with women. 300 male and 167 female managers were asked to assess 92 descriptions and rate whether they were like men in general, women in general or successful middle managers. The Schein Descriptive Index (SDI) as it became known found that the analysis for both male and female respondents linked conclusively the ratings of men and management, and a non-significant relationship between women and management. Schein's early studies (1973, 1975) thus proved that 'psychological barriers' existed, in essence stereotypical perceptions about men and women's managerial abilities which made it difficult for women to progress in managerial work.

A repeat of Schein's work by Brenner et al. (1989) in the US found similar results as the original studies for male respondents. However female responses indicated managerial effectiveness as being related to female qualities. A similar conclusion was reached by Schein when she repeated her study in 1994 (Schein et al., 1996). Powell (1993) notes that while the perceptions of women managers have changed, they have not changed for male managers. This finding is significant. Although it indicates that male managers' attitudes and values have not changed, it marks a change for women's status and career aspirations for themselves as women. Clearly the feminist movement and the influence of anti-discriminatory legislative power and affirmative action in the United States has given women a stronger voice and confidence to compete with men on more equal terms. More recent studies by Schein et al. (1996) however indicate that the managerial sex-typing hypothesis is confirmed by females in every country except the US. Her study of 361 male and 228 female management students in Japan and China was compared to previous studies in the US, Great Britain and Germany (again using the SDI) and revealed that sex role stereotyping and 'think manager-think male' is a global phenomenon. Both men and women managers perceived that characteristics associated with managerial success were more likely to be held by men than women.

A different approach to exploring the nature of managerial stereotypes was taken by Butterfield and Powell (1979 in Powell, 1993) who focused not on masculine/feminine but on androgynous management styles. The study reported that 70 per cent of women and men respondents associate masculine traits with descriptions of a good manager. Less than 20 per cent of individuals described a good manager as androgynous and virtually no-one preferred a feminine good manager (Powell, 1993). A significant aspect of their work explored managerial effectiveness in terms of workers' and managers' stereotypical perceptions. They found that senior personnel were more likely to favour masculine traits, whereas subordinates preferred a more supportive work environment favoured by feminine traits. This provides one clear indication as to why women are so under represented at senior and executive levels in organizations.

It appears there is no escape from the sex trap. The attitudes of male managers are still prevalent at senior levels, and these deeply embedded sex-role prescriptions may well impact women's corporate and leadership development. Schein et al. assert that the think manager, think male phenomenon can foster bias against women in managerial selection, placement, promotion and training decisions' (1996: 34). Given this, several studies have attempted to evaluate whether men are more likely to emerge as leaders; and to investigate the effects of gender role on leadership emergence.

Megargee's (1969) classic study used gender neutral tasks and masculine and feminine tasks to assess emergent leadership patterns. Using the California Personality Inventory subjects were selected by their dominance scale rating (higher dominance indicating stereotypically masculine traits). Megargee allocated gender neutral tasks and found that in mixed groups with high dominance men and low dominance women, the men emerged as leaders 88 per cent of the time. However in groups of high dominance women and low dominance men the women emerged as leaders only 25 per cent of the time. The same patterns emerged when a masculine task was used: men were more likely, irrespective of the group make-up, to emerge as leaders.

There are clear perceptions then about what women can do and achieve in a leadership position. The study implies women lead according to sex-role expertise, by utilizing appropriate feminine qualities (Megargee, 1969). A phenomenon of the 1980s and 1990s is the emergence of sexual expertise in relation to female leadership (Wentworth and Anderson, 1984; Calas and Smircich, 1993; Fondas, 1997). Women are seen to assume a leadership position where 'feminine' qualities such as diplomacy and counselling are called for. However men by comparison, are seen to assume leadership positions just because they are men. This is different to saying that female leaders display leadership effectiveness. Research thus indicates men are rated higher than women in leadership tasks, and that leadership emergence is directly related to perceived masculine characteristics (Kent and Moss, 1994). On the one hand there is evidence of women's leadership skills being valued. On the other it still appears leadership theorizing is still embedded within the framework of a masculine discourse.

The discussion so far has highlighted how research has focused on male management even when the subject is female. Rosener's (1990) research is heralded as a breakthrough study of American corporate leaders. Her work clearly identified differences in male and female leadership styles. Her research focused on a group of successful male and female leaders and how they enacted their managerial role. Both men and women in the study were in the same pay bracket and had endured similar work/family friction. She found that transformational leadership was associated with women who encouraged participation; shared information; praised employee performance and whose managerial style worked at building a conciliatory approach thereby fostering mutual respect. In contrast masculine or transactional styles embraced a more functional approach based on competitiveness and power, where relations were reduced to commodities of exchange and business transactions. Men used rewards for effective performance and services rendered, and punishment/ retribution for inadequate performance. Rosener (1990) argues that originally the first wave of female executives adhered to many of the established male 'rules of conduct' and the behavioural and attitudinal styles that men equated with success. However she believes that the rising generation of women leaders are successful not because they follow the characteristics and styles of men but because they are 'drawing on the skills and attitudes they developed from their shared experience as women' (Rosener, 1990: 120). Bass and Avolio's (1997) work supported Rosner's finding's. Using the Multi-Factored Leadership Questionnaire (MLQ) they found that women were rated higher on transformational qualities than men. They attributed this to the fact that for observed differences in leadership women tend to be more nurturing, interested in others, and more socially sensitive. As a consequence they are likely to be seen as more 'effective' (Bass and Avolio, 1997: 208) by both their female and male followers. Yet surely this approach appears to reinforce stereotypical representations of female qualities rather than advance our understanding of the skills, attitudes and behaviours of successful and unsuccessful leaders?

Like Dammateo (1994) we would argue that Rosener's (1990) studies are flawed as they support sex-role management identity, something which management theorists are trying to explain and conceptualize. Rosener, by emphasising 'soft' or relationship skills being associated with women, and 'hard' or transactional skills with men, neglects the way the construction of masculinity and femininity is organizationally constituted (Parkin, 1993; Hearn and Parkin, 1995). Nor does she acknowledge how the connection between sexuality, gender and power occurs in organizational structures and processes. As we highlighted earlier it is sex-role orientation, not biological sex, that determines leadership behaviour. Gender cannot represent only a dual classification; gender identities must be seen as complex and contextually defined (Hearn and Parkin, 1995; Collinson and Hearn, 1994).

The overall conclusion seems to be that the masculine is dominant and where we essentialize difference as in the case of Rosener (1990), the implication is that women lead not like men, but are lesser than men or men with a lack (Oseen, 1997). Women generally are evaluated unfairly in terms of leadership ability because people hold sex stereotypical beliefs and attitudes (Alimo-Metcalfe, 1994a, 1994b; Luthar, 1996). As we attempt to demonstrate, the gendered nature of managerial discourse is more complex than a focus on the simple dualisms of masculinity and femininity, and public versus private, since sexualities are never static but shift in accordance with organizational, historical and social processes, the personal construction of sexual identity, as well as sex-role perceptions of managerial/leadership competence. The following two sections on masculinity and management and the feminization of management attempt to unravel a greater critical sensitivity to the nature of the unities, differences, and interrelations, between men and women and leadership theorizing.

Masculinity and management

Throughout this chapter we have discussed leadership theorizing and its implications/consequences for women. The discourses about management activity and managerial power and their effects rarely question the ways in which gender relations and managerial and leadership practices can often be mutually constituting and reproducing. Although we have highlighted that studies reveal that leadership skills are inherently related to masculine traits, this does not advance our understanding of the socially constructed notion of gender and its relationship to leadership activity. We also need to consider how specific masculinities are reproduced within, and between men, at senior levels in organizations; or indeed, the role masculinity plays in maintaining the elite power of managers in organizations (Collinson and Hearn, 1994; Hearn and Parkin, 1995).

Kanter's seminal study *Men and Women of The Corporation* (1977) illustrates the organization dynamics through which the power of men and managers can be reproduced. She uses the term 'homosexual reproduction' (1977: 48) to describe the practices that exclude women from managerial posts. These practices include men selecting men in their own image because they perceive them to be more reliable, loyal and committed. The corporate expectations depict men as a head of the household and a family breadwinner. The importance of marriage and a supportive wife as a man progresses in the organization is an example of how men relate to, and identify, with specific management selection criteria. 'Homosocial reproduction' explains the ways individual men and managers are recruited in relation to their skill to be able to demonstrate appropriate social (manly?) characteristics. However the criteria for effective managerial performance is 'White and male, with a certain shiny, clean cut look' (1977: 42). Kanter suggests that this managerial profile unifies those male managers who invariably went to an elite school, and are Protestant and Republicans. The restricted social criteria thus serve to exclude and devalue different/shifting types of masculine social identity in organizations. Kanter's concepts of homosexual and homosocial reproduction are useful in depicting how men use their power *with* and *over* men, and how the differences between men themselves can also characterize the nature of gendered discourses, networks and practices of management and organizations.

A more recent study of men and management and organizations by Collinson and Hearn (1994) outlines a variety of different practices and discourses that illustrates how masculinities are shaped contextually and highlights what brings men together and what differentiates them. These include: i) authoritarianism, in which aggressive and violent behaviour by men is reinforced; ii) paternalism, in which traditional roles/co-operation are emphasized. This can include for example younger men separating themselves from women and identifying with older men, and attempts to position women in a supporting role; iii) informalism, where informal relationships and contacts are emphasized either through sport or drinking; iv) careerism, in which concern for competition and achievement are clear signifiers of image and success and of being a man.

The studies by Kanter (1977) and Collinson and Hearn (1994; 1996) reveal how particular forms of masculinity are constructed and exist in relation both to femininity and other forms of masculinity. In this sense we can see how different masculinities are shaped and embedded in organizational practices that may be classified as 'hegemonic or subordinate'. As Hearn and Parkin state 'these masculinities are not fixed, but continually shifting. They have been shown to be culturally and historically contingent' (1995: 6).

The mention of cultural, historical and contingent factors is important if we consider the evolutionary process of management and leadership practices and of the 'preferred or complementary' behaviours required to support specific relations of production. The following section explores the issues surrounding the debate on the 'Feminization of Management' which has been presented as a cultural force influencing the management professional, and is particularly suited to new economic/work structures.

Feminization of management

The increased emphasis on new wave management techniques highlighting the importance of employee involvement, interpersonal and teamworking skills, and empowerment have highlighted personal characteristics and behaviours such as counselling, coaching, nurturing, and collaborating. These characteristics are traditionally associated with women with growing evidence pointing towards business requiring a more feminine approach to management (Lee, 1994; Lorenzon, 1996; Fondas, 1997). These developments towards feminized leadership styles reassert the feminist voice that men's competitive behaviours and attitudes need to change. Lee goes as far as to assert that there is a new model emerging, one that emphasizes 'persuasion over power, co-operation over competition, and inclusion over exclusion' (1994: 4).

The process of feminization however is not so clear cut. What is it that feminization really means? In the context of leadership it refers to the tendency by organization theorists and management practitioners to describe managerial work in terms of qualities defined as traditionally feminine. However as Lee asserts 'identifying a talent to nurture participation and inclusion as a female strength is not the same as assigning that ability to the exclusive domain of women' (1994: 28), and in no way does the feminization of management mean that women's style is more effective. Rosener (1990) comments significantly that when a participative style was considered deficient, it was considered female, but that now it is seen as effective we see it as 'non-gender related'. This critique is built upon by Fondas (1997) who argues that the 'unveiling' of the feminine has not been explicitly named by organizational scholars.

Fondas' (1997) analysis is significant; she acknowledges writers such as Peters (1987), Kanter (1989) and Champy (1994) who advocate supporting, nurturing and mentoring qualities, and the adoption of more interactional, relational and participatory styles; however she writes they do so by concluding that females are suited to managerial work in contemporary organization settings and that males also need to develop more female leadership traits. Fondas (1997) proposes that there are characteristics that are culturally associated with females appearing in descriptions of managerial work in the texts of contemporary writers, and that these texts function as carriers of a 'feminine ethos' to practising managers.

This is different to saying that managers need to adopt a more feminine leadership style. Fondas (1997) reveals how the unnamed 'feminine ethos' is embedded within contemporary management practices. Fondas explores through textual analysis three management texts. *Managing for Excellence* (Bradford and Cohen, 1984), *Leading Self Directed Work Teams* (Fisher, 1993) and *Re-engineering Management* (Champy, 1994) and uncovers a number of feminization themes. She highlights how managers are 'told' not to command and control but to nurture and support people. This involves sharing power, often associated with femininity, and relinquishing power over people, traditionally equated with masculinity. Managers are also 'told' via those feminized cultural messages to focus on helping and developing others in order to demonstrate their responsiveness and sensitivity to people's needs and motivations. This role incorporates the movement away from self interest towards relationship building, characterized by mutuality, co-operation and affiliation. A third theme that Fondas draws from the texts is the need for managers to build a connected network of relationships where managers work *with* subordinates in achieving shared goals and also in developing mutually supportive partnerships. This female culture of 'affiliation and collaboration' is in direct contrast to the male culture of 'competition and hierarchy' (Fondas, 1997: 268).

Fondas' analysis is important as she provides examples of writers 'invoking' feminine qualities in their descriptions of managerial work. These texts represent 'cultural carriers' that 'legitimise the feminine ethos, thereby initiating its institutionalisation as managers and organizations adapt the practices the writers describe' (1997: 269).

In the early texts on management first referred to in this chapter (Whyte, 1957; Dalton, 1959; Bennis and Nanus, 1985), it was rare to find practices that hinted at feminization because they were probably not acceptable. By contrast throughout the 1990s and on the brink of the millennium the social organization of work emphasizes partnership and non-hierarchical work modes where specific feminine traits are admired. As Calas and Smircich (1993) highlight, global competition is the context within which feminine characteristics are socially acceptable in men and women. Fondas rightly argues 'Why are the authors willing to use potent feminine imagery but not the name?' (1997: 272). The emphasis on the feminization of management reinforces traditional masculine discourses on management, because feminine identity is constructed under patriarchy 'extending patriarchal family's female role from the private to the public domain' (Calas and Smircich, 1993: 74). Fondas asserts that to recognize and name feminization is a 'complete reversal of femininity to masculinity in management discourse' (1997: 273). In this sense we should be sensitive to the difference between describing a feminized manager or a managerial role and the way that role is executed. Thus women can be themselves in a managerial capacity *only* because men perceive it is beneficial to patriarchal and organizational systems. We would argue therefore that feminization has not elevated the status of women's abilities and qualities, and that women and their special qualities are still being defined and constructed in relation to, and in support of, men and leadership. As Wajcman (1996) argues, the revaluing of the female style will not necessarily improve women's prospects of success. Men will probably adopt these female qualities to complement their traditional male ones, and 'Whereas men will be seen as adding new qualities to those they are already deemed to have, women will continue to be seen as only offering these qualities' (1996: 347).

The following biblical tale in particular draws on the nature of feminine traits and how they can support men in leadership positions.

Deborah and Barak

The story of Deborah is significant in the historical narrative on leadership as it is the first recorded account in the old testament of a woman leader. The Bible, of course, is the single most influential text in the making of Western civilization. It is therefore of interest to follow through the narrative closely and reflect on the position of the narrator vis-a-vis the question of leadership and gender. By doing so we gain an insight into the gendering of leadership, perhaps at its very inception. The story is set in the period immediately following the settlement of the ancient Hebrews in the land of Israel, about 1200 BC. That period was characterized by a loose tribal confederation without a central unifying authority. From time to time Judges (as they become to be known) rose to rule over some of the tribes in their regions as well as to lead them to war with their enemy and become spiritual figures who spoke the Word of God. Figures like Gideon, Samson and Samuel are among the most notable leaders in the Old Testament. Deborah stands out as the only woman leader in the triple role of judge, prophet and warlord. This is how the Bible tells her story.

> After Ehud died, the people of Israel sinned against the LORD again. So the LORD let them be conquered by Jabin, a Canaanite King who ruled in the city of Hazor. The commander of his army was Sisera, who lived at Harosheth-of-the Gentiles. Jabin had 900 iron chariots, and he ruled the people of Israel with cruelty and violence for twenty years. Then the people of Israel cried out to the LORD for help.

Now Deborah, the wife of Lappidoth, was a prophet, and she was serving as a judge for the Israelites at that time. She used to sit under a certain palm tree between Ramah and Bethel in the hill country of Ephraim, and the people of Israel would go there for her decisions. One day she sent for Barak son of Abinoam from the city of Kedesh in Naphtali and said to him, 'the LORD, the God of Israel, has given you this command: "Take ten thousand men from the tribes of Naphtali and Zebulun and lead them to Mount Tabor. I will bring Sisera, the commander of Jabin's army, to fight against you at the River Kishon. He will have his chariots and soldiers, but I will give you victory over him."'

Then Barak replied, 'I will go if you go with me, but if you don't go with me, I won't go either'.

She answered, 'All right, I will go with you, however, you won't get any credit for the victory, because the LORD will hand Sisera over to a woman.' So Deborah set off for Kedesh with Barak. Barak called the tribes of Zebulun and Naphtali to Kedesh, and 10,000 men followed him. Deborah went with him.

In the meantime Heber the Kenite had set up his tent close to Kedesh near the oak tree at Zanannim. He had moved away from the other Kenites, the descendants of Hobab, the brother-in-law of Moses.

When Sisera learnt that Barak had gone up to Mount Tabor, he called out his 900 iron chariots and all his men, and sent them from Harosheth-of-the-Gentiles to the River Kishon.

Then Deborah said to Barak, 'Go! The LORD is leading you! Today he has given you victory over Sisera.' So Barak went down from Mount Tabor with his 10,000 men. When Barak attacked with his army, the LORD threw Sisera into confusion together with all his chariots and men. Sisera got down from his chariot and fled on foot. Barak pursued the chariots and the army to Harosheth-of-the-Gentiles, and Sisera's whole army was killed. Not a man was left.

Sisera ran away to the tent of Jael, the wife of Heber the Kenite, because King Jabin of Hazor was at peace with Heber's family. Jael went out to meet Sisera and said to him, 'Come in, sir; come into my tent. Don't be afraid'. So he went in, and she hid him behind a curtain. He said to her, 'Please give me a drink of water; I'm thirsty.' She opened a leather bag of milk, gave him a drink, and hid him again. Then he told her, 'Stand at the door of the tent, and if anyone comes and asks you if someone is here, say no.'

Sisera was so tired that he fell sound asleep. Then Jael took a hammer and a tent peg, went up to him quietly, and killed him by driving the peg right through the side of his head and into the ground. When Barak came looking for Sisera, Jael went out to meet him and said to him, 'Come here! I'll show you the man you're looking for.' So he went in with her, and there was Sisera on the ground, dead, with the tent peg through his head.

That day God gave the Israelites victory over Jabin, the Canaanite king. They pressed harder and harder against him until they destroyed him.

The Song of Deborah and Barak

On that day Deborah and Barak son
of Abinoam sang this song:
Praise the LORD!
  The Israelites were determined to
    fight;
  the people gladly volunteered.
Listen, you kings!
  Pay attention, you rulers!
I will sing, I will play music
  to Israel's God, the LORD.
LORD, when you left the mountains
    of Seir,
  when you came out of the region
    of Edom,
  the earth shook, and rain fell from
    the sky.
  Yes, water poured down from the
    clouds.

The mountains quaked before the
    LORD of Sinai,
  before the LORD, the God of Israel.
In the days of Shamgar son of Anath,
    in the days of Jael,
caravans no longer went through the
    land,
  and travellers used the side roads.
The towns of Israel stood
    abandoned, Deborah;
  they stood empty until you came,
  came like a mother for Israel.
Then there was war in the land
  when the Israelites chose new gods.
Of the forty thousand men in Israel,
  did anyone carry shield or spear?
My heart is with the commanders of
    Israel,
  with the people who gladly
    volunteered.
  Praise the LORD!

Tell of it, you that ride on white
    donkeys,
  sitting on saddles,
  and you that must walk wherever
    you go.

Listen! The noisy crowds round the
    wells
  are telling of the LORD's victories,
  the victories of Israel's people!

Then the LORD's people marched
    down from their cities.
Lead on, Deborah, lead on!
  Lead on! Sing a song! Lead on!
Forward, Barak son of Abinoam,
  lead your captives away!
Then the faithful ones came down to
    their leaders;
  the LORD's people came to him
    ready to fight.
They came from Ephraim into the
    valley,
  behind the tribe of Benjamin and
    its people.
The commanders came down from
    Machir,
  the officers down from Zebulun.
The leaders of Issachar came with
    Deborah;
  yes, Issachar came and Barak too,
  and they followed him into the
    valley.
But the tribe of Reuben was divided,
  they could not decide whether to
    come.
Why did they stay behind with the
    sheep?
  To listen to shepherds calling the
    flocks?
Yes, the tribe of Reuben was divided,
  they could not decide whether to
    come.
The tribe of Gad stayed east of the
    Jordan,
  and the tribe of Dan remained by
    the ships.
The tribe of Asher stayed by the coast,
  they remained along the shore.
But the people of Zebulun and
    Naphtali
  risked their lives on the battlefield.

At Taanach, by the stream of Megiddo,
  the kings came and fought;

the kings of Canaan fought,
   but they took no silver away.
The stars fought from the sky;
   as they moved across the sky,
   they fought against Sisera.
A flood in the Kishon swept them
   away ---
   the onrushing River Kishon.
I shall march, march on, with strength!
Then the horses came galloping on,
   stamping the ground with their
   hooves.
"Put a curse on Meroz," says the
   angel of the LORD,
   'a curse, a curse on those who live
   there.
They did not come to help the LORD,
   come as soldiers to fight for him.'

Be blessed, of all women Jael,
   the wife of Heber the Kenite -
   be blessed of women who
   live in tents.
Sisera asked for water,
   milk she gave;
   Brought him cream in a
   masters bowl.
She took a tent peg in one hand,
   a workman's hammer in her right;
she struck Sisera and crushed his
   skull;
   she pierced him through his temple.
Between her legs,
   he sank to his knees;
   fell down and lay between her legs,
   he fell to the ground, slayed.

Sisera's mother looked out of the
   window;
   she gazed from behind the lattice.
'Why is his chariot so late in
   coming?' she asked.
   'Why are his horses to slow to
   return?'
Her wisest ladies answered her,
   and she told herself over and over,

'They are only finding things to
   capture and divide,
a women or two for every soldier,

rich cloth for Sisera,
embroidered pieces for the neck of
   the queen.'

May all your enemies die like that,
   O LORD,
   but may your friends shine like the
   rising sun!

And there was peace in the land for
40 years.

Source: Good News Bible (1994),
American   Bible   Society,
HarperCollins   Publishers   UK,
published   with   permission   of
HarperCollins.   Alterations to match
the Hebrew original made by the
second author.

Discussion and conclusions

Deborah, as formidable a figure as she was, is set within a males' universe. To start with, she is presented as someone's wife; which is the proper naming in the bible of women in a patriarchal society (and, in that respect, is no more than a naming). The careful reader will note that Lappidoth, Deborah's husband, is mentioned only once in the text. Significantly, the expression 'a Lappidoth's wife' has in Hebrew become synonymous with a resourceful and outgoing wife. Still, the bible does not ungender Deborah. She is presented clearly as a 'woman prophet', though this is implicitly clear from both her home and her position as married to a man (the tale makes a point she is a woman). She is a prophet, a judge, but, how interesting, not quite a combatant. Though she heralds the war against the Jabin and commands it strategically, the assistance of Barak her male counter-part is required to execute the actual battle plan. This is presented as a state of symbiosis in what became a key-phrase of the narrative. Barak says to Deborah; 'I will go if you go with me, but if you don't go with me, I won't go either' (verse 8). Deborah's reply is significant; 'All right, I will go with you, however you won't get any credit for the victory because the Lord will hand Sisera over to a woman' (verse 9), alluding to the second heroine figure of the tale: Jael. Jael, the wife of Heber the Kenite, complements Deborah in the tale through her active involvement in the slaying of Sisera, the commander-in-chief of Jabin's army, thereby contributing to the decisive victory of the Israelites.

The story of Deborah and Barak, and of Jael raises important issues regarding women's experience of leadership and management. Although the women are clearly represented as courageous, and, as such heroines, the tale hallmarks the confines of a female in a battle (organization) context. Deborah and Jael clearly do not challenge the conventional malestream and hierarchical notions of leadership. The bible's position is clearly spelled out. A woman can become a leader in her own right, and may assume most, but not all of a man's leadership roles: there is a domain, that of war, which is an all male domain. Is there much difference if we draw comparisons between the male executives in the boardroom in contemporary organizations? There is an inference that Barak by virtue of his manly strength has appropriate characteristics associated with leadership success, and in the modern corporation the persistence of organizational power relations reinforces dominant workplace masculinities. Throughout this chapter we have stressed that discourses of management frequently reflect masculine power and identity. Indeed throughout the history of management thought and practice there has been a recurrent association between gender hierarchy and organization on the one hand, and militarism and warfare on the other (Collinson and Hearn, 1996). Barak's warrior profile is a prime example of how management writers have tended to draw on military experience and language when formulating leadership theory (Grint, 1997).

The tale is also significant since it displays sexualized imagery pertaining to women, and also indicates the limitations of women's leadership ability in respect of her sexual identity. Deborah is portrayed as 'the mother of Israel' and provided her country and its people with appropriate nurture and support. The image of the 'mother' figure is of particular importance, Deborah can be seen to represent fertility, growth, sensitivity and warmth; she offers hope and a sense of rejuvenation as her people lament over their years of suffering:

> The towns of Israel stood
> abandoned, Deborah;
> they stood empty till you came,
> came like a mother for Israel.

Her leadership style is depicted as participatory and supportive, she 'listens', she was appointed by the Lord God of Israel. In direct contrast the persona of Sisera is perceived as dictatorial and hard; his reign was characterized by pain and misery:

> the earth shook, and rain fell from the sky.
> Yes water poured down from the
> clouds.

Sisera uses 'cruelty and violence' to rule the land. We can draw some comparisons with the work of feminist scholars who articulate men and women's different leadership styles by reference to stereotypical descriptions of male and female behaviour (see discussion on Rosener, 1990 above). Deborah can lead and help rebuild a nation, acknowledging women's reproductive and self-renewal qualities, but in more tough, competitive times she must submit to the strength and authority of a man, in the same way that women can be personnel managers or middle mangers today, but the battles in the boardroom must remain the domain for men.

The story of Sisera's assassination and the role of Jael in defeating him is equally alive with sexualized and traditionally feminine imagery:

> *Between her legs*
> he sank to his knees
> fell down and lay *between her legs* (author's emphasis)

Sisera's manly prowess is lost by seeking refuge in a woman's tent and hiding behind a curtain: his cowardly behaviour is manifested by association with a woman's world; inversely thus empowering Jael to command strength and be his match. Jael by seducing Sisera 'Come in, Sir; come into my tent', enchants him with her female allure. The reference to how Sisera fell 'between her legs' communicates powerful sexualized messages of how women can be successful if they use their sexual talents to win over men. The way Sisera 'sank' to his knees and 'fell down' emphasizes how men are seduced slowly, by female sexual power. Her role is that of seductress and her special talents her female sexual energy and vitality. Many commentators have noted that female sexual power is the most defining feature of women's presence in organizations, their place is of aesthetic accessory or indeed through her sexedness, a femme fatale (Burrell, 1986; Hearn and Parkin, 1995). Even where female talents are valued and praised the story of Deborah and Barak does so in a way that confines women's role and abilities. Deborah is strong in a supportive sense, she assists but does not direct Barak's war plan. Jael is presented as a sexual commodity. Through creating feminized imagery the biblical tale of Deborah and Barak succeeds in essentializing the differences between men and women and supports gendered stereotypes of men and women.

Conclusion

If stereotypical perceptions are still prevalent long after the first ever recorded account of a woman leader what can we conclude? Can we ever expect women to be equal when theorizing about leadership ability and effectiveness? The chapter has revealed that the link between leadership style and effectiveness is a tenuous one. Whereas previously management practitioners and organization consultants apparently preferred command-and-control type leadership approaches, the emphasis today on flatter organization structures, decentralization, and more advanced forms of open and two-way communication enhances the profile and status of more democratic and participatory styles. This is not to suggest of course that autocratic styles are not effective given the many examples of successful dictatorial leaders (both men and women, Marco Pierre White and Margaret Thatcher for example) in contemporary organizations.

And yet it appears that there is a silence about sexuality within management practices and discourses reinforcing supposed gender neutrality through organizational logic. When we 'unveil' (Fondas, 1997) the ways gendered identities are reproduced in management texts and practices men and masculinity appear to be privileged. This is particularly the case when we attempt to analyse leadership behaviour in organization settings. The literature discussed in this chapter linked management effectiveness and perceptions of management effectiveness to men and masculinities. The case of Deborah and Barak reinforced the unequal power relations between men and women and reduced women's role as an accessory to man, and as a sexual object supporting men. Will women continue to be treated as sexual commodities and tokens? And will they be able to challenge the conventional malestream notions of management and leadership? It could be argued that women are trapped in a male culture where both women and men are socialized for certain roles and managers need to develop male characteristics. Marshall suggests that the question of differing abilities between the sexes will never be resolved until we move beyond the 'foundations in male experience and sex role stereotypes,' (1995: 858). As Calas and Smircich (1993) and Marshall (1995) emphasize, the 'presence' of women in management may not be enough to break down the deeply entrenched attitudes that link masculinity to managerial power and status. Attempts to undo these stereotypes have primarily focused on the special (and different to men) qualities that women leaders possess, (Vinnicombe, 1987; Rosener, 1990; Alimo-Metcalfe, 1994a, 1994b). Where feminine qualities and skills are given pre-eminence they are done so under the veil of patriarchy, an issue Fondas (1997) highlights effectively. By preferring the feminine in contemporary texts we problematize the privileging of masculine in all areas of organization and management theory.   We cannot be gender neutral since gender is part of the conceptualizations of management. Calas and Smircich suggest that we can only move forward when we begin to understand female sexuality by theorizing it in its own right, not in relation to men so that we 'recognize that gender no longer equals women – therefore the implicitly male gendered organizational theorizing practices get noticed – and recognizing that the implicitly male gendered organizational theorizing has kept women's voices silent – therefore women's voices begin to be written into organizational theorising' (Calas and Smircich, 1991: 235).

References

Adair, J. (1973) *Action-Centred Leadership*. London: McGraw-Hill.

Alimo-Metcalfe, B. (1994a) 'Waiting for fish to grow feet! Removing organizational barriers to women's entry into leadership positions', in Tanton, M. (ed.) *Women in Management: a Developing Presence*. London: Routledge.

Alimo-Metcalfe, B. (1994b) 'Women in management: organizational socialization and assessment practices that prevent career advancement', in Mabey, C. and Lles, P. (eds) *Managing Learning*. London: Routledge.

Bass, B.M., and Avolio, B.J. (1997) 'Shatter the glass ceiling: women may make better managers', in Grint, K. (eds) *Leadership, Classical, Contemporary and Critical Approaches*. New York: Oxford University Press.

Bennis, W. (1990) *Why Leaders Can't Lead*. San Francisco: Jossey-Bass.

Bennis, W. and Nanus, B. (1985) *Leaders*. New York: Harper and Row.

Blake, R. and Mouton, J.S. (1964) *The Managerial Grid*. Houston, Texas: Gulf Publishing Co.

Bradford, D.L. and Cohen, H.R. (1984) *Managing for Excellence*, New York: Wiley, cited in Fondas, N. (1997) 'Feminization unveiled: Management writings in contemporary texts', *Academy of Management Review*, 22 (1): 257-82.

Brenner, O.C., Tomkiewicz, J., and Schein, V.E. (1989) 'The relationship between sex role stereotypes and requisite managerial characteristics', *Academy of Management Journal*, 32 (3): 662-69.

Burke, R.J. and McKeen, C.A. (1996) 'Do women at the top make a difference? Gender proportions and the experiences of managerial and professional women', *Human Relations*, 49 (3): 1093-1104.

Burrell, G. (1986) 'No accounting for sexuality', *Accounting Organizations and Society*, 12 (1): 89-101.

Calas, M.B. and Smircich, L. (1991) 'Voicing seduction to silence leadership', *Organization Studies*, 12 (4) 227-53.

Calas, M.B. and Smircich L. (1993) 'Dangerous liaisons: the feminine in management meets globalisation', *Business Horizons*, March–April: 73-83.

Champy, J. (1994) *Re-engineering Management: The Mandate for the New Leadership*. London: Harper Collins.

Champy, J. (1995) *Re-engineering Management: The Mandate for the New Leadership*, London: Harper Collins, cited in Fondas, N. (1997) 'Feminization unveiled: Management writings in contemporary texts', *Academy of Management Review*, 22 (1): 257-82.

Collinson, D.L. and Hearn, J. (1994) 'Naming men as men: implications for work organization and management', *Gender Work and Organization*, 1 (1): 2-22.

Collinson, D.L. and Hearn, J. (1996) 'Men managing leadership! Men and women of the corporation revisited', *International Review of Women and Leadership*, 1 (1): 1-24.

Dalton, M. (1959) *Men Who Manage*. New York: Wiley and Sons.

Damatteo, L.A. (1994) 'From hierarchy to unity between men and women managers? Towards an androgynous style of management', *Women in Management Review*, 9 (7): 21-33.

Drucker, P.F. (1973) *Management*. London: Heinemann.

Eagly, A.H. and Johnson, B.T. (1990) 'Gender and leadership style: a meta-analysis', *Psychological Bulletin*, 108: 233-56.

Eagly, A.H., Makhijani, M.G. and Klonsky, B.G. (1992) 'Gender and the evaluation of leaders: a meta analysis', *Psychological Bulletin*, 111: 3-22.

Fiedler, F.E. (1967) *A Theory of Leadership Effectiveness*. New York: McGraw-Hill.

Fisher, K. (1993) *Leading Self-directed Work Teams*. New York: McGraw-Hill.

Fondas, N. (1997) 'Feminization unveiled: Management writings in contemporary texts', *Academy of Management Review*, 22 (1): 257-82.

Grint, K. (ed.) (1997) *Leadership, Classic, Contemporary, and Critical Approaches*. New York: Oxford University Press.

Hearn, J. and Parkin, W. (1995) *Sex at Work: The Power and Paradox of Organization Sexualities*. London: Prentice Hall/Wheatsheaf (revised).

Hellriegal, D., Slocum, J.W., Woodman, R.W. (1995) *Organizational Behaviour*, Minneapolis, Wets Publishing Company.

Hersey, P. and Blanchard, K.H. (1984) *The Management of Organizational Behaviour*. 4th Edition. Englewood Cliffs, NJ: Prentice Hall.

Johnson, J.E.V. and Powell, P.L. (1994) 'Decision making risk and gender: are managers different?', *British Journal of Management*, 5 (2): 123-39.

Kanter, R.M. (1977) *Men and Women of the Corporation*. USA: Basic Books.

Kanter, R.M. (1989) 'The new managerial work', Harvard Business Review, 67 (6): 85-92, cited in Fondas, N. (1997) 'Feminization unveiled: Management writings in contemporary texts', *Academy of Management Review*, 22 (1): 257-82.

Kent, R.L. and Moss, S.E. (1994) 'Effects of sex and gender and role on leader's emergence', *Academy of Management Journal*, 37 (5): 1335-47.

Korabik, K. (1990) 'Androgyny and leadership style', *Journal of Business Ethics*, 9, 283-92.

Lee, C. (1994) 'The feminization of management', *Training*, 31 (11): 25-32.

Lorenzon, Z. (1996) 'Female leadership: some personal and professional reflections', *Leadership and Organization Development Journal*, 6 (9): 24-32.

Luthar, H.K. (1996) 'Gender differences in evaluation of performance and leadership ability: autocratic versus democratic managers', *Sex Roles*, 35 (5/6): 335-52.

Maddock, S. and Parkin, D. (1993) 'Gender cultures: women's choices and strategies at work', *Women in Management Review*, 2 (2): 3-9.

Marshall, J. (1995) 'Gender and management: a critical review of research', *British Journal of Management*, 6 (4): 553-63.

Megargee, E.I. (1969) 'Influence of sex roles on the manifestation of leadership', *Journal of Applied Psychology*, 53: 377-82.

Moore, H. (1994) 'Divided we stand: sex gender and sexual difference', *Feminist Review*, 47 (Summer): 78-95.

Oseen, C. (1997) 'Luce Irigaray, sexual difference and theorising leaders and leadership', *Gender, Work and Organization*, 4 (3): 170-84.

Parkin, W. (1993) 'The public and the private: gender sexuality and emotion', in Fineman, S. (ed.) *Emotion in Organizations*, London: Sage: 167-89.

Peters, T. (1987) *Thriving on Chaos*, New York: Knopf, cited in Fondas, N. (1997) 'Feminization unveiled: Management writings in contemporary texts', *Academy of Management Review*, 22 (1): 257-82.

Powell, G.N. (1993) *Women and Men in Management*. London: Sage.

Remuneration Economics (1998) *National Management Salary Survey*. London: Remuneration Economics and Institute of Management.

Rosener, J. (1990) 'Ways women lead', *Harvard Business Review*, November-December: 119-25.

Rosener, J. (1997) 'Sexual static', in *Leadership, Classic, Contemporary, and Critical Approaches*, in Grint, K. (ed.), New York: Oxford University Press.

Schein, V.E. (1973) 'One relationship between sex-role stereotypes and requisite management characteristics among female managers', *Journal of Applied Psychology*, 57 (2): 95-100.

Schein, V.E. (1975) 'Relationships between sex-role stereotypes and requisite management characteristics among female managers', *Journal of Applied Psychology*, 60 (3): 340-44.

Schein, V.E., Mueller, R., Lituchy, T. and Liu, J. (1996) 'Think manager, think male: a global phenomenon', *Journal of Organizational Behaviour*, 17: 33-41.

Siedler, V.J. (1994) 'Men, feminism and power', in Hearn, J. and Morgan, D. (eds) *New Masculinities and Social Theory*. London: Unwin Hyman.

Silverman, D. (1970) *The Theory of Organizations*. London: Heinemann.

Telford, L. (1996) 'Selves in bunkers: Organisational consequences of failing to verify alternative masculinities', in Cheng, C. (eds) *Masculinities in Organisations*. Thousand Oaks, California: Sage.

Tosi, L.H., Rizzo, J.R. and Carrol, S.J. (1990) *Managing Organizational Behaviour*. New York: Harper and Row.

Vinnicombe, S. (1987) 'What exactly are the differences in male and female working styles', *Women in Management Review*, 3 (1): 13-21.

Wajcman, J. (1996) 'Desperately seeking differences: is management style gendered?', *British Journal of Industrial Relations*, 34 (3): 333-49.

Wentworth, D.K. and Anderson, L.R. (1984) 'Emergent leadership as a function of sex and task type', *Sex Roles*, 11: 513-23.

White, B., Cox, M. and Cooper, C. (1997) 'A portrait of successful women', *Women in Management Review*, 12 (1): 27-34.

Whyte, W. J. Jr. (1957) *The Organization Man*. London: Jonathan Cape.

Yukl, G. (1994) *Leadership in Organizations*. 3rd Edition. Englewood Cliffs, NJ: Prentice Hall.

Zuboff, S. (1989) *In the Age of the Smart Machine*. Oxford: Heinemann Professional Publishing.

7   Teamworking

Elizabeth Sondhaus and Mary Beth Gallagher

Introduction

No one knows the true impact of the profound and dramatic changes business is experiencing today. In most companies business practices will never be the same, but what about their underlying organizational structures? Companies across the globe are facing tremendous pressures to continuously innovate and improve their business practices in order to remain competitive (Trent, 1996). At the same time that they introduce innovations, many still cling to traditional organizational values such as strong, individualistic leaders; different degrees of hierarchical control, authority, direction, and planning; and entrenched differences in pay, authority, status and power. This hidden agenda helps explain why many apparently promising new ideas do not work and why workers often feel so cynical about the sincerity of change attempts in their organizations. Many companies seem to want to have their cake and eat it, too: they want to change their operations so they can compete more effectively, yet they want to keep the power structure intact. They fail to accept the idea that innovations cannot thrive without fundamental structural changes.

The dilemma created by this dual agenda is glaringly evident in the team-based model of operations. Teams are one of the most popular innovations to date. In fact, some report that 'over the past decade, teaming has become a way of life in virtually all American companies' (Hayes, 1995). Organizations are highly committed to the team-based model because they believe teams offer benefits to everyone. In theory, businesses gain improved quality, productivity, reduced operating costs, increased efficiency and satisfied employees. Workers gain an opportunity to participate, to learn different job skills, to grow, and to experience empowerment and fulfillment (Wellins et al., 1991). However, in reality, teams often do not hit the mark. The question is 'why not?' The answer, at least in part, can be found in an analysis of gender, power and hierarchy.

Over the last decade, theorists have been paying more and more attention to the gendered nature of organizations, (Acker, 1990; Ely, 1995; Ferguson, 1984; Fletcher, 1998; Iannello, 1992; Itzen and Newman, 1995; Karsten, 1994; Savage and Witz, 1992). Only a few articles, however, have specifically addressed the impact of the team model on issues of hierarchy and power within organizations (Pinchot, 1992) and they fail to make any reference to gender. This chapter addresses this lack through a feminist analysis of team-based organizations. Of particular interest is whether the use of teams in the workplace has influenced the gendered distribution of power and position in modern organizations.

It is true that in many instances the team model has reduced the level of hierarchy in organizations while simultaneously increasing egalitarianism and employee empowerment.   However, this chapter argues that team-based organizations have fallen short of their potential for reducing organizational hierarchy and redistributing power since most organizations remain fundamentally gendered in their culture, structure and operation. Using the so-called 'gender lens' (Williams and MacAlpine, 1995) to view organizational power relationships not only makes these issues visible and subject to analysis, but also provides the understanding needed for change to occur.

Understanding organizations from a feminist perspective

In recent years, feminist thought has begun to influence organizational theory and practice, starting with the seminal works of Kanter (1977) and Ferguson (1984). This influence can be seen as the incorporation of key feminist concepts such as caring, voice, collaboration, empowerment, and egalitarianism into popular management trends such as organizational learning, teamwork, and participative leadership. In fact, some believe 'organizational cultures based on feminist values ... will more effectively empower their members to learn these skills than will cultures based on Western patriarchal masculine norms' (Schor et al., 1994). It is interesting to note that in most cases the feminist origins of these concepts go unacknowledged, which is a comment perhaps on the ongoing struggle for the feminist voice to be heard within the wider organizational world. For example, one of the most important feminist contributions to organizational theory, the idea that organizations are 'gendered' has been misunderstood by many popular approaches to organizational restructuring. It has been taken to refer to the number of men versus women holding certain (Lewis and Morgan, 1994) rather than the more complex understanding that masculine values tend to dominate many organizations (Lewis and Morgan, 1994). This gap in understanding helps explain why so many of the attempts at changing the nature of organizations have not been completely successful.

The issues related to defining the term 'gender' have been introduced elsewhere (Wilson, in this volume). For the purposes of the current discussion, it is useful to add Acker's description of gender as 'an analytic category' and 'a process by which human activities, practices and social structures are ordered in terms of differentiations between men and women' (Acker, 1992: 565 quoted in Lewis and Morgan, 1994: 642). It is in this sense that gender can be seen to permeate the ideas and practices of modern business organizations, since so much of how power and position are distributed in businesses is based on gendered beliefs about who should hold power (most commonly those who ascribe to masculine values), which behaviours and values are acceptable/

unacceptable within the organization (masculine) and even what language should be used to describe organizational behaviour (Maier, 1997). Maier (1997) describes what he sees as the key dimensions of this 'corporate masculinity'. These characteristics include: 1) 'No Sissy Stuff': the stigma of anything vaguely feminine (emotions, self-doubt, intuition) influencing behaviour at work which should be masculine (logical, rational, data-driven); 2) 'the Big Wheel': always striving for success, status and the need to be number one; 3) 'The Sturdy Oak': always appearing tough, confident and in control; and 4) 'Give 'Em Hell': maintaining an aura of violence, toughness and daring. It is important to recognize that the masculine practices alluded to (dominance, ranking, status, authority, intimidation, hierarchy, top-down decision-making, reckless bravado, and excessive involvement with work) are only considered masculine because they have traditionally been more typical of the patterns men engage in than women. So-called 'feminine' practices (empowerment, participation and linking, connection, intimacy, egalitarianism, inclusion and consensus) are only seen as feminine because they are currently more commonly seen in women. However, none of these approaches are inherently male or female.

Gherardi (1994) emphasizes the socially constructed nature of gender, seeing it as embedded in everyday social interactions as well as in deeply held cultural metaphors and beliefs. To her, femininity and masculinity are 'symbolic universes of meaning which derive from an implicit and explicit opposition. Affirming one entails denying the other, imagined to be antithetical to it' (Gherardi, 1994: 592). This dichotomization of masculinity and femininity (as discussed in Newell in this volume) represents the classical Western way of thinking, in which concepts such as masculine/feminine, public/private, reason/emotion, competition/collaboration, individualism/community are paired and in opposition to one another. These pairs are both antithetical and, as Gherardi (1994) indicates, their interdependence is hierarchical: the first terms are superior, the second ones inferior. This dichotomous thinking has been persistent in organizations. All of the 'superior' terms have been associated with what is most important in business: the public domain (real work), reason, competition, and individualism. It is becoming clearer that this dualistic model is fundamentally wrong since it fails to recognize the systemic way most organisms, teams and organizations actually operate. Every person within a team and every team within an organization is a vital part of the whole. Dualism also fails to address the reality that most of these paired constructs actually co-exist and complement each other. For example, successful businesses today need to use both the rational and emotional skills of their employees and they must support both the public and private aspects of people's lives in order to be successful.

The persistence of the traditional view of organizational structures and processes as gender neutral has made it difficult to accept the idea of gendered organizations. The gender-neutral paradigm arises when men in organizations as well as in the broader society equate their behaviour and perspectives with universal human attributes. Therefore, organizational structures and processes based on these masculine values are seen to be gender neutral since they are presented as being based on fundamental human attributes (Acker, 1990). Qualities such as objectivity, competition, rationality, ambition, decisiveness, unemotionality, and commitment to rules, order and hierarchy are all part of the 'masculinist' culture that dominates most organizations (Maier, 1997). It is these qualities that make organizations 'gendered' in the way they operate and in the values they espouse.

Organizations may also have failed to embrace the importance of gender due to the influence of so-called 'organizational humanism' which began in the humanist movement of the 1950s and 1960s (Ramsey and Calvert, 1994). Humanism initially emphasized respect, freedom, the recognition of individual worth, and the full development of human potential. However, according to Ramsey and Calvert (1994), organizational humanism, while maintaining the original humanistic rhetoric, distorted these original values and goals in order to accomplish organizational goals and manage the 'bottom line'. Organizational humanism requires that organizational needs subsume those of individuals and that individual differences be homogenized. Organizational humanist methods which emphasize similarities rather than differences, the inevitability of hierarchy and competition, and the importance of individualism and autonomy may have to this point overshadowed the feminist approach. The rapidly changing demands of the current and future workplace make it imperative to shift away from organizational humanism and instead to incorporate feminist principles into the process of organizational change.

Acker (1990) makes a strong argument for the importance of understanding gender and organizations. She cites the following reasons: 1) gender segregation of work which is partly created by organizational structures that keep most women and minorities at the bottom and most men at the top; 2) male/female income and status inequality that is also partly created by organizational processes which lock in salaries for men and women in analogous positions at different levels; 3) the role organizations play as major arenas for the invention and reproduction of cultural images of gender, such as strong men as individualistic hero leaders and strong women as overly aggressive; and 4) the need to make organizations more democratic and humane (Acker, 1990). Until recently, the gendered nature of organizations remained invisible. Only by making these issues both visible and open to discussion can a recognition of the outdated and dysfunctional nature of a solely masculine organizational ethos be attained. As Maier (1997) argues, 'it is only by abandoning this [masculinist] script, that organizations will promote not only gender equity, but optimum performance.'

Power (which is more fully discussed in Green et al., in this volume) is often understood to mean domination or the ability of one person to get another to do what he/she would not ordinarily do (Iannello, 1992). However, power can also mean the ability to act and accomplish goals. When power exists in the first sense, it supports a hierarchical organizational structure with a few people at the top of an organization having control over the actions of the majority of others. In this configuration, most of the people in the organization feel thwarted both in their ambitions and in their actions. As a result, inefficiency and delays grow and motivation and productivity decline. Also, power as the 'dominant control system creates bottlenecks, and squeezes a lot of intelligence out of the picture' (Pinchot, 1992). When power is the ability to act without being controlled from above, people can maximize their abilities and energies and thereby expand the resources available to the organization as a whole (Iannello, 1992). The currently popular term 'empowerment' means the power to do or accomplish something by exercising control over oneself. Teams are often described as 'empowering' their members to perform in a way they could not within traditionally structured organizations, since through empowerment they are meant to truly have control over their own activities.

Until recently, hierarchy as an expression of power relationships characterized most modern business organizations. Team-based organizations arose as a response to the increasing difficulties traditional hierarchical organizations had navigating the modern business environment. Historically, the concept of hierarchy developed from the need to define organizations which operated with a top-down delegation of power and function (Iannello, 1992). As with the term gender, power when used to connote domination is central to the most common definition of hierarchy as which describes hierarchical systems as those system that involve systematic and unequal distributions of power, privilege and authority (Iannello, 1992).

The most common defence for the use of hierarchy in organizations is its perceived efficiency. It is believed to offer a clear structure, formal rules and specific roles so as to create a stable and consistent work environment. However, some have argued that the true goals of hierarchical work organizations are not technical efficiency but rather accumulation and control (Ramsey and Calvert, 1994). From this perspective, one of the major reasons for the development of hierarchy was the wish of those in power 'to maintain their position without threat from those at lower levels' (Iannello, 1992). Therefore, hierarchy itself can also be seen to be a social construction, in that it is not an inevitable or 'natural' means of organization, but rather one that serves particular social and political ends. It follows that hierarchy can also be altered with changes in the prevailing ideology and values. Although there is no single feminist position regarding hierarchy, some argue that people must accept the reality of hierarchical institutions and work within them to bring about equality. Others argue that viable alternatives to hierarchical organization do exist and should be implemented where, for example, different members could take turns sharing leadership positions and responsibility (Iannello, 1992).

Team-based organizations

Teams have been a hot topic in business in the US for some time. But what exactly are they? The simplest definition of a team is 'any group of people who need each other to accomplish a result' (Senge et al., 1994: 354). Katzenbach and Smith (1993: 14) say a team is 'a small number of people with complementary skills who are committed to a common purpose, performance goals, and approach for which they hold themselves mutually accountable.' One very popular team model is the self-directed team, which is based on the idea that small groups of people be given the power to manage themselves and their daily work (Wellins et al., 1991). Self-directed teams handle their job responsibilities, plan and schedule their work, make production-related decisions, take action to solve problems, and share leadership responsibilities. The underlying assumption here, of course, is that teams have the power to do these things.

From these definitions it is clear that, at least in theory, the team model is based on the principles of collaboration, empowerment, reduced hierarchy and open communications (Pinchot, 1992), all of which are basic feminist ideals. Additionally, there is data that indicates that from a traditional management point of view teams can be very effective (Banker et al., 1996; Frohman, 1995; Ortiz, 1998). The key benefits of teams from this vantage point include: a faster response to technological change; fewer, simpler job classifications; better 'buy-in' by workers to organizational goals and values; innovative and effective problem-solving; skill development and cross-training of staff; improved quality and customer service; and increased productivity and profitability (Harrington-Macklin, 1994). In fact, a 1991 survey of executives in 340 American companies indicated that for 'the three most serious problems [facing those organizations] – customer service, cost reduction, and product quality – teamwork was cited consistently as one of the most important solutions being used' (Frohman, 1995: 21).

Despite these positive evaluations, many observers do not believe teams have been as effective as they could be for a variety of reasons (Koze and Masciale, 1993). Although not explicitly drawn from a feminist model, many of these concerns involve issues fundamental to feminist organizational theory. For example, the results of a recent survey of 4,500 teams at 500 organizations suggest that 'many companies are hindering performance by not changing their organizational structures to support their teams' (American Management Association, 1993: 24). The majority of respondents in this study indicated that organizational and individual factors were the main obstacles to effective team performance. Only 15 per cent of those surveyed reported that team-specific factors, such as group problem solving, meeting and conflict management, interfered with team functioning (American Management Association, 1993). Problems were most frequently attributed to reward/compensation programmes; performance appraisals; top management; organizational cultures; and organizations that require staff to work on as many as three of four teams simultaneously, thereby reducing both productivity and team cohesiveness (Koze and Masciale, 1993). A brief review of some of these traditional organizational practices will help to illustrate why many team-based organizations miss the mark.

Reward and compensation programmes can be one of the most influential practices within an organization (Lawler, 1994). Reward systems identify behaviours that are valued by the organization from those that are not. When well designed and implemented, reward systems align employee behaviour with organizational objectives. The impact reward systems have on individual and group behaviour is most commonly understood from the perspective of the expectancy theory model (Vroom, 1964). The model suggests that behaviour is initiated and guided by the belief that behaviour will create outcomes, that the outcomes will be rewarded, that the rewards will be valued, and that the desired performance is possible (Vroom, 1964; Lawler, 1973). Applied simply to organizational behaviour, an individual's level of effort and ability leads to performance. The performance results in an outcome, the outcome is rewarded and the reward influences future behaviour (Lawler, 1994). Therefore, the outcomes that are rewarded within an organization motivate and influence behaviour. If, for example, rewards are based upon individual contributions, the organization will be dominated by individualists who seek to differentiate themselves from their colleagues in order to be rewarded. Most organizations remain inherently individualistic as rewards continue to be allocated based upon individual performance, despite the recent advent of teams. A recent study cited by Koze and Masciale (1993) indicated that 80 per cent of those surveyed stated that their reward and compensation programmes focused on individual performance, ignoring team performance altogether. Since individual behaviour is being rewarded, there is little impetus to perform well as a team, which undermines the fundamental principles and benefits of team-based organizations.

Another common problem confronting team-based organizations is the disconnection of senior managers from the rest of the organization. As teams continue to become the preferred business unit within organizations, senior leadership groups continue to function in what Katzenbach (1997: 51) describes as 'the single-leader mode'. Although teams are touted as being capable of outperforming individuals, especially when confronted with complex business problems, most executives function from a position of power and status that a traditional hierarchy provides (Katzenbach, 1997). Therefore, senior management groups prefer to operate as individuals and not as teams because they have mastered the dynamics of a traditional pyramid hierarchy. In fact, most traditional management education espouses the benefits of obtaining power and control in order to influence the performance of subordinates (Thomann and Strickland, 1992). To function as a member of a team would compromise the very skills and strategies that got managers to the top.

The phenomenon of individuals rather than teams at the top of an organization sends a mixed message to the rest of the organization about the value of teams. Most teams are implemented in organizations under the guise of improving organizational effectiveness through self-direction and empowerment. However, in many instances those at the top continue to work as individuals and to retain ultimate power and control over budgetary issues, the flow of information and other valuable resources (Pinchot, 1992). For example, after much deliberation work teams will frequently develop a work plan only to have the proposal vetoed by a senior vice president. Although team-based organizations are an attempt to decentralize decision making in order to deal with a rapidly changing work environment, rarely is participative management an organizational norm (Thomann and Strickland, 1992). Since power and control have been the true currency of organizations for decades, relinquishing these valued 'possessions' will not come easily, especially for those at the top (Block, 1999). For team-based organizations to truly utilize collective knowledge, resources and expertise in order to create a competitive advantage, collaboration will need to replace positional power throughout the organization (Thomann and Strickland, 1992).

Since many organizational leaders tend to possess an autocratic management style and rewards tend to be based upon individual contributions, the prevailing culture within many team-based organizations is the antithesis of teamwork. Developing team-based organizations is intended to create empowered decision making, flatten hierarchies and create a collaborative work environment as a means of creating a more adaptive and flexible organization. If, however, the prevailing organizational culture rewards the acquisition of power and control via promotion, salary increases are predicated upon individual assessments, and executives behave as solitary powerful leaders, the work environment advocates competition not collaboration. Morley and Garavan (1995: 10) point out that 'culture assumes significance usually because the strategy of the organization, the type of people in power and its structures and systems reflect the dominant managerial ideology or culture'. Therefore, managerial practices should be aligned with stated organizational objectives: improved quality, productivity, reduced operating costs, increased efficiency and satisfied employees, which is the impetus for implementing teams. Furthermore, these practices should support the structural design of the organization, which is team-based. When the culture values winning and individuals are rewarded for out-performing one another, teams are destined to fail. All of the problems discussed above essentially stem from a failure to change organizational ideology and practice, largely because traditional organizational structures remain in place which compete with and undermine the team-based model.

In addition to the need to fundamentally shift organizational culture and structures in support of team-based organizations, the prevailing management literature regarding teams also needs to be re-evaluated. Consider, for example, the popular team development model of forming, storming, norming, performing and adjourning (Tuckman, 1965). This model suggests that there is a universal progression that all teams experience (Robbins, 1996). Using the 'gender lens' (Williams and MacAlpine, 1995), once again the themes of hierarchy and power come into focus. Tuckman's model highlights the interpersonal conflicts associated with team work – the forming, storming and norming stages being characterized by experiences of testing, intragroup conflict and defining acceptable group behaviour respectively – while postulating that once the power struggles are resolved within each stage, the group progresses to a higher level of performance. This seems to be a very 'masculine' view of team development – focusing on power and hierarchy – while ignoring other aspects of team development such as the impact of organizational context on team development (Robbins, 1996). The airline industry provides an example of the importance of organizational context on the development of work teams. Flight crews meet and disband daily and their ability to quickly come together and work as a team is vital to the safety of all those onboard (Robbins, 1996). In this situation, there is no time for the power struggles and other interpersonal conflicts associated with prevailing team models. In order for team models to act as resources in the development of team-based organizations, the models must reflect the complexity of the team experience.

Several individual factors also limit the effectiveness of teams. Many of these stem from differences in work and interpersonal styles, ethnicity, gender, race and power. These include: team members who are unwilling or afraid to set aside position and power and to give up past practices; differences in levels of skill, education or training that may result in some team members having to take more responsibility than others; difficulties individual team members have when faced by challenges to their personal beliefs (Koze and Masciale, 1993); a lack of team-based skills in issues such as conflict management, group decision making, problem-solving, dealing with differences and even understanding the team development process which make working in a team setting very difficult; and recognition by individual team members that the organization is not truly committed to sharing leadership and power. Obviously, it is not only organizations that need to change their basic orientation to business arrangements. Many of the people employed by companies have nothing but the traditional hierarchical paradigms from which to work. For example, for all but the youngest workers, the workplace has traditionally been hierarchically structured with rigid roles, rules and structure. Many people were also raised in families that were hierarchical. When people are put into a different paradigm like the team-based approach and given more autonomy and empowerment, they do not know what to do or how to act. They also do not know whether or not to trust this change as being real and safe. A more thorough analysis of these factors is now in order to fully understand both the implications of the present state of team functioning and the possibilities for change.

A feminist analysis of team-based organizations

There have been a number of discussions recently regarding the establishment and operation of feminist organizations (Ferguson, 1984; Iannello, 1992; Itzen and Newman, 1995; Morgen, 1994; Riger, 1994; Savage and Witz, 1992; Schor et al., 1994). Most deal with traditional women's organizations, such as social service agencies and women's health care. Others address the issues raised by a feminist analysis of more traditional male dominated workplaces, such as law offices, engineering firms and the publishing industry (Ely, 1995; Farrell, 1994; Fletcher, 1998; Maier, 1997). Although many of these studies refer to teams, none specifically investigate team-based organizations using a feminist approach. The need for this analysis is especially pressing since the team model is now so widely used in business and yet is so often unsatisfactory. Because the parallels between team theory and feminist organizational models are very strong, these models can be used not only to understand but to improve the functioning of team-based organizations.

In their critique of organizational humanism, Ramsey and Calvert (1994) raised a number of points germane to the analysis of team-based organizations. To begin with, although the development of teams stemmed largely from the need to compete successfully in a rapidly changing business environment, at least some of the push towards a team model came from a desire to counteract the damage done to individuals by traditional organizational structures. Unfortunately, however, most companies that employ teams often remain fundamentally hierarchical and bureaucratic in nature. Teams and other innovations are simply meant to improve rather than change existing forms. Status and power still emanate from certain positions within the organizational hierarchy. Rigid rules and procedures govern much of daily activity. Individuals are given the 'right' to control others based solely on their hierarchical rank within the organization, rather than basing leadership on differences in skill, knowledge or experience, as the team-based model indicates. When power structures remain the same, teams feel powerless and they fail to thrive. In the optimum situation, control comes not from above but from the collaboration and open communication within and between teams in an organization. Effective team-based organizations 'redistribute and balance the power and spread intelligence and responsibility more widely' (Pinchot, 1992: 3).

Most often, hierarchical positions are highly gendered in that they have traditionally been associated with masculine ideals. Corporate leadership is still dominated by the myth of the hero. The heroes are males, usually white males, and, as such, they are both more entitled and more qualified to hold power (e.g. 'father knows best'). Due to the power of these myths, although women and minorities are now more visible in organizations and may play important roles on teams, they continue to hit a 'power ceiling' when it comes to getting access to positions of greater power within the higher ranks. In effective team-based organizations, woman and (ethnic) minorities would be as empowered as all other workers. Women and minorities would also make an even greater contribution and reach equal status 'given structures and processes to balance the power, and given excellent education and training [for] all' (Pinchot, 1992: 5). One bureaucratic idea that some employees must be controlled by others in order to be productive also persists. From this perspective, 'teams created as "add-ons" are still embedded in hierarchical structures; they are created as better ways of being productive within their own areas, not to challenge or make changes in the larger system' (Ramsey and Calvert, 1994). Clearly, this effort represents an ad hoc process rather than a truly systemic approach to change.

A feminist critique would suggest that permanent power relationships could be replaced by temporary and shifting ones. These transitory power relationships would be based on differences in expertise, professional development, knowledge or commitment and would exist only as long as needed to accomplish specific goals (Ramsey and Calvert, 1994). In teams, leadership roles could be transferred from member to member, depending on the particular need of the team at the time and the particular skills of its members. In addition, the hierarchical model would be replaced with one based on the principals of inclusion and connection. Hierarchical ranking would be replaced by linking, where people's different but interrelated roles or responsibilities would no longer be equated with either inferiority or superiority. Pay inequities based solely on rank would be replaced with pay based on experience, expertise and skill. Huge pay gaps between upper management and other employees would be eliminated since positions based on rank would no longer be overvalued. In fact, the very notion of 'upper' management and 'lower' level employees would disappear since that language is based on hierarchical thinking.

Leaders would still be necessary in team-based organizations but rather than being seated at the top of a power pyramid, they would be seen as the center of webs of relationships. Their job would be to 'draw others closer to the center, developing and strengthening interrelationships' rather than organizing or controlling those with less power (Ramsey and Calvert, 1994). The most effective leaders would give 'unprecedented freedom to people to select their own goals and then figure out their own system of doing work' (Pinchot, 1992: 4). They would act to maintain fairness in opportunities and rewards, facilitate communications and decision making, demand higher levels of communication, and ensure diversity of representation on teams.

In such a scenario, we suggest a need for capable leaders to emphasize and encourage the interconnection between various teams and model the way people are to be treated with respect within an organization. These leaders would move individual teams away from narrow, self-interest 'to serving the common good and shared vision and mission of the organization' (Pinchot and Pinchot, 1996: 18). The best leadership makes the common purposes inspirational and surrounds the collaborations with strong values, mission and standards (Pinchot, 1992). Leadership can also be seen not only as a position but as an approach to work, with the goal of eliciting leadership capacity throughout the organization. Everyone would participate in leadership and everyone would be responsible for his or her own learning, growth, commitment and contribution.

As mentioned above, power and hierarchy are closely linked. In a hierarchical system, power is still defined as 'power over' and those with power are seen to be of greater value to the organization than those without it. Often, in team-based organizations power sharing is still based on the idea that the power to be shared is located in certain positions and can be 'given' to other positions. For example, many team models describe shifting the power traditionally held by middle management to teams with respect to many of the aspects of day-to-day work, such as scheduling, hiring/firing, problem-solving and production-related decision making. In addition, some problems with team success have been attributed to middle management's resistance to their loss of power. Feminists would argue that power received under these conditions is not really power, 'it is only a loan of the temporary ability to act in tightly circumscribed ways' (Ramsey and Calvert, 1994). Therefore, one of the reasons teams have not been as successful as they might have been is because they have not really attained power within the organizational framework. In order to truly equalize power, management and workers must share 'responsibility with' rather than 'responsibility for' each other. This means 'responsibility for one's own development within relationships supportive of mutual development, where power relationships, and hence hierarchy, are fluid' (Ramsey and Calvert, 1994: 89). This is the process by which teams would be most effective. It is very similar to what Joyce Fletcher (1998) called the 'creating team' aspect of the relational practice of work. The process of creating team involves creating the background conditions in which group life can flourish by both attending to the needs of the individual and attending to collective needs. The underlying belief is that when individuals feel understood, accepted, appreciated or 'heard,' they are more likely to provide those same benefits to others, adding strong interaction and connection to their group life (Fletcher, 1998). In addition, this practice is rooted in the belief that it is valuable to understanding of problems or situations from a collective perspective, using everyone's ideas and input (Fletcher, 1998). All of these values form the basis for the collaborative organization.

A case study – teamwork in the masculine mode

The following case study illustrates the problems and pitfalls encountered when a conventional, hierarchical North American company tries to implement a team model in a traditionally structured organization. In order to protect the confidentiality of this organization, its name and certain identifying information has been omitted from the discussion, which follows. The company is in the hospitality industry, employing tens of thousands of people and serving millions of customers each year. After a quality problem was discovered several years ago, the company moved to implement a team model as part of a total quality management initiative. At the company's headquarters alone, there were almost 100 cross-functional teams involving hundreds of employees working on a variety of projects. Teams were led by managers and they usually included employees from multiple departments. These teams, in turn, were generally managed by higher level directional teams. Team leaders were recruited by department heads from the departments responsible for the various projects. They were assigned as team leaders according to the strength of their individual job performances as well as for their past experience as team leaders. Therefore, the same set of individuals was often repeatedly assigned to the team leader role. Although individual teams were given some responsibility for decision making regarding their projects, upper management maintained ultimate control. All final decisions were made in regular meetings of the upper management team.

Individuals within the company identified several organizational problems stemming from this arrangement. These difficulties arose in the following areas: first, training – limited and inadequate training was provided for team members and team leaders regarding both team functions and how to operate within a team framework. Training efforts provided by the organization were disjointed and fragmented. Second, workload was a problem: employees, especially team leaders, felt overworked and underpaid. Employees typically served on several teams (an average of four) while also being required to meet the demands of their individual work roles. Third, the quality of management support was raised: most employees perceived a lack of executive level support for the team process. Many key executives still seemed to view teams as a necessary evil needed to address a specific organizational problem (quality) and not as an asset to the company. Finally, performance appraisals and rewards were based on individual performance instead of team performance.

The problems experienced by this traditional North American company can be readily understood when analysed from a feminist perspective. In this setting, as in many others, teams were introduced in response to a pressing business need and not from any desire to change the fundamental structures of the organization or to empower individual employees. Like many companies that institute the team model, this one remained fundamentally hierarchical and bureaucratic in nature (Ramsey and Calvert, 1994). Teams, as an organizational tool, were implemented solely to improve particular functions rather than to change existing forms. Status and power in this organization still came from upper management positions within the organizational hierarchy. Team leaders had significant power based on their individual positions as managers and by their selection by their own supervisors. They were given the 'right' to manage the teams based on their hierarchical position within the organization, rather than on their skills or knowledge. Problematically, as Ramsey and Calvert (1994) indicate, when power structures remain the same as in this case, teams feel powerless and they fail to flourish.

In the present study, power and hierarchy were entwined. Within any hierarchical organization, power is defined as 'power over' and those with power are more highly valued than those without it (Ramsey and Calvert, 1994). In our example the idea of power sharing in this organization (via the team model) stems from the belief that power comes from management positions and can be 'given' (or, perhaps more accurately, 'loaned') to the teams in order for them to accomplish their tasks. Yet, the teams never truly had power, since all final decisions continue to be made by upper management. Also, if one accepts the notion that knowledge is power, one can see how teams remain disempowered in this organization in other ways as well. Employees complained that the training they are provided to assist team functioning was inadequate. They did not learn how to best function in a team nor how to handle common challenges that impede team effectiveness. Being denied the tools necessary to function effectively in a team environment, they were also kept from maximizing the power that teams would ideally provide. In this way, those in power within the organization attempted to reap some of the benefits of teams without facing the danger to their own positions within the hierarchy that could arise if they truly empowered their workforce.

The desire to maintain the power status quo was also evidenced by senior management's perceived antipathy to teams and lack of action in changing other organizational structures to support team functioning. For example, team performance was not included within the performance evaluation process (which was still individually based) and rewards were based on individual rather than team performance. In part because employees were required to serve on a number of teams in addition to carrying out their individual job duties and in part because they were only rewarded for their individual performance, team members complained of being overworked and underpaid. In this sense, team members with less power than managers continued to be viewed as less valuable to the organization. Pay inequities based on rank remained entrenched in the organizational structure and huge pay gaps persisted between upper management and other employees.

As previously discussed, most often hierarchical positions are highly gendered in the sense that they are strongly defined by masculine ideals (Maier, 1997). The masculine hero myth still dominates much of American and Western European thinking about leadership in the corporate world. As discussed above, women and ethnic minorities rarely break through the 'power ceiling' that separates them from the positions of highest authority and influence. In the present case study, the company strongly adhered to the male hero myth. Of all the top executives, only one was female. The company's male CEO was characterized as a tough loner who ran the organization with a tough, 'no nonsense' style and who was rarely accessible to employees. Even the corporate logo which was widely influential both within and outside the company is male, providing an image meant to convey important masculine traits such as confidence, daring and control. Despite the presence of teams, this organization remained fundamentally masculine in its image and structure.

The collaborative organization

Teamwork has been conceptualized and touted as an effective strategy for dealing with the complexities of an ever-changing business environment. However, a team as 'any group of people who need each other to accomplish a task', more often than not remains just that, a group of people simply focusing on a task (Senge et al., 1994: 354). What is often missing is what Haskins et al. (1998: 34) refers to as a 'collaborative work environment'.

Collaboration is a 'work ethic that recognizes that work gets done through people' (Marshall, 1995: 13). The emphasis is on a shared ethic, not a shared task. Where teams often convene to create a new software product or recommend a course of action, collaboration is a value-based concept that permeates an entire organization. It is the way in which an organization conducts business – serves the customer, treats employees and allocates resources – in an on-going manner.

Teamwork, on the other hand, tends to be 'transactional' and this is, in part, what can be so problematic (Haskins et al., 1998). A team comes together for a finite amount of time and it is within this discreet business unit that work gets done. Although effective teams must learn to work together on some level, the learning often remains within the team or work group. Since the nature of teams is temporal, the high level of performance that may have been achieved within the work group dies when the team disbands (Haskins et al., 1998). An organization that is driven by an ethos of collaboration and cooperative work processes is often better able to sustain the higher level of functioning espoused in team-based organizations.

Team-based organizations, as the name implies, tend to be reductionistic, focusing on a piece of the organization – the team – instead of the system. If all work is instead conducted in the spirit of 'two heads are better than one', and each employee is trained to work collaboratively, the entire organization is aligned and is better able to capitalize on the strengths of its human resources. As developed economies continue to shift to service and information-based industries, successful companies will use this approach and employ a workforce that is innovative, able to see the world from diverse perspectives and ready to adapt to dynamic work environments.

The valuing of an organization's workforce is critical to its success. A collaborative organization demonstrates this valuation by sharing power. Therefore, collaborative organizations are antithetical to hierarchical organizations where the ultimate power resides with status, organizations committed to and driven by a dedication to collaboration share decision making, resources, values and vision. In doing so, collaborative organizations transcend individual contributions and create a system that exceeds the sums of its parts. Ideally, the unification of the organization under a shared ethos of collaboration transcends the 'male gendered organization' – the rational, rugged individualistic culture still prevalent in, for instance, many US corporations – into a 'gender neutral' organization. Although collaborative organizations are conceptualized as relational – traditionally a female gendered trait – collaborative organizations are committed to a systemic valuation of all human traits, the rational/emotional, the public/private, and the individual/collective. In this context, the relational organization eliminates dichotomies and creates a culture based upon shared values where the 'managerial concern is the creation of an organizational context conducive to positive inter-group dynamics' (Haskins et al., 1998: 35).

Positive inter-group dynamics guided by collaboration implicitly value differences. Each individual brings a unique set of skills and experiences, that in concert with others, creates a compilation of shared ability. Haskins et al., (1998) use the following example to illustrate this phenomenon:

> Relational collaboration is not like an all-star group of dancers brought together to stage a Balanchine ballet. It is more like the long-standing dance ensemble that presents ballets with such mutual passion, joy, artistry and harmony that they create experiences for audiences that go beyond an acknowledgment of the dancers' technical expertise – the dancers are felt, not merely seen (Haskins et al., 1998: 36).

Collaborative intra-group dynamics are compelled by a desire to bridge individual capabilities in order to build shared capabilities. This enables an organization to adapt, to change and to deploy human resources quickly and effectively in response to a changing business environment. Since heterogeneous teams have been demonstrated to out-perform homogeneous groups in complex problem solving, it can therefore be concluded that collaborative organizations seek and embrace diversity as a means to enhancing the capabilities of the workforce (Thomas, 1999).

Enhancing the 'resources' of the workforce, in addition to training employees on how to manage conflict, problem solve, build consensus, work cooperatively, means seeking out a variety of opinions, points of view, and experiences (Koze and Masciale, 1993). This valuing of differences and an organizational culture that expects individuals to work cooperatively inherently promotes and embraces diversity. Women, people of color, and the disabled-groups that have historically been marginalized in patriarchal organizations-are expected to contribute their unique perspective and skills to the workplace. In doing so, they push the organization and challenge the status quo (Koze and Masciale, 1993). This pushing process challenges homeostasis and may act as an impetus for the organization to grow and change. Furthermore, these internal 'growing pains' may provide the transitional organization with an opportunity to 'rehearse' responses to internal and external threats, which can provide an organization with strategic insights regarding strengths, weaknesses and opportunities.

Collaborative organizations are emerging throughout service and information-based industries. Technology companies, in particular, are fostering collaborative work environments where innovation and knowledge sharing are critical success factors. During a time when the U.S. and other Western labour forces are shrinking, technology continues to change rapidly and the global economy has created an extremely competitive marketplace, effective employee and knowledge management creates a competitive advantage. Collaborative teamwork and 'consensus engineering', for example, are effective strategies for dealing with workforce and knowledge management. Consensus engineering and collaborative teamwork encourage each individual to share ideas which can then be integrated into a high quality product that the workforce can support and 'own' (Constantine, 1993).

Health care is another industry where collaboration and shared decision making are well on the way to becoming industry standards. An American west coast health care company, for example, is in the process of vertically integrating six hospitals, two convalescent homes and a physician network into a value-based system that is committed to 'putting the patient first' in a collaborative work environment. Each health care worker is 'empowered' to make patient care decisions in concert with co-workers where every action is guided by the values of the organization. These are not just teams of people working together, but an integrated workforce that believes that in order to achieve 'excellence and provide patient, physician and employee satisfaction, each individual in the organization must have the information, resources, knowledge, and *support* they need in a collaborative work environment to accomplish their work objectives' (Gann, personal communication 1999). It is important to note that both quality patient care and the satisfaction of employees are equally valued. It is believed that not only will these values result in a higher level of quality patient care, but also employees will continue to feel passionate about caring for others as well as remaining a member of this particular health care community.

Relational collaboration is an organization wide circumstance. Haskins and colleagues (Haskins et al., 1998) explain this phenomenon as an:

> Organizational strategic intent and infrastructure, as well as decision-making, reward, and recruiting systems involve and connect each individual with the whole, in a process that we have likened to nuclear fusion – the joining of atom (p. 46).

It is a re-connection not just of people, but of systems that collectively 'release power', exceeding the summing of parts. Reaching this objective requires that an organization behave as one inter and intra-connected, empowered, high performing team (Haskins et al., 1998).

Conclusion

A feminist framework has been used to analyse team-based organization with particular attention being paid to power, hierarchy and the gendered organization. This chapter has argued that most team-based organizations do not go far enough in reducing hierarchy, shattering the power glass ceiling and redistributing power. Although some organizations have, in fact, reduced the levels of hierarchy within their organizations and have sought to 'empower' employees, most of these organizations remain fundamentally 'male gendered', with power allocated to position and status.

Male gendered organizations have traditionally segregated work with women and ethnic minorities in a 'one down' position. Although team-based organizations bring people together to work shoulder to shoulder, the glass ceiling remains firmly in place. Furthermore, team-based organizations tend to stress the importance of a task and not the process used to achieve a desired outcome. Therefore, a collaborative, team-based organizational model has been suggested as a preferred alternative. It is suggested that organizations that stress the importance of teamwork and collaboration as system wide initiatives far outperform traditional hierarchical organizations as well as many team-based organizations. Although teams, especially if they represent diversity as well as collaboration, offer many exciting possibilities for change, much additional information is needed before their effectiveness can be assured (Wilson and Iles, 1996). With further investigation, it is hoped that stronger theory and data will provide the means necessary to fulfill the promise teams hold to fundamentally change the gendered nature of organizations.

References

Acker, J. (1990) 'Hierarchies, jobs, bodies: a theory of gendered organizations', *Gender and* Society, 4 (2): 139-58.

American Management Association (1993) 'Work teams have their work cut out for them: teamwork survey', *HR Focus*, 70 (1): 24-25.

Banker, R., Field, J., Schroeder, R. and Sinha, K. (1996) 'Impact of work teams on manufacturing performance: a longitudinal field study', *Academy of Management Journal*, 39 (4): 867-91.

Block, Peter (1999) *Flawless Consulting*. San Francisco: Jossey-Bass Pfeiffer.

Constantine, L. (1993) 'Work organization: paradigms for project management and organization', *Communications of the ACM*, 36 (10): 34-43.

Ely, R. (1995) 'The power of demography: women's social construction of gender identity at work', *Academy of Management Journal*, 38 (3): 589-634.

Farrell, A. (1994) 'A social experiment in publishing: *Ms.* Magazine 1972-1989', *Human Relations*, 47 (6): 707-30.

Ferguson, Kathy (1984) *The Feminist Case Against Bureaucracy*. Philadelphia: Temple University Press.

Fletcher, J. (1998) 'Relational practice: a feminist reconstruction of work', *Journal of Management Inquiry*, 7 (2): 163-86.

Frohman, M. (1995) 'Do teams…but do them right', *Industry Week*, 244 (3): 21-24.

Gann, C. (1999) 'Shared decision-making concept paper', unpublished.

Gherardi, S. (1994) 'The gender we think, the gender we do in our everyday organizational lives', *Human Relations*, 47 (6): 591-611.

Harrington-Macklin, D. (1994) *The Team Building Tool Kit: Tips, Tactics, and Rules for Effective Workplace Teams*. New York: American Management Association.

Haskins, M., Liedtka, J. and Rosenblum, J. (1998) 'Beyond teams: toward an ethic of collaboration', *Organizational Dynamics*, 26 (4): 34-50.

Hayes, C. (1995) 'The new spin on corporate work teams', *Black Enterprise*, 6, 6-30-1995: 5-9.

Iannello, Kathleen (1992) *Decisions Without Hierarchy*. New York: Routledge.

Itzen, Catherine and Newman, Janet (1995) *Gender, Culture and Organizational Change: Putting Theory into Practice*. London: Routledge.

Kanter, R.M. (1977) *Men and Women of the Corporation*. New York: Harper Collins.

Karsten, Margaret (1994) *Management and Gender*. Westport, Connecticut: Quorum Books.

Katzenbach, Jon R. (1997) *Teams at the Top*. Boston, Massachusetts: Harvard Business School Press.

Katzenbach, Jon R. and Smith, Douglas K. (1993) *The Wisdom of Teams*. New York: Harper Collins.

Koze, S. and Masciale, E. (1993) 'Why teams don't work and how to fix them', *Canadian Manager*, 18 (1): 8-9.

Lawler, Edward E. III (1994) 'Effective reward systems: strategy, diagnosis and design', in Howard, Ann (ed.), *Diagnosis for Organizational Change*. New York: Guilford Press. pp. 210-38.

Lawler, Edward E. III (1973) *Motivation in Work Organizations*. Monterey, CA: Brooks/Cole.

Lewis, J. and Morgan, D. (1994) 'Gendering organizational change: the case of Relate', *Human Relations*, 47 (6): 641-64.

Maier, M. (1997) 'Gender equity, organizational transformation and Challenger', *Journal of Business Ethics*, 16 (9): 943-62.

Marshall, E. (1995) 'The collaborative workplace', *Management Review*, 1: 13-17.

Morgen, S. (1994) 'Personalizing personnel decisions in feminist organizational theory and practice', *Human Relations*, 47 (6): 665-84.

Morley, M. and Garavan, T. (1995) 'Current themes in organizational design: implications for human resource development', *Journal of European Industrial Training*, 19 (11): 3-13.

Ortiz, L. (1998) 'Union response to teamwork: the case of Opel Spain', *Industrial Relations Journal*, 29 (1): 42-58.

Pinchot, E. (1992) 'Balance the power', *Executive Excellence*, 9 (9): 3-5.

Pinchot, G. and Pinchot E. (1996) 'Creating space for many leaders', *Executive Excellence*, 13, (4): 17-18.

Ramsey, V. and Calvert, L. (1994) 'A feminist critique of organizational humanism', *Journal of Applied Behavioural Science*, 30 (1): 83-97.

Riger, S. (1994) 'Challenges of success: stages of growth in feminist organizations', *Feminist Studies*, 20 (2): 275-301.

Robbins, S. (1996) *Organizational Behaviour*. New Jersey: Prentice Hall, Inc.

Savage, Mike and Witz, Anne (eds) (1992) *Gender and Bureaucracy*. Oxford: Blackwell Publishers.

Schor, S., Van Buskirk, W. and McGrath, D. (1994) 'Caring, voice and self-reflection: feminist values and organizational change', *Journal of Organizational Change Management*, 7 (6): 34-48.

Senge, Peter, Kleiner, Art, Roberts, Charlotte, Ross, Richard and Smith, Bryan (1994) *The Fifth Discipline Fieldbook*. New York: Currency Doubleday.

Thomann, D. and Strickland, D. (1992) 'Managing collaborative organizations in the 90s', *Industrial Management*, 34 (4): 26-29.

Thomas, D. (1999) 'Cultural diversity and work group effectiveness: an experimental study', *Journal of Cross-Cultural Psychology*, 2 (2): 242-63.

Trent, R. (1996) 'Understanding and evaluating cross-functional sourcing team leadership', *International Journal of Purchasing and Materials Management*, 32 (4): 29-36.

Tuckman, B. (1965) 'Developmental sequences in small groups', *Psychological Bulletin*, 63 (6): 384-99.

Vroom, Victor (1964) *Work and Motivation*. New York: Wiley.

Wellins, Richard, Byham, William and Wilson, Jeanne (1991). *Empowered Teams*. San Francisco: Jossey-Bass.

Williams, G. and MacAlpine, M. (1995) 'The gender lens: management development for women in "developing countries"' in Itzen, Catherine and Newman, Janet (eds), *Gender, Culture and Organizational Change: Putting Theory into Practice*. London: Routledge.

Wilson, E. and Iles, P. (1996) *Managing Diversity: Critique of an Emerging Paradigm*. Proceedings of the British Academy of Management Conference, 12-14 September, Aston.

8   Organizational Design

Margaret Dale

Introduction

The concepts of 'organization' and gender are introduced in the opening chapter. This chapter will develop these concepts to gain greater insight into how the underpinning principles and philosophies drive design and operation of organizations and how they continue to reflect traditional paradigms. Are organizations male inventions as suggested by Mills and Murgatroyd (1991)? Are there female organizations? Are organizations gender neutral and dominated by factors other than those emanating from gender concerns?

These issues raise a number of subordinate questions: What is an organization? What is its origins? How did the tradition form emerge? Why does it continue to dominate? If women were left to their own devices without the influence of men and male dominated systems, language and society, how would they achieve tasks that require the combined effort of several people? Would they do it differently?

Much of the writing on organizational analysis has been described as being 'gender blind'. Although some of the more recent texts acknowledge the existence of the issue, Wilson (chapter 1 in this volume) suggests these are gender myopic. The difficulties experienced by researchers trying to untangle what is caused by gender or the interplay of other similarly complex factors cannot be underestimated. Studies are made more difficult as sadly there are very few (if any) organizations that can be described as being totally 'female', immured from the masculine influences that shape and dominate so much of society. The comparison between balanced opposites is virtually impossible.

There are some notable organizations, F International, The Bodyshop and Stagecoach, which were started and are controlled by women. However these organizations are comparatively young, having become established in the post-women's liberation world. Inevitably, as companies, they are constrained by the world in which they function and the systems within which they are obliged, by law as well as accepted practice, to operate. Unlike male dominated organizations, they are heavily influenced by members of the opposite sex, they operate in contexts controlled by men and the assessment of their success is carried out according to traditional criteria.

Similarly, female dominated occupations are found in organizations controlled by men, nursing and primary school teaching being examples. Whether the differences between the behaviour of men and women in organizations are products of nature or nurture or a combination of the two is discussed elsewhere (Wilson, chapter 1 in this volume). There is little doubt that there is an imbalance in the power distribution attributable to gender, and differing patterns of behaviour and approach by men and women can be seen.

The way in which theorizing on gender in management prior to the influx of women managers was ignored, is critiqued by Calas and Smircich (1990). It is difficult to pin down a point in time when women managers were first found in organizations. There have been examples of influential women throughout history. These tend to be few, exceptional, and are often remembered for their display of masculine characteristics. As in other fields such as science and literature, many more will have been forgotten, their impact invisible to the eye of the historian. Nevertheless it is fairly safe to assume that due to lack of evidence to the contrary, the degree of their influence was confined by what was allowed within the structure and culture of organizations, organizations designed by and for men using design principles characterized by factors that lie within the parameters of what can be labelled as masculinity.

Well-established theories of traditional organization design are widely recorded (e.g. Buchanan and Huczynski, 1997) and so there is no need to redefine them here but their relative merits, limitations and influence on women will be discussed.

Organization design

The word 'organization' has its roots in the classical languages. The Oxford Diction of Current English roots *Organ* in the Greek *organon* and the Latin *organum* is defined as meaning a tool. 'Organize' is to

> give an orderly structure, to systematise; bring the affairs of (another) into order, make arrangements for another; arrange for or initiate (a scheme); provide, take responsibility for; enrol in a trade union, political party etc, form and group; make organic, make into a living being or tissue.

An organization is

> the act or an instance of organising, the state of being organized, and organized body, especially a business, government department, charity etc; systematic arrangement, tidiness.

For thousands of years people have come together to carry out activities aimed at achieving common tasks. Typically activities were (and still are) divided on the grounds of gender, frequently justified by biological differences. The contributions made by men and women may have been different but each group needed and relied on the other. As societal forms became more sophisticated and larger, the rules and divisions became more complex and diverse. Historical accounts show a division between the sexes and the ways in which the value of the different contributions made by men and women were recorded unequally. For example, how much is known about the roles of women in the Capitol? We know Caesar's wife had influence and authority, but was this personal or a product of her husband's position? Perhaps one of the reasons for this inequality is the predominance of military adventures and campaigns.

The origins of management

Garratt (1994) traces some modern management techniques to Greek culture. The concepts of strategy and policy, he argues, have grown from the Greek approach to governance, democracy and warfare. 'Policy' is rooted in *politeia* or citizenship and 'politics' is the art and science of government or the process or principle affecting authority and status. A 'strategist' denotes a commander-in chief. In Athens, this was a chief magistrate. 'Strategy' is derived from 'command of a general or generalship. The art of projecting and directing the larger military movements and operations of a campaign'. This is distinguished from 'tactics'; the art of handling forces in battle or in the immediate presence of the enemy. The Romans divided themselves into units and sub units of ten for the conduct and defence of their conquests. The language of the Roman hierarchical system is still used by contemporary management writers, who defined the optimum chain of command and span of control.

The beginnings of bureaucracy were evident in Europe in the breakdown of feudalism and the remnants of the Classical World. The Christian Church developed a hierarchy based on seniority and authority, state governance moved from warlords to politicians, and the military developed separate systems for control. Government moved gradually from the monarchy and aristocratic control through landowners and money owners into forms of democracy. The role of civil servants, officers and the growing dependence on administration supported the separation of decision making and implementation. The Roman Catholic Church, often cited as the most enduring organization, is notable for its male domination, which has only recently been challenged.

Management is a comparatively recent construct, administration being a more familiar notion in early organizations. The administrator ensured that the systems and procedures needed to carry out the instructions of others were in place and ran smoothly. An administrator tended to be of lowly status. Management, on the other hand contains notions of decision making and control. Garratt (1994) identifies two origins for the word: *manège* or the breaking horses and *ménage* or housekeeping and the harnessing resources. It was only in the 1950s that the distinct role of manager was recognized and the status of the occupants increased.

Traditional organizational design

The late 17th century saw the beginnings of industrialization in Britain, and the end of cottage industries and agricultural way of life. The separation of work and family life for the masses began. As organizations increased in size and their operation needed more control, the owners began to delegate responsibility and authority to others to act on their behalf. The military and church achieved this through layers of appointed officials; companies and landowners used agents, secretaries and servants. The move from a rural economy during the Industrial Revolution in Britain and then other countries saw women moving from the countryside and the home into factories, the weaving shed, down the mines, in domestic service and in the fields. They and children were used to undercut men's wages and undermine attempts at unionization, and women became the invisible backbone of the largely gender segregated Victorian economy. The fundamental principles of the British employment contract were laid down, based on the master/servant relationship, where the worker would carry out all reasonable requests and the employer would give a fair day's pay for a fair day's work (both hotly contested).

  Bureaucracy was described by Weber (1947) as a rational way of organizing and controlling joint endeavours. Its characteristics include the use of written, formal records, formal and exclusive decision making, the functional division of labour, promotion on merit, and control systems run by those deemed to possess expertise and authority. As organizations became bigger, more complex and diverse, different ways of organizing and running them were tried. However, most of the variations centred on the principles of bureaucracy. Even if organizational structures were changed from functional specialism, to product based, to location, they still depended on hierarchy, formalized decision making and the functional division of labour.

  Over the years Weber's (1947) ideas may have been augmented and slightly modified, but the early thinking has endured into modern working practices and current ideas on how best to design and construct organizations. For example Gulick and Urwick (1937), proposed eight principles of design, seven of which were concerned about the exercise of control and Lodge and Cushway (1993) discuss principles of good organizational design. These start with structure, the purpose of which is to support the achievement of strategy; organize resources; provide for the effective division of tasks and accountabilities; ensure effective co-ordination; enhance and clarify lines of communication; allow for effective monitoring; provide mechanisms for coping with changes; facilitate handling of crises; help to motive, manage and give job satisfaction, and provide for managerial succession.

  The typical organization structure is represented as a linear model, compartmentalizing and dividing functions. The structure denotes a hierarchy that gives status and authority to those located at the 'top' over the work and effort of those at the 'bottom'. There is a semblance of rationality and logic to the shape of the organization, the organogram, which deters challenge. The designs tend to look good on paper, appearing neat, clear and functional. Making them work in practice may not be as easy. As well as vertical gender segregation by occupation, the traditional organization embodies horizontal segregation.

Smith (1776) explored the concept of division of labour and the possibility of increasing productivity and efficiency by breaking down a task into its component parts. Taylor (1911), the father of Scientific Management, drawing from Smith's work and the notion of Rational Man, proposed that a man would work harder if he were able to improve his economic lot (note use of the term he). According to Taylor (1911) the Principles of Scientific Management state that economic advantages can be gained by breaking tasks into their elemental parts. Having staff skilled in particular functions obtains high levels of production. Once the organization is broken into units, the co-ordination of activities becomes important. The units are placed on the line of command according to the degree of responsibility allocated to the function. Each is simultaneously superior and subordinate to another. Those higher up the line tend to be general, those lower down become more specific and specialized. Control over the activities of the unit is exercised by a supervisor or manager whose position in the hierarchy is determined by degree of expertise, representing status, authority and power. Such a structure requires formalized systems and procedures to make it work. Without the systems and procedures, the structure does not become operationalized. Unless they are obliged by the rules to follow them people will find their own ways of working together. The flow between divisions and between the line and staff is limited, sometimes on a need to know basis, and sometimes as part of the mechanisms used to control.

People do not naturally group themselves in the same sorts of units as those produced by rational organizational design. As formal organizations cut across human relationships and subjugate interests other dynamics take over and begin to operate. Thus the organization moves from being functional to dysfunctional. Parochialism, conflict and goal displacement occur from compartmentalization, labelling and separating people into forced categories. Developing shared values and maintaining the commonality of purpose, the very reason why the organizational members come together in the first place, become organizational tasks in their own right.

Consequently there is a need to devise mechanisms to co-ordinate the activities of different divisions to ensure that efficiencies are achieved and that there is no duplication or waste of effort. The rules and systems for the whole organization need to be established and enforced across the divisions. Co-ordination and rule making is typically carried out by the central core of the organization. Originally this was made up of those with the highest stake in the organization, but latterly, this has become the function of employees, professionals who have developed the skills of co-ordinating, controlling, planning and directing the activities of others. They also provide the support services required equally by each of the lines. In this way specialisms have developed which in turn have become professions in their own right. Personnel is the classic example of this.

The co-ordination of the activities of each unit is carried out at the joining points in the line, the nodes where the subordinate units report to the next level up. As these get higher in the organization they come together to form an apex, where the senior management team or executive is located. Centralization of decision making at the apex allows it to be concentrated amongst a small group of people who, it is believed, possess the required knowledge and ability and are concerned for the organization's long term well being. They are overwhelmingly men.   This group is responsible for determining the overall direction the organization is to follow and leading the other members of the organization along this route. Directions are passed back down the line though the chain of subordinate managers.   The authority possessed by an individual and the amount of choice they are able to exercise over their actions are defined by their position within the hierarchy.   By implication the required attributes for decision making and ability to accept responsibility do not exist at the lower levels of the hierarchy.   Operational staff in direct contact with the customer, who are more likely to be women, are usually found at the bottom of a hierarchy in non-managerial roles.   Their scope for decision making is usually inversely proportionate to their direct accountability to customers.

Decision making, as described by writers such as Cooke and Slack (1984) and Wilson (1993) make it seem an open, rational and effective process. Despite the semblance of so doing some well accepted management books (e.g. Child, 1984) seldom give a true representation of how decisions really are made or the impact of internal politics, personal relations and gender on the processes. In reality, decisions are often made in ways that are neither open nor rational. Structural rigidity may make the organization backward looking, with a consequent reliance on a limited range of solutions known to work in the past. The formality and power dynamics exclude those who know what is happening at the interface with the customers and have the real knowledge about how the operations function. Moreover, the denial of involvement in decision making reduces employees' commitment to the organization.

The definition of the jobs and decisions about who does what are also made on the basis of history. Jobs are described as lists of tasks to be completed and their purpose outlined in general terms. The human performing the tasks is regarded as an automaton devoid of feeling or emotion. Until the advent of the competencies movement the attributes needed for successful performance were rarely described in human terms, except perhaps the attributes needed for leadership and these are modelled on the images of previously successful leaders. Metcalfe and Altman (in this volume) discuss this issue more fully. Other jobs tend to be based on the notion of full-time occupants with few other demands on their time. It is assumed they will dedicate themselves fully to the job and the organization. However their degree of ownership and involvement in decision making is limited by their position in the structure and the level of acceptance extended to the individual.

At its very worst, the formalized 'masculine' organization is secretive and exclusive. It is hypocritical about its decision making processes, pretending to have rational structures and delegated authority. In reality, decisions are made outside the formal structures. It is not uncommon to find them being made by a sub-group meeting in other places and times. Formal meetings merely confirm private decisions and give a semblance of involvement. Large bureaucratic organizations often have a public face, there to display openness and participation. The private reality is about internal politics, expediency, personal preferences and hidden agendas. In many such organizations, *Gamesplay,* a phrase coined by Berne (1964), is rife and can be brutal. It uses fear, the control of decision making and regulation of people.

Many of the studies into organizations and management thinking suggest that the working world is peopled exclusively by men. Acker (1990) draws attention to the way in which men have constructed organizations for men to manage, for men to earn their living, and for male researchers and thinkers to develop theories to fit the masculine experience. She notes that some, but only a few, management gurus and researchers have questioned the paradigm that had gone largely unchallenged for nearly a century (Acker, 1990). Very few writers drew attention to the sexuality of organizations and gender issues until the 1970s and even when it is considered there is a tendency to miss the issue of male dominance. The Hawthorne Studies are a case in point.

A few exceptions have begun to question received opinion about organizations. Morgan (1986) challenged some of the accepted mores by framing organizations as metaphors and others such as Peters and Waterman (1982) and notably Kanter (1989) put forward models different to the traditional form of hierarchy. But, as Acker (1990) notes, Kanter misses the effect of masculine hegemony. Many of the writers who consider the impact of gender on organizational life are labelled as feminist and their work classified as being about women's experience and issues. Indeed many consider the political dimensions of gender, especially the disadvantage caused to women and their real life experiences. However even writers whose work explores women's perspective on work find themselves catalogued away from the main body of management and organization literature.

The most often cited alternative structure to the hierarchy is the matrix. In this people from different parts of an organization are drawn together to work on specific projects, often for short periods of time. A leader is appointed to be responsible for the achievement of the task and the management of the team members on a day to day basis. However, it is likely that they will continue to report, professionally or functionally, to a line manager. Other bureaucratic principles tend to be present, for example formalized decision making by an elite and the functional division of labour. Thus the matrix may give some flexibility and appearance of difference without necessarily challenging the underpinning philosophy of organizational design (see Sondhaus and Gallagher in this volume).

Galbraith (1973) also took a different view. He saw organizations as systems for processing information generated from the environment in which they exist. He discussed matrix organizations where relationships and linkages operate across the formal lines of authority and described ways in which the rigidity of the bureaucracy could be reduced. However his ideas were not as widely known as some of the other writers on the subject and generally attention is given to the straightness of the lines of control and the width of the span of command than the strength of interlinkages and connections. Perhaps the widespread use of information technology and the increased volume and speed of communications and their implications on working practice might restore interest in his work.

Women, even though they have been ever present in organizations, have been denied access to positions of influence and power. Even in those where women were in the majority, men find their way to the higher levels in the hierarchy. The processes of discrimination are reported elsewhere, and despite nearly thirty years of equal opportunity legislation, are still present and in many quarters condoned. Indirect discrimination is prevalent, and cultural bias deeply ingrained into every aspect of society. The long hours culture in the private and public sector (Wajcman, 1996; Maddock and Parkin, 1994) can make excessive demands on all managers. Some women opt to leave organizations, including those who have attained middle and senior management positions, in an attempt to gain some balance in their lives (Marshall, 1994). A rejection of male dominated organizations is thought to be one motivation behind the rise in businesses managed by women (Vokins, 1994).

The numbers of women in senior management support this assertion. Despite the efforts of many to improve their position and that of other women, the numbers of women at the top have failed to rise to reflect their increased level of participation in the workforce and the greater presence in the middle ranks. At the end of the 1990s little seems to have changed. The Roffey Park 1999 Annual Management Survey reveals that employees are well aware of the changes happening in organizational life but organizations are not taking advantage of the opportunities being offered. Advances in new technology are creating different forms of team-working but in turn these are reinforcing divisions based on gender as women continue to be clustered in part-time low paid jobs and men occupy full-time, higher paid roles Examination of government statistics published in New Earnings Survey each year clearly show the enduring trends.

Organizational design: emerging themes

Fifty-two per cent of the population is female. More women than ever before are in the labour force. This is by choice, as well as economic necessity. Since the Second World War, social, educational and economic expectations have increased. Women want to work in jobs that reward them financially as well as providing job satisfaction. They also want to advance, and are no longer prepared to be merely labourers in a male dominated world.

As the proportion of women in the workplace was increasing, the shortcomings of organizations noted above were being recognized. Greater attention is now given to their dysfunctional effects on the achievement of organizational aims and quality of working life for men as much as women. Handy (1989) said

> Organizations used to be perceived as gigantic pieces of engineering, with largely interchangeable human parts. We talked of their structures and their systems, of inputs and outputs, of control devices and of managing them as if the whole was one large factory. Today, the language is not that of engineering but of politics, with talk of cultures and networks, of teams and coalitions, of influence or power rather than control, of leadership not management. It is as if we had suddenly woken up to the fact that organizations were made up of people, after all, not just 'hands' or role occupants.

He discusses the idea of the web or network organization, which he calls a shamrock. In such an organization, the core consists of essential executives and others whose work is critical for organizational success. They are supported by external contractors whose relationship with the organization can vary in degree of tightness; they are not employees but providers of service. They may simultaneously work for other organizations in similar or different ways and have a long lasting or short-term relationship. Handy (1989) hoped that new technology would allow this new organizational shape to be used to good effect. Email and electronic communications would enable people to work together on joint enterprises without ever meeting in the flesh. The notion of the virtual organization was born.

However he does not discuss their gendered origins. The pressure to change and compete in a global economy are held responsible for the blame culture and the long working hours noted by Hirsh (1997). The move towards temporary and short term contracts, part time working and outsourcing of services is put down to economic realities and global competition. Many of the 'new' jobs in the service industries, traditionally 'women's' jobs, are on these sorts of contracts while many of the 'new' jobs in the high tech and finance sector are occupied predominantly by men, and thus gender segregation is reasserted and realigned.

The recessions of the early 1990s have caused traditionally structured organizations to strip out levels of management. Sometimes this has been done on the pretence of improving effectiveness, enabling decisions to be made closer to the customer, and increasing job satisfaction as a result of the empowerment of staff. In reality, much of the pressure for flatter, leaner structures has come from the need to reduce costs. Improving customer service as a way of improving competitive advantage comes second. Despite the flatness of many organizations, the paradigms used to determine the shape of the new structures, relationships, communication flows, the loci of power and involvement in decision making are predicated on traditional, masculine models of straight lines and rational problem solving.

The statistics indicate that the trend towards female self employment described by Hirsch (1997) is happening. Increasingly women are moving out of corporate life to start their own businesses. They are following the example of women such as Steve Shirley (F International) and Anita Roddick (The Body Shop) and find they can design and run their own organization in their own way. Shirley's F International was built from the idea of women working in their own homes, networked and networking through technology, marrying domestic responsibilities with interesting work. Shirley, Roddick and others have had significant impact on the thinking about how companies can be organized and managed. But these cannot be treated as 'women's' organizations. They are governed by the same laws and need to operate in the male world. They are not immured from the traditions and pressures that determine organizational success or failure.

As information technology has advanced, the possibility of working from home has become a reality for many more. Electronic communications has made it easy for an individual to be employed but rarely physically present in the employer's premises. Alternatively the individual can be self-employed, with contracts from several organizations. Several organizations can form a federation, with a small central core of key employees carrying out common tasks. The organization can have links of varying degrees of formality to self employed, part-employed, contracted or sub-contracted individuals and other organizations. The binding thread is mutual self-interest and commitment to the achievement of some shared goals.

It is not easy to describe this sort of organizational structure. It is fluid and capable of rapid transmogrification. Many of the available paradigms seem somewhat inadequate, perhaps indicating the need for an alternative language. Representing such an organization on paper is not easy. The image is of linking cells or units, simultaneously independent and interdependent. The honeycomb is a useful comparator, its cells sitting close, interlinking and capable of growth, with both strength and flexibility. If one part of the structure is removed, the remainder can survive. But the walls of the comb suggest a redundant rigidity and the structure is only two-dimensional. The spider's web is also inadequate but nearer. It too has the strength and flexibility, but again is two-dimensional. Perhaps the androgynous organization is a three-dimensional web.

In such organizations, new ways of organizing are essential. Functional division of labour, formal communication systems and job specific training lead to lack of understanding, skill shortages and inflexibility. Modern organizations require wise workers who are able to move across sections. The sections exist to serve a purpose or achieve specific objectives. Once the job is done the section breaks down and the staff move to other areas of work. The difference between this and the matrix is that there is no return to former positions at the end of the project and reporting to two managers for its duration does not happen.

Employees in the new type of organization, need the ability to learn continuously and are prepared to be adaptable. Because they understand the business and are competent in their own sphere of operation they do not need line managers to tell them what to do. The individuals who are part of such an organization, employees or others, are treated as members. They are not jobholders working to tightly defined job descriptions with a list of tasks to complete. They are role holders, often occupying a number of roles within the organizations. The role is defined in broad terms, often describing the results to be achieved. Everyone is aware of the fact that their roles will change. Emphasis is placed on doing what is needed to be done to contribute to the success of the organization's (shared) objectives. Because the individual understands what is expected, and is equipped and trusted to get on with it, the degree of management control required is that of only the lightest touch. The members' opinions are valued and sought and their efforts rewarded according to the value of their contribution.

The way in which the efforts of the individuals are co-ordinated is through the flow of information and participative decision making. The role of managers shifts from command, control and directing to one within which emphasis is placed on enabling, developing and guiding. Individuals are aware of the context in which they are working and are close to the people they are serving. Different section divisions within the organization are not enemies whose main role is to get in the way of each other; they are colleagues, partners in a joint venture. The central core's key role is to keep everyone's focus sharply on the shared goals and to remove obstacles that stand in the way of achievement. The achievement of success is dependent on the health of the workforce and the strength of the team.

These ideas are not new. Similar notions were being put forward by Mary Parker Follet (1940) an American sociologist. She argued that a person was a whole entity, existing both in and outside work. Treating the individual as such and allowing a total contribution to be made was a more productive and effective use of skill and abilities. She also argued that leadership could be found in different places at different times. It was not the preserve of the Boss. Conflict, she stated, is a fact of life and should therefore be used productively not squashed. Above, all everyone has a legitimate interest and the giving of orders is unnecessary; decision making should be a shared activity. Central control should mean a correlation of many controls rather than a superimposed control (Follet, 1940).

Follet (1940; see also Graham, 1989) described management as a social process in which importance of the individual's participation in the work and management of the organization required due recognition. The definitions of power current then (and probably now) were concerned with power-over people, groups, organizations. She argued another form of power is possible. Power-with, a jointly developed power, a co-active, not a coercive power. An organization formed on such principles makes it possible for influence to be exerted through joint interactions and integration. Such power cannot be delegated as it is a capacity that is grown. Therefore opportunities that enable individuals to develop their power can be created.

Follet was not labelled as a feminist even though she was working in the 1930s when the women's movement in Britain was undergoing an ideological shift. Brittain (1980) describes how one faction wanted to continue with social and political reforms; others argued successfully that attention should focus on reproductive and similar issues confronting women. The Second World War diverted attention from these issues. Since then it has been largely left to the feminist movement to explore the real nature of the different approaches adopted by women and men in organizations. For example Spender (1981) argues that women are seen as deviant men and any difference in approach or view was attributed to this deviation. Anyone disputing the model is treated as being unreasonable. Gilligan (1982) explains how the differences in male and female perceptions are articulated.

Cockburn (1991) uses the words of women to explain their contribution to organizational life and how the effectiveness of their performance is constrained by the dominance of the masculine view. This dominance does not just stem from sexism; it comes from the fact that organizations are constructed on only a partial understanding. By focusing exclusively on the male way of being they exclude the female experience and thus represent only part of the human race. As such they are impoverished. Spender (1981) described how women understand their own reality and, because they are obliged to function within it, they are able to see (if not understand fully) the reality of men. By contrast many men do not see the female world and often reject its existence.

There are some signs to suggest that thinking is changing. Although some of the leading thinkers are seen to be gender blind, they are drawing attention to some of the inadequacies of traditional organizational form and alternative views are being expressed with a growing force that is becoming increasingly difficult to ignore. As a result more and more men are questioning the masculine hegemony implicit in hierarchical structures and the ways in which work is divided. In this questioning, they are listening to the voices of women and, in hearing, are beginning to understand that different approaches may be possible.

Schein (1978), Leary (1985) and Bem (1974) are amongst those who have identified the different ways in which women and men approach organizational life and the management of processes and people. Whether these differences are the produce of genetics or socialization is a matter for debate elsewhere. Suffice it to say here the differences exist and are documented. Rosener (1990) and Alimo-Metcalfe (1995) discuss the difference between transformational and transactional leadership and give recognition to their comparative merits. Like Spender (1981) before them, they can see both the male and the females perspectives. Wilson (in the opening chapter, this volume) questions whether these are positions on a binary divide, poles on a continuum, or overlapping clusters of constructs. In a way it does not really matter for it is known that rules in organizations affect men and women differently, and women and men adopt different ways of working within them.

Do these differences affect the way in which women organize? Finding female organizations to compare to male dominated ones has been surprisingly difficult. Many occupations are regarded as the preserve of women and women are in the majority. Teaching, librarianship, nursing, cooking all spring to mind. Yet almost without exception, when men have joined their body, they have progressed through the levels. Even when men are in the minority they have become the decision makers and holders of power. Despite tending to earn less than men in masculine professions, according to Millward and Woodland (1995) they still do better on average than the majority of female members. Is this simply another example of the way in which men take over and women, for many complex reasons, allow them to do so?

Even the organizations led by strong and successful women are not totally within their exclusive control. It would be wrong to deny the mark made by these outstanding individuals. But the very fact that they are remarkable and so few is a statement in itself. Their freedom for action is in any case externally controlled. The reality is that businesses run by women are obliged to operate by masculine rules encapsulated in the law and regulation and the demands of finance houses and the market. Other organizations that could be called feminine include, perhaps, women's religious orders and single sex sections of organizations. They are, however, adjuncts to masculine organizations and mirror the masculine structures.

There was a hope at the beginning of the 1990s that the pressures on organizational life would bring about the changes being forecast by writers such as Handy (1989) for the benefit of men and women alike. The investment in new technology would make virtual organizations, networking and home working real. This would remove the heavy pressure imposed by the weight of the hierarchy. Employees would have more choice and would be better able to balance their personal and organizational lives. Working lesser hours would result in more job opportunities for the under employed and the up turn in the economy would bring more leisure opportunities.

The Roffey Park 1999 Annual Management Agenda found that organizational change continues unabated into the new century. The trend towards flatter structures, mergers and formation of strategic alliances remains a feature of organizational life. New ways of working and different forms of team working are evident. Employees are well aware of the pressures being faced by their employers but ensuring continuity of employment means working longer hours and putting the job before personal life. Although employees are confident about their own abilities to remain in employment and are developing their own skills, they are also becoming less tolerant of the excessive burdens being placed upon them.

The report highlighted five ironies. First despite the use of IT, technology is failing to fulfil its promise of reducing working loads. E-mail has reduced face to face contact and increased the sense of isolation. Second, although organizations claim to want quick and innovative responses, many reinforce the status quo through the reward structures and blame culture. Third, employers are dependent on the skills of their employees; their employees are less dependent on their employer. Fourth, employees have been encouraged to see their manager as a mentor and coach, but the manager is too pressurized to fulfil this role. Last, organizations want employees to share information and ideas for the benefit of the business but when they do they may find they have not necessarily acted in their own best interests.

The shape of the new organization may appear to be a network on paper. It may have the form of a spider's web or look like a representation of a shamrock, but is it anything other than a different manifestation of older forms? If change has not happened, why not? One reason could be that there are very few examples of how to design an organization in any other way. The case study explores just one such example.

Case study: The Women's Institute

The Women's Institute (WI) has been in existence for 100 years. It was started in Canada by Mrs Hoodless. She had suffered the tragedy of losing her first child, largely, she later realised, because of her own ignorance of food hygiene and proper feeding methods. In a public speech to urge other women to learn how to improve the quality of their domestic practice, she suggested that they should come together to copy the men's Farmers' Institute. The early days of the new body were heavily influenced by Erland Lee who obtained State Government support for the movement. However, much of the organizational planning and implementation was left in the hands of women. The idea of the Institute was imported into Britain in 1913. Again, its early days were in the shadow of male influence and control, as it was run firstly from the Agricultural Organization Society and then by the Board of Agriculture. However in 1919 it became an independent body.

One might question what relevancy has such an organization on 21st century organizations. The answer is that the WI has survived for nearly 70 years, has

300,000 members and, in 1993, a turnover of £10.5m. To celebrate its centenary, the WI published its history by Garner (1998). The WI is not one organization; the national body is a federation of nearly 9,000 separate institutes whose membership number between 15 and 150. And despite its popular image the WI is not all 'jam and Jerusalem':

> It is not a trade union, although it supports the advancement of women's rights. It speaks up as strongly for children, health issues and the protection of the environment. Over the years its firm, informed voice has been raised on a wide variety of social issues. Never strident, never aggressive, it carries its point by the common sense of its approach and the solid background of factual homework which goes into the presentation of each case. The National Federation of Women's Institutes is not a pressure group: it owes allegiance to no political party, subscribes to no particular religion and is open to all women - and girls- with no top limits! What all have in common is a sense of belonging, a joy in companionship, in sharing skills and pursing knowledge and in enjoying themselves ... A young male colleague once complained that men too needed something like the WI but had not got it 'We need friends, and safe space too. We've nowhere to go for that kind of support (Garner, 1998).

The WI is run on democratic principles and over the years has waged fierce battles to ensure it remained independent. The movement has its own College and a history of campaigning to rival the most militant of organizations. But the tactics and actions are very different from those adopted in men's wars. Its organizational structure is not a network, rather a network of networks. Each institute is self supporting financially and elects a small committee to run its affairs. Each WI belongs to a County or Island Federation, nominates candidates to the executive committee and votes for the latter's selection. The Federation executive committee chooses its chairman from among its members and appoints sub-committees to cater for the interests of WIs. The National Federation of Women's Institutes (NFWI) is the link between Federations. There is a strong bond of communication and continuity between the WIs, County and Island Federations and National Committee is provided by Voluntary County Organizers.

The annual meeting is the forum where the major decisions are made on the basis of delegates' votes. 10,000 delegates were present at the last Triennial General Meeting, 'making it the largest general meeting of any national organization in the United Kingdom'. Resolutions suggested by local Institutes are discussed at special meetings to decide whether they are worthy of conference time and significant efforts are made to involve members in their consideration and amendment. The topics of these resolutions are wide ranging covering the ground from domestic to highly political, but they all have one thing in common; they can be actioned.

The Women's Institute does not often appear in the lists of large organizations nor stand in the ranks of activists. Yet it is an employer, a provider of education and a profitable business. Perhaps a measure of its success has been its ability to remain a preserve of women and out of the limelight, until it wants attention. The WI has fought hard to retain its unique identity yet has adapted to deal with the societal and economic changes that have threatened its survival. It may not be the most attractively modern of organizations. However, it continues to succeed in attracting members of all ages and interests from rural and urban communities, with a common pursuit of wanting to make improvements.

The work of those writers who describe the preferred ways of women can be seen in the characteristics of the WI. The single institute is not a branch, a cell, a unit or a division. It is the centre of the whole and is part of an interlinking network, bound together by similar interests, common values and shared priorities. The shape of the structure above is markedly different from the hierarchy used by most organizations. It is three dimensional and iterative. It is formed of the linkages between all parts of the networks. It is inclusive and allows for discussion, consultation and participative decision making.

Its college provides a dedicated forum for learning and the Institute in itself is and in its functions provides the workplace in which the individual can hone her skills. In neither do women have to fight to make their voices heard. The WI's independence and financial viability provide a safe haven in which the women can conduct their business and prepare to argue their cases in the potentially hostile world. Thus the members of the WI have been able to develop their confidence and abilities in private.

Many women's organizations face considerable problems in winning credibility in a male world and gaining access to resources. The WI had male allies in its early days and made full use of its members with money and influence. However, it quickly gained its own financial viability and it was noted for its ability to run its affairs efficiently. In 1930 the West Lancashire Evening Gazetter commented 'they are punctual, systematic, rigorously obedient to the rules of debate, one had only to see them at the conference to discover how much they could teach many a male congress that thinks it knows all about running an affair like this'. The most abiding feature of the WI has been its tenacity.

There are many lessons that can be learnt by other organizations from the WI's enduring and successful qualities. The fact that to many it is a mockery and parody of times gone by, may be advantageous. The facade conceals the latent power of women, who when mobiliZed can provide a force resisted by only the foolhardy.

Perhaps the challenge is to take the example provided by the WI and the thinking of feminist writers and promulgate them into main stream. The separation of women's views on experience of organizations is no longer good enough. The Women's Institute, despite the size of its membership and turnover, tends not to be seen as a major organization and seldom is referred to as a example of alternative organizational design. The issues implicit in the design of organizational structures effect everyone and the way they impact people should be given more attention. Certainly the debate on institutional discrimination and the way in which structural dysfunctions adversely effect the way people, especially women, merits far more serious consideration that that currently given.

Conclusions

What has this discussion of organizational design shown? It has raised the question as to whether there is a way forward which can eliminate the dysfunctional aspects of the classical, traditional models, and replace them with more human, inclusive and less punishing forms that facilitate both organizational and individual performance and allow for learning and growth.

The option to do nothing is not a real choice. The traditional models contain flaws that in the longer term could prove to be fatal. They have served their purpose in a world that was more stable and predictable. Then, change was gradual and came at a pace that could be managed. The conditions now are more complex and multi-faceted; some of the changes cannot be predicted. The speed of communications and development of ideas are so fast that their dissemination cannot be controlled. There are too many players with such different expectations; managing the processes are beyond the scope of one omnipotent leader.

There is now an increasing need to look for practical examples of different organizational design that take account of gender. This will enable women's values and preferred ways of working to be identified and included as models of good practice. Research and the ideas of the leading thinkers, such as Handy (1989) and Kanter (1989) suggest that alternative ways are possible. Most of these are hypothetical but more and more organizations are experimenting with different ways of organizing themselves. Most of these are being proposed tentatively in response to pressures to find different ways of working. Many are gender blind but the examination of the Women's Institute demonstrates that organizations built on female paradigms do work successfully and are enduring.

Perhaps the ideal organizational structure is one that values and reflects the values of women and men, allows for the preferred behaviours of both, recognizes the contributions of all to the organization's objectives, and strives to achieve the common good. This ideal should result in organizations that are flexible, humane and inclusive.

References

Acker, J. (1990) 'Hierarchies, jobs, bodies: a theory of gendered organizations', *Gender and Society*, 2 (4): 139-58.

Alimo-Metcalfe, B. (1995) 'An investigation of female and male constructs of leadership and empowerment', *Women in Management Review*, 10 (2): 3-8.

Bem, S. (1974) 'The measurement of psychological androgyny', *Journal of Consulting and Clinical Psychology*, 42 (2): 259-68.

Berne, E. (1964) *Games People Play*. Harmondsworth: Penguin.

Brittain, V. (1980) *Testament of Friendship*. Fontana.

Buchanan, D. and Huczynski, A. (1997) *Organizational Behaviour: An Introductory Text*. 3rd Edition. London and New York: Prentice Hall.

Calas, M. and Smircich, L. (1990) 'Reinventing gender into organizational theorizing: directions from feminist perspectives', in Reed, M. and Hughes, M. (eds) *Rethinking Organization: New Directions in Organizational Analysis and Research*. London: Sage. pp. 227-53.

Child, John (1984) *Organization: A Guide to Problems and Practice*, 2nd Edition. London: Harper and Row.

Cockburn, C. (1991) *In the Way of Men's Resistance to Sex Equality in Organsizations*. Houndsmills: MacMillan.

Cooke, S. and Slack, N. (1994) *Making Management Decisions*. Englewood Cliffs: Prentice Hall.

Follet, M. P. (1940) *Dynamic Administration: the Collected Papers of Mary Parker Follet*. Edited by H.C. Metcalf and L. Urwick. New York: Harper and Row.

Galbraith, J. (1973) *Designing Complex Organizations*. Reading, Mass: Addison-Wesley.

Garner, G. (1998) *Extraordinary women: a history of the Women's Institutes*. Crediton: WI Books.

Garratt, B. (1994) *The Learning Organization*. 2nd Edition. London: Harper Collins.

Gilligan, C. (1982) *In a Different Voice: Psychological Theory and Women's Development*. Cambridge, Mass, London: Harvard University Press.

Graham, P. (1989) 'Follet - the pre-emptive manageress', *Education and Training*, Jan/Feb.

Gulick, L. and Urwick L. F. (eds) (1937) *Papers on the Science of Administration*. New York: Columbia University.

Handy, C. (1989) *The Age of Unreason*. London: Arrow.

Kanter, R.M. (1989) 'The new managerial work', *Harvard Business Review*.

Leary, M. (1985) 'Men and women: what are the differences and does it matter', *Management Education and Development*, 16 (2).

Lodge, D. and Cushway, B. (1993) *Organizational Behaviour and Design*. London: Kogan Page.

Maddock, Su and Parkin, Di (1994) 'Gender cultures: how they affect men and women at work' in Davidson, Marilyn and Burke, Ronald *Women in Management: Current Research Issues*. London: Paul Chapman. pp. 29-40.

Marshall, Judi (1994) *Women Managers Moving On: Exploring Life and CareerChoices*. London: Routledge.

Mills, A. and Murgatroyd, S. (1991) *Organizational Rules: a Framework for Understanding Organizational Action*. Milton Keynes: Open University Press.

Millward, N. and Woodland, St. (1995) 'Gender segregation and male/female wage differences', in Humphries, J. and Rubery, J. (eds) *The Economics of Equal Opportunities*. Manchester: Equal Opportunities Commission. pp. 221-44.

Morgan, G. (1986) *Images of Organizations*. New York: Sage.

Peters, T. and Waterman, R. (1982) *In Search of Excellence: Lessons from America's Best Run Companies*. New York: Harper and Row.

Rosener, J. (1990) 'Ways women lead', *Harvard Business Review*, 68: Nov/Dec. 119-25.

Schein, V. (1978) 'Sex role stereotyping, ability and performance: prior research and new directions', *Personnel Psychology*, 31 (2): 259-68.

Smith, A. (1776) *The Wealth of Nations*. Ed E. Cannan (1937) New York: Modern Library.

Spender, D. (1981) *Manmade Language*. London: Routledge.

Taylor, F. (1911) *Principles of Scientific Management*. New York: Harper & Row.

Vokins, N. (1994) 'The minerva matrix women entrepreneurs: their perception of their management style' in Allen, S. and Truman, C. *Women in Business: Perspectives on Women Entrepreneurs*. London: Routledge. pp. 46-56.

Wajcman, Judy (1996) 'Desperately seeking differences: is management style gendered?', *British Journal of Industrial Relations*, 34 (3): 333-49.

Weber, M. (1947) *The Theory of Social and Economic Organizations*. New York: Free Press.

Wilson, G. (1993) *Problem Solving and Decision Making*. London: Kogan Page.

9   Organizational Culture

Elisabeth M. Wilson

Introduction

This chapter looks at the concept of organizational culture. Culture can be conceived in many different ways: as societal or national culture, as corporate culture, and as a homogenous or heterogeneous organizational culture. Subcultures can be identified within the boundaries of an organization, and may be based on or across departments, or on occupations or other interest groups, for instance within the managerial group. Similarities can also be seen across organizations (Turner, 1971). This is a rich, complex and potentially confusing field, and this chapter will therefore provide a selective overview of the topic.

Turner (1971) was an early influential writer on culture within organizations. He coined the phrase 'the industrial subculture', to describe the similarities which could be observed across a number of industrial concerns. In describing this as a subculture he distinguishes it from the host society in which it is situated, although noting that there is no clear-cut distinction between culture (national, societal) and subculture (industrial, organizational). He defines the industrial subculture as a distinctive set of shared meanings, maintained by socializing new members (Turner, 1971). What he describes collectively across a number of organizations as the industrial subculture, would today be described in relation to a single organization as (the) organizational culture. Turner (1971) writes about a number of features of organizational culture, which have been developed subsequently. These include: the use of symbols to convey meaning; the rites and rituals of organizational life; the use of specialized language within particular concerns; socialization and norms; the moral code transmitted by the organization; and attempts to manipulate culture. Following Turner (1971) the field developed and fragmented into a number of different, sometimes overlapping perspectives. These can however be divided into two main groupings, which are outlined in the next section

Organizational culture is generally written about as if it were gender neutral, a view contested by this chapter, which considers most writing in organizational studies as gender blind. The gendered nature of organizational culture is demonstrated daily by a multitude of differences and differentiations predicated on gender, for instance, job segregation, pay, promotion and status. Most discussion of culture within organizational behaviour and even more so within popular business and management texts relies on 'corporate culture', a variant of the functionalist approach. This popular conception will be discussed and critiqued. An alternative approach to the functionalist paradigm is a symbolic perspective. This approach is more sympathetic to gender as one aspect in a plurality of approaches. The chapter ends with a case example of a company in the financial sector.

Functionalism and symbolism

In an influential paper Smircich (1983) drew attention to the main divisions and subdivisions within the field of organizational culture. Reviewing the meaning of organizational culture, Smircich (1983) identifies two main uses, the first regarding organizational culture as an independent variable, that is something separate from other features of the organization such as structure and technology, and the second perceiving it as a root metaphor. The phase root metaphor needs some explanation. Smircich (1983) reviews work suggesting that both managers and organization theorists use metaphors or images as a way of understanding organizations and organizational life. Thus stating that an organization is a culture is a way of stating that it can be understood *as if it were* a culture. As with other metaphors, the word culture is used so often in organizational parlance that it is easy to forget that its usage is metaphorical.

To put these two meanings of Smircich (1983) into other terms, the first view treats organizational culture as something which may be influenced, changed and manipulated, and that in turn influences, changes and manipulates members and features of the organization. Thus the number and hierarchical positions of women employees could be seen as an outcome (a dependent variable) of the organizational culture (the independent variable). The second broad approach, where culture is viewed as a root metaphor, regards the number and hierarchical positions of women employees as one of many manifestations of organizational culture. It is a facet of organization that throws more light on a situation without assuming a cause and effect argument. The purposes of these two approaches can be seen respectively to promote managerial action, and to aid broader understanding (Alvesson, 1993). These two approaches have more simply been described by Schultz (1995) as functionalism and symbolism. In functionalism the organization is seen as a natural system, and culture is viewed as necessary for its survival, hence the name functionalism. The functionalist 'seeks to discover the role which each aspect of cultural practice plays in sustaining the culture as an ongoing system' (Morgan et al., 1983: 19). By contrast, symbolism is concerned with shared meanings, and the aim of the researcher is to understand these meanings (Schultz, 1995).

Schultz (1995) summarizes the main theoretical and methodological differences between functionalism and symbolism as follows. The key analytical question for functionalism is concerned with answering the question of what function culture plays in the organization. There is an assumption that culture develops through problem solving within the organization, what Schein (1992) refers to as the problems of external adaptation and internal integration. In functionalism a universal framework for culture is suggested that envisages different levels of culture (Schein, 1992) and is applicable to all organizations (Schultz, 1995). These cultural elements are therefore listed according to the categories/levels within which they fall, and the researcher's task is to find the relations between them. The functionalist approach is primarily diagnostic, and the results produced between organizations are comparable and potentially generalizable, as they are using the same theoretical framework (Schultz, 1995).

By contrast the symbolist approach takes a social constructionist view that culture is about the construction and reconstruction of meaning, which is necessarily specific to the organization and its particular context (Schultz, 1995); meaning may even be specific to a small part of the organization. Research findings are the result of qualitative investigation, where there is a search for associations between meanings (Schultz, 1995). Rather than a model being produced, the aim is to achieve understanding, and what is forthcoming is a narrative text, uniquely describing the organization (Schultz, 1995). Although culture is seen in a pattern in both perspectives, in functionalism the pattern is seen as shared, whereas in symbolism there may be shared or non-shared webs of meaning (Schultz, 1995).

Both perspectives assume that depth and surface manifestations are stable (Schultz, 1995). Symbolism is similar to functionalism in viewing culture as an integrated pattern, but it is more sympathetic to the local creation of meaning, that is, subcultures (Schultz, 1995). In symbolic perspectives it is acknowledged that there may be different views of reality, whereas in functionalism culture is assumed to be objectively real and discoverable. In symbolism reality is defined as subjective and multi-dimensional, with the possibility of different meanings attached to the same phenomenon; conversely the same meaning may be conveyed by different phenomena (Schultz, 1995). It follows that culture from a symbolic perspective can never be totally understood and explained, and must be discovered through interpretation (Schultz, 1995).

Despite the extensive academic literature about organizational symbolism, the most popular conceptions of organizational culture are based on the functionalist paradigm.

Popular conceptions of culture

In this section three popular and influential conceptions of organizational culture are described and discussed, all within the functionalist paradigm: first, Handy (1985), a British author and otherwise management guru, second, Deal and Kennedy (1982) US writers who popularized the idea of 'strong' culture as necessary for good performance, and third, Schein (1992), also from the US, one of the best known writers in this field. This is followed by a critique of 'corporate culture'.

Handy

Handy (1985) popularized the fourfold typology of power, role, task and person culture, which was originally described by Harrison (1972). He describes a power culture as one where there is a single source of power, meting out rewards and punishments. Employees are expected to anticipate what is required and act accordingly (Handy, 1985). With no or few procedures, judgement is by results, and communication by telepathy or conversation. This type of culture depends crucially on control by selection of key individuals, and is dependent on the founder. By contrast a role culture, according to Handy (1985), has the features of a typical bureaucracy, where roles are more important than individuals, and there are rules for everything, including how to settle disputes. Power relates to position in hierarchy with co-ordination by a narrow band of managers at the top. Communication is by memo. Technical expertise is more highly prized than innovation. In a task culture influence is based in expert power, and more widely dispersed throughout the organization. Project or task are more important than hierarchy, and control is by allocation of tasks and resources, but this can also lead to competition when resources are scarce. Teamwork is more important than individual effort. In a person culture the organization exists to serve the individual, and this model is only thought to persist in modern organizations which are professional partnerships or similar, although Handy (1985) states that it is sometimes found in pockets of large organizations. Control and hierarchies are only possible by mutual consent, and influence is shared and based on expertise (Handy, 1985).

Handy's (1985) typology falls closely within the functionalist paradigm, as he explicitly evaluates each culture type in terms of its ability to carry out the overt functions of the organization, to grow and prosper. What he ignores are the covert agendas within organizations, particularly those of people in powerful positions. Reference is made to power in each culture type he describes, but not to the gendered nature of that power, concentrated generally in the hands of white, heterosexual, able-bodied males. Nor does he discuss the processes by which gendered roles and gendered inequality are perpetuated. The relationship between power and gender is discussed more fully in Green et al. (in this volume).

Handy (1985) acknowledges criticisms of earlier editions of his book that it was sexist and offensive. However, he falls back on the linguistic convention of suggesting that whereas 'he' may be read as standing for 'he or she' this cannot be the case for 'she'. His text is therefore littered with references to 'man' and 'he', and it is often unclear whether he is referring merely to men, or to men and women. Going beyond linguistic considerations, gendered assumptions creep into his chapter on culture. When discussing the parameters and variations in culture, he writes: 'What about expense accounts and secretaries, stock options and incentives?' (p. 186). This appears to class secretaries (usually female) as managerial perks. There is a similar reference to clerical and secretarial assistance in person cultures. These employees seem adjuncts or commodities, rather than participants in the culture. Elsewhere in his book (chapter 12) he makes some references to feminism, and the business arguments for increasing women managers, but also uncritically mentions 'supportive wives' (p. 383) who help their husbands' career progression.

Deal and Kennedy

Deal and Kennedy (1982) were among the first writers to popularize the 'culture-performance' link (Alvesson, 1993), the other well-known pair being Peters and Waterman (1982). They investigated successful companies for their secrets of success, and state 'the secret is as American as apple pie' (p. 5), revealing a recurrent ethnocentric bias.   Their book is offered both as a diagnostic tool to assess the relative strength of an organization, and also as a recipe for successful culture management.

   They suggest a series of causal links.   Proposing that companies that are market leaders have 'strong cultures' (p. 1), they state that in many cases the distinctive cultural features can be traced back to the influence of the founder, or a top manager who took charge at a crucial time in the organization's history. A 'strong' culture is a system of informal rules, underpinned by superordinate beliefs.   They quote a selection of 'values' (p. 7), all of which pertain to products or services.   They assert that heroes are important in exemplifying culture, and that rites and rituals demonstrate desired behaviour.   Because people feel better in a strong culture, so the argument goes, they are therefore more likely to work harder, hence company performance is enhanced.   Deal and Kennedy (1982) propose a fourfold typology.   The 'tough guy/macho' (p. 107) culture is individualistic, and high risk, and receives quick feedback from the environment.   The 'work hard/play hard' (p. 108) is fun, active, takes few risks and receives quick feedback from the environment.   'Bet your company' (p. 108) cultures are high risk but slow feedback, typically having to risk large investments into the future.   'Process' (p. 108) cultures are what Handy (1985) describes as role cultures, and what elsewhere are recognized as bureaucracies.

   In looking at Deal and Kennedy (1982) from a gendered perspective, there is an unselfconscious use of language which carries gendered implications, such as the tough guy/macho culture.   In one company identified in this culture it was acceptable to swear and shout, but not to cry, offering a model of masculinity that Deal and Kennedy (1982) acknowledge encourages immature behaviour.   It is interesting to focus on their account of heroes (never heroines – almost all of those mentioned are men).   The lasting success of heroes is in providing an internal role model that indicates that success is possible, by setting standards of performance, motivating employees, and preserving what makes a company special.   That is, heroes may be inspirational, but their inspiration is functional.

   Despite a largely ethnocentric (focused on the US) and masculinist outlook, Deal and Kennedy (1982) acknowledge that the assimilation of (ethnic) minorities and women is problematic, as there are no comparable rituals to those that ease in the traditional corporate entrant, by implication the white heterosexual male.   Instead women and minorities are met with taboos.   They are excluded from old boys' networks, informal consultations, and after work socializing (Deal and Kennedy, 1982).   Despite this perceptive analysis, Deal and Kennedy (1982) are unable to make critical links with the nature of the 'strong' cultures they describe, so that this critique is marginalized.   Instead of making more fundamental suggestions about changing culture, as is recommended in the case of lacklustre financial performance, they propose a series of human resource management/development initiatives.   They see no contradiction between this critique and their comment that secretaries who have accompanied a manager's rise through the organization are good sources of inside information, implicitly acknowledging the helpmeet role (Roper, 1994).

Schein

Schultz (1995) suggests Schein (1992) is the main protagonist of the functionalist approach, although noting that he is not a pure functionalist. Alvesson and Berg (1992) suggest that his main assumption is that culture is a system of shared values and beliefs. Thus culture is related to meaning, where it is seen as a sense making device, both influencing and controlling behaviour. Schein (1992: 12) describes culture as:

> A pattern of shared basic assumptions that the group learned as it solved its problem of external adaptation and internal integration, that has worked well enough to be considered valid and, therefore, to be taught to new members as the correct way to perceive, think, and feel in relation to these problems.

This definition is criticized by Alvesson (1993) as normative, implying that norms are imposed on group members, rather than left to the individual to work out. However, to be fair to Schein (1992) he is not totally committed to a functionalist approach, as is discussed below. Schein (1992) makes clear his preference for an instrumental approach, stating that any concepts formulated must be of use to practitioners. Schein asserts that 'leadership and culture are two sides of the same coin' (1992: 1), indicating his is a top-down approach. He therefore tends to assume that top managers can give an accurate account of culture, although there is an acknowledgement of the existence of subcultures and the possibility of varying viewpoints (Schein, 1992).

In his theoretical work on organizational culture and leadership Schein (1992) writes about the difference between espoused values, those appearing publicly in mission statements, policies and charters, and the underlying assumptions which are rarely articulated and may conflict with espoused values and even with each other. What Schein (1992) calls espoused values, others might extend to include norms and expectations. Evidence for these may be found in slogans, mission statements, minutes of meetings, and policy and other official documents. More subtly, norms may be conveyed verbally and non-verbally in an informal way. The third element of Schein's (1992) model is artefacts, not merely physical objects, but anything that may be observed, such as behaviour and processes.

There are three ways in which the relevance of gender can be examined in Schein's work. First, he makes some overt references to gender as significant features of culture. Second, there are aspects of his theorizing that can be extended and extrapolated to explain gendered phenomena. Third, there are gendered assumptions that are not critically examined. These will be discussed in turn. This discussion is based on the first seven chapters of Schein's (1992) book, his principal contribution to this field.

First, among Schein's (1992) overt references to gender there are one or two occasions when he abandons the male pronoun in favour of the female, as when discussing some aspects of time. The leader as female also appears at the end of chapter seven, an unusual use in a book that uses 'he' and 'man' unselfconsciously. Some of the debate about race and gender is addressed. In one particular discussion on the relative importance of work, home, and personal concerns, Schein refers to Hofstede's (1980) findings on the degree to which countries distinguish masculine and feminine roles. He adds with some sensitivity that this typology is based on Western assumptions about self as separate from society. He discusses race and gender-related assumptions prevalent in US organizations that engender both stereotyping and career barriers. This short entry could be developed and related to other debates that are not examined.

The second topic in this critique is examination of those aspects of Schein's theory that can be extended and extrapolated to explain gendered phenomena. In the preface Schein (1992) states that 'cultural analysis illuminates subcultural dynamics within organizations' (p. xii). This could be used to look at the dynamic of relationships between the categories of women and men in organizations. This is reinforced by his observation that the power of shared assumptions derives from their operation outside of consciousness. Awareness of gender differences and appropriate roles and behaviour are examples of societal assumptions that are imported into organizations, but this is not explicitly picked up by Schein. Noting that not all organizations develop integrated cultures, he does not address the extent to which differentiation might be on gender lines. In discussing the distribution of power and status, Schein notes that members new to the organization, both men and women, may have varying amounts of power and authority attributed to them. He fails to follow up this comment with the observation that gendered assumptions mean that women are less likely than their male colleagues to have power and authority attributed to them.

He identifies that significant movement within organizations can occur in three directions: laterally, from task to task or function to function; vertically, through the ranks; and last inclusionary, from outsider to insider. As has been discussed by Bartol (1978) all these movements may be problematic for women. This can occur because of gendered job segregation, the 'glass ceiling', and exclusion from informal networks, respectively.

Schein appears to acknowledge a social constructionist view of individual reality, indicating that what a person has learned from experience may not be shared. This allows for a much more differentiated view of culture, one that may be shaped by gendered experience. Surprisingly, when he discusses the rules for love and intimacy, he misses the opportunity to extend this to an examination of consensual and non-consensual sexual relations.

Schein points out that attempts to change organizations may founder when some assumptions are amended but others left unaltered. His comment that culture provides a 'primary source of resistance to change' (p. xiv) is highly relevant to the failure of equal opportunity policies in organizations.

Third, there are a number of gendered assumptions in Schein's theory that are not critically examined. Despite Schein's (1992) acknowledgement that different groups in an organization may have different perception of the culture, there is an absence of gender analysis. Schein recognizes that it would be both difficult and misleading to suggest that any particular cultural analysis is totally objective, and suggests that included in the primary data should be the investigator's emotional reactions and biases. This he has signally failed to do in relation to his own cultural biases towards gender. He correctly points out that in some organizations being emotional means one is regarded as unfit for higher management. The dual standard in assessing similar behaviour by men and women has been well documented (e.g. Tannen, 1995), but Schein draws no conclusions. Thus the writer cannot accept his contention that culture is 'morally neutral' (p. 48). On the level of language, Schein draws attention to the fact that in relation to his example 'Multi' he uses 'he' to refer to managers because he did not meet any female senior managers. On first sight this comment appears gender aware, but closer reflection suggests that he apparently did nothing to remedy this information bias. The 'rituals of deference and demeanour' (p. 119) between subordinate and boss may also have a gendered content.

Schein appears both gender and race blind in implying that status and position in the US are related only to accomplishment, and that this therefore makes puzzling other societies that rely on birth, family background, school and other criteria. This appears to assume a flawless meritocracy in the US, a country where the ascription of gender and race from birth is an important determinant of career outcomes (Carr-Ruffino, 1996).

Critiques of 'corporate culture'

Corporate culture is the most extreme form of functionalism, in that it is principally, often solely, concerned with economic performance. Deal and Kennedy (1982) is typical of this genre, which will now be examined in more detail. It is the most popular current conception of culture, in which culture is seen as a manipulable accessory to performance. Corporate culture puts extreme emphasis on culture as a variable, and hypothesizes culture as a product of the organization as much as goods and services (Smircich, 1983), and as a sub-system comparable to other sub-systems such as technology or strategy (Alvesson and Berg, 1992). Anthony (1994) points out the instrumentality of the corporate culture approach. Schultz (1995) suggests that there are two main measures of culture; first, strong or weak, as in Deal and Kennedy (1982), and second efficient and inefficient as in Peters and Waterman (1982).

Corporate culture has a number of features, which are summarized in this paragraph. First it is assumed that culture is unitary and homogenous, with impermeable boundaries. It is said to give to individuals a sense of identity, evoking commitment, and increasing social stability. The most important claim is the link with performance, where culture is seen as strongly influential both of organizational performance and individual behaviour. Although there is sometimes a view that it is static, paradoxically it is also seen as something, which can be changed easily. The underlying ontology (theory of being) is that corporate culture is real, and it is described in anthropomorphic terms (e.g. healthy, happy). These points will be discussed in turn.

The first aspect of corporate culture mentioned is its integrity or cohesiveness. Corporate culture is described as unitary and homogenous (Alvesson, 1993), and with impermeable boundaries. Meyerson and Martin (1987) characterized this as the integrationist perspective, where culture is perceived as an all-embracing social glue. This view has been criticized for ignoring the internal diversity of organizations and denying the existence of subcultures (e.g. Anthony, 1994). It is also challenged by the concept of the industrial subculture (Turner, 1971), as discussed above. A unitary corporate culture may thus be understood as a desired state of affairs, rather than necessarily a description of what is there. This unitary view ignores differences such as gender and race.

The second aspect of corporate culture concerns individuals: it is said to give a sense of identity, evoke commitment, and increase social stability (Smircich, 1983). Although many employees derive an important component of their sense of identity from their employing organization, organizational membership is not the only, or necessarily the principal, influence on identity, which can be derived from extra-organizational factors such as gender, race, ethnicity, class (Bell and Nkomo, 1992) and sexuality. Differential outcomes may decrease rather than increase commitment on the part of disadvantaged organizational members. It is asserted that corporate culture evokes commitment, and therefore encourages employees to function on the basis of internal rather than external controls. However, there may be a difference between outward compliance and inner disagreement.

The most important argument about corporate culture is the third aspect considered here, the culture-performance link (Alvesson, 1993), which is based on assumptions of causality between leadership and culture, and culture and performance. Culture is said to influence and control behaviour, and hence individual and organizational performance. Managers are urged to understand, manage, and even create culture, and a cursory glance at much popular management literature will reveal exhortations for quality cultures, learning cultures, people cultures and so on. As well as Deal and Kennedy (1982) writers such as Peters and Waterman (1982) powerfully advocated the efficacy of culture in promoting superior performance. Strength and efficacy are therefore two measures of success (Schultz, 1995). Anthony (1994) questions whether top managers really want a change in culture, or are simply seeking a change in employees' behaviour. The management of change is discussed more fully in Foreman (in this volume).

Corporate culture adherents write about it in an anthropomorphic fashion, that is, as if culture were alive. Good corporate cultures are described glowingly as 'strong' and 'healthy', which implies a value judgement. Meek (1988) criticizes the notion that strong cultures are better than weak ones, and rejects the identification of culture with management's interests, what Alvesson (1993: 90) calls 'management-centric' culture. Meek (1988) points out that the concept of culture used has been imported from one particular branch of social anthropology, the structural-functional paradigm, which sees societal culture as primarily purposeful, as opposed to an alternative paradigm, which views culture as a means of creating meaning (Meek, 1998). These two paradigms can be seen as conceptually related to functionalism and symbolism respectively.

Corporate culture is gendered whilst being overtly gender blind, at the same time as glorifying a heroic corporate culture, by the retelling of tales of corporate heroes, a way of glorifying male dominance (Aaltio-Marjosola, 1994). Some corporate cultures do have equal opportunity policies, but these vary in the extent to which these are implemented. Their efficacy may be judged by the fact that despite 20 years of equal opportunities legislation in the UK there are still disparities in male and female pay and male dominance of management (Maddock and Parkin, 1993). Corporate culture may subscribe to ideas on managing diversity where a diverse workforce is seen as instrumental in helping economic performance, but the managing diversity approach has been criticized for ignoring equity and power issues (Wilson and Iles, 1996).

Overviews of the topic

This section looks at two general overviews of organizational culture, Alvesson (1993) and Brown (1995). Alvesson had the benefit of writing his review of this field at a time when there had been considerable proliferation and exploration within both perspectives, and he addresses both.

In reviewing the functionalist perspective, Alvesson (1993: 90) critiques what he terms the 'culture-performance link'. A more general critique of this can be found in the section above on corporate culture, incorporating Alvesson's criticisms as well as others'. Alvesson suggests that some of the problems associated with exploring causality within the functionalist paradigm can be avoided by adopting the approach of culture as root metaphor, a symbolic approach. Interpretation and description are then the principal concerns. In examining culture as metaphor, he suggests this can have both illuminating and shadowing effects. Alvesson points out that whilst metaphors can be seen simply as an illustrative device, dangers lie in the choice of poor, oversimplified and superficial metaphors.

Alvesson writes about the taken for granted nature of Western managerial culture, and warns against ethnocentrism. In discussing approaches to investigating organizations. Alvesson suggests broadening the field of enquiry, and treating organizational features and phenomena as located in a particular historical, geographical and political context. Alvesson suggests that studies of culture can be prompted by emancipatory interest, for instance exploring the asymmetrical power relations within organizations. He states that the process of casting light on basic taken-for-granted assumptions may help to oppose ethnocentric bias. Clearly the same process could help to oppose gendered bias, but this is not specifically mentioned by Alvesson. He suggests that gender disparities in organizations should be confronted, and that this is one route to challenging taken-for-granted assumptions.

Alvesson uses the phrase 'cultural traffic' (p. 80) to describe the reciprocal influences of organizations and their environments. He lists gender relations as among those influences that affect both inside and outside workplaces. Alvesson proposes that there is necessarily a degree of ambiguity in organizational culture, largely because of cultural traffic with the host culture. Gender, as well as class, ethnic and national origins, and professions are among those elements subject to cultural traffic.

Alvesson's review of organizational culture can be seen to include considerations of gender that are easily incorporated into his general understanding of culture.

Brown's (1995) contribution is more recent than Alvesson (1993). It differs from Alvesson (1993) in being a textbook rather than a monograph, and hence is aimed at a different audience. Having said this the approach is disappointing. The cover clearly indicates that the main part of the book is devoted to the culture-performance link (Alvesson, 1993), and the book has a strong functionalist bias, for instance stating that the function of organizational culture is to reduce conflict, co-ordinate and control, reduce uncertainty, increase motivation and hence competitive advantage. Although rejecting the idea that culture is an independent variable affecting strategy, a dependent variable, Brown states that either may impact on the other. Typologies quoted, such as Quinn and McGrath (1985) and Scholz (1987) deal principally with performance.

Similarly to Deal and Kennedy (1982), Brown discusses the role of heroes, who are all men. His only significant mention of gender is a reference to the classic Hofstede (1980) study, although he points out the incongruence of supposedly Equal Opportunity employers who lose sex discrimination cases, and refers to the myth that women are unreliable. His recognition of subcultures, conflict, and the importance of power resources are not linked to any gender analysis. This book is a safe, unexciting and largely uncritical overview of the functionalist field.

Gender and organizational culture

A number of writers on culture give clues as to where culture may be coloured by gender considerations, such as Hofstede's (1980) account of the dimension of masculinity/femininity between different nationalities, and Schein's (1992) reference to gender subcultures in organizations. The gendered nature of cultures within organizations can be seen in the fact that many companies with espoused 'woman friendly' policies are exposed by their organizational underbelly: women daily experience that they do not fit. Some writers suggest that all organizations are gendered (e.g. Gherardi, 1994). Alvesson and Due Billing (1992) point out two different ways in which organizations may be considered gendered: first, one could take a simple head count of the numbers of each sex in a particular job; second they point to jobs and organizational areas having an 'aura' which they consider as more persistent than mere head counting. Gendered culture can be seen in hierarchical and patriarchal features (Itzin, 1995), gendered social divisions (Newman, 1995), gendered departments (Roper, 1994), gendered jobs and roles (Kanter, 1977), gendered personnel processes (Alimo-Metcalfe, 1993), gendered outcomes in terms of promotion (Davidson and Cooper, 1992), gendered pay (Symons, 1992), gendered discourse, sexualized environment (Itzin, 1995), gendered bullying, gendered power (Itzin, 1995) and gendered dominant and subordinate subcultures.

It is suggested that culture at almost any level or angle may be viewed as gendered. As Acker (1990) states:

> To say that an organization, or any other analytic unit, is gendered means that advantage and disadvantage, exploitation and control, action and emotion,

> meaning and identity, are patterned through and in terms of a distinction between male and female, masculine and feminine. (p. 146)

It is helpful to draw a distinction between 'gender cultures' where culture is addressed solely or principally in terms of gender, and 'gendered cultures', the extent to which all organizational cultures are integrally and invisibly cast in terms of gender (Hearn et al., 1989). The distinction is essentially one of approach or intention. When gender cultures are investigated the researcher is seeking those aspects pertaining to gender. On the other hand any investigation of culture is inevitably one of gendered cultures, whether this is highlighted by the investigation or not.

The next part of this section will discuss the different sites and levels of gender, starting with gender as externalities, which relates to national or societal culture. Hofstede's (1980) study has already been mentioned, where he contends there are long-standing and pervasive differences to the extent to which nationalities perceive differences between masculine and feminine. The influence on societal culture is developed by Mills and Murgatroyd (1991) who assert that we know about gender rules before we enter the organization, as this starts at birth and continues in family and school through the socialization process. As an example they state that boys learn to play games, which involves learning rules, rule negotiation, roles, teamwork and leadership, all of which prepare them for the public world of work (Mills and Murgatroyd, 1991). On the other hand, girls are prepared for domestic work at home, and are discouraged from learning technical skills (Mills and Murgatroyd, 1991). Case (1994) noted that girls are more concerned with relationships than rules in play. Gherardi (1995) suggests that familial archetypes are carried over into organizations; relationships replicated include complementary work roles such as boss and secretary, which reproduces the subordination of women.

Second, a number of studies demonstrate that there are similarities between organizations in respect of their treatment and processing of gender, which supports the contention that one of the elements of the industrial subculture is its gendered nature. Gendered activities and processes can be found commonly across a variety of organizations. For instance, Cockburn (1991) studied four different organizations, all with good reputations for equal opportunities, and in each, to differing extents, men resisted the advancement of women. At a symbolic level, Gherardi (1995) points out the frequency with which take-overs and mergers are described in terms of love affairs, marriages and rape. In order to explain the pervasiveness of gender in organizations, Gherardi (1995) draws principally on a symbolic and social constructionist perspective to explore organizational culture and gender, suggesting that gender relations are present both as practice and as patterns of thought. Gherardi (1995) suggests that we think about 'natural' differences between men and women, and that this in turn reproduces these differences.

Third, the managerial subculture in most organizations is gendered both in terms of numbers and status of women (Davidson and Cooper, 1992). Marshall (1994) describes the managerial culture experienced by senior women, where they were a minority or tokens, as hostile, aggressive, status conscious and isolating. She expressed her surprise that her findings were similar to those of Kanter (1977) when she described women managers twenty years earlier at lower levels of the organization. Itzin (1995) in a study of three departments of a local authority described the gendered culture as hierarchical and patriarchal, based on a sex segregated, sexual division of labour in the home. There was sex stereotyping, sex discrimination, sexual harassment, resistance to change, and gendered power (Itzin, 1995).

Fourth, departmental subcultures are described as gendered by Roper (1994). He found that engineering was regarded as masculine, and personnel as feminine. This also applied to sections of departments. For instance within personnel, a feminine department, industrial relations is seen as tough and masculine compared to other softer, feminine 'welfare' parts of personnel management (Roper, 1994). According to Gherardi (1995) gender relationships in the workplace reflect, create and amend the symbolic order of gender in society. The symbolic order of gender is expressed through male and female domains in organizations, and accompanying differences in, for instance, status and pay (Gherardi, 1995). Job segregation recognizes the separate symbolic worlds of male and female (Gherardi, 1995). However, gender is not a category tied unequivocally to sex, as Gherardi (1995) points out that some organizations have more female positions than there are women to fill them. Thus some work positions have gendered attributes, even though occupied by men. Gherardi (1995: 131) writes about 'second sexing', to describe the way organizational members, usually women, are relegated to an inferior and subordinate position. She notes that men may belong to the second sex because of age or lack of status.

Fifth, given that organizational cultures as experienced by men and women are in many cases respectively dominant and subordinate, certain counter culture subcultures inhabited by women may be gendered but in different ways to the dominant culture. Aaltio-Marjosola (1994) describes a female subculture in a technological manufacturing company where women felt discriminated against, and wore clothes which differentiated them from their male colleagues.

Gherardi (1995) suggests that the dual presence, the presence of both men and women in the workplace, is a breach of the symbolic order of gender. This is why ceremonial work, celebrating gender identity, and also remedial work, doing restitution for offences to the symbolic order of gender, are necessary (Gherardi, 1995). In ceremonial work the symbolic differences are stressed (Gherardi, 1995). It starts by ascertaining gender differences on meeting someone, and therefore cannot be avoided. Ceremonial work includes behaviour that is thought proper for one's own gender, and for acknowledging the gender of other according to expectations. Ceremonial work can include elements of courtship, but this is an affirmation of gender identity and attractiveness, a means of reassurance rather than a route to sexual pairing. Chivalric rituals, the traditional courtesy shown to women at work, are a confirmation of their subordination, as the sexes are in an asymmetrical position (Gherardi, 1995). Remedial work is necessary for women to apologise and make reparations for their presence in the workplace (Gherardi, 1995). For instance one remedial ritual is using the interrogative form: 'Can I ask you...?' (p. 140). Lack of assertiveness may be another reparative ritual. Sometimes women accepted into a man's world are treated as one of the boys, and therefore accepted as people, but devalued as women. They therefore have to choose between being honorary men, or stay female and ignore the acceptance offered (Gherardi, 1995).

The evidence reviewed at all these different levels of organizational culture indicates that gendering is ubiquitous. The majority of this gendering is at the behest of the dominant, masculine culture, working to their advantage. Having argued the case that all cultures are gendered, the next section will look at descriptions of culture in purely gender terms.

Typologies of gender cultures

One of the popular descriptions of gender cultures currently used is macho management (Personnel Management Plus, 1994). Cornwall and Lindisfarne (1994) note that 'macho' is often associated with heterosexism, the use of physical force and the suppression of emotion. The expression macho management is currently used to describe a highly aggressive, ruthless management style. Macho management is often described as if it were gender neutral (e.g. Personnel Management, 1994). Despite the repeated criticisms of the effectiveness of this management style (e.g. Personnel Management Plus, 1994), it seems remarkably persistent. Whilst it is clearly damaging to most subordinates, it may be conjectured to be particularly so for women, who are more likely to be in subordinate positions.

There are some descriptions of cultures that are identified primarily in terms of gender, such as Maddock and Parkin's (1993) account of the types of gender cultures within the UK public sector. They suggest a typology of gender cultures which appears equally applicable to private sector organizations. First is the Gentleman's Club, which is polite, civilized, and patronizing towards women, acting in a paternalist manner. Women are kept in their (subordinate) place, and survive as long as they conform. By contrast the Barrack Room has an atmosphere of bullying, is hostile towards any kind of identifiable difference, and is built on an authoritarian power culture; women and other disadvantaged groups are rendered invisible. In the Locker Room there are common assumptions and agreements between men, much talk about sex and sport, and exaggerated body language; women are excluded from the inner circle. The Gender Blind culture asserts that there is no difference between men and women. Because of this it ignores women's identity and reality that denies obstacles and can lead to the superwoman syndrome. In the Lip Service/Feminist Pretenders culture there are good policies, but little happens. This type of culture may have equality experts, and there may be hierarchies of oppression, where different disadvantaged groups vie for attention and resources. Lastly, there is the Smart Macho, which Maddock and Parkin (1993) say is particularly prevalent in the UK National Health Service. This is very competitive, and although overtly in favour of equal opportunities will discriminate if someone cannot deliver 80 hours a week. Maddock and Parkin (1993) suggest that in all types of culture men in powerful positions are reluctant to relinquish power.

More specifically, Gherardi (1995) describes how women can find themselves in a variety of different positions when they enter a previously all-male culture. Women entering certain occupations, professions and management are entering the symbolic territory of maleness.   Although officially members of the organization, females are trespassing on male territory. Women may enter either a friendly or hostile culture. First, they may be in a friendly culture where they are treated as the guest. Despite its privileges this position however hinders equality, and women remain subordinate. The second culture is friendly and the woman has the position of a holidaymaker. Women are treated as just passing through. Not being in ownership of the territory they cannot do things their way. The third culture is friendly and the woman has the position of a newcomer. Her femininity may evoke fear, even if she is not a femme fatale. The newcomer's position is defined by the host culture, and she is judged on her capacity to conform and integrate. The fourth culture is hostile, and the woman marginalized, as is anyone noticeably different. The fifth is hostile and the woman has the position of the snake in the grass. She is seen as a threat, and her inability or unwillingness to confirm leads to irreconcilable differences. Lastly, there is a hostile culture where the woman is cast as intruder. The intruder is other, and she and the intruded upon are complementary in their hostility (Gherardi, 1995).

Both these typologies describe the pervasive and persistent gendering of culture.

Case study: *Finco*

Finco was a company in the turbulent financial sector, with core competencies in marketing, financial skills, and IT. Sources of competitive advantage were its reputation, recent downsizing, and market response that included the development of niche products. Its mission included being the best in the industry, working to the highest standards, including quality of service, making profit, and being an excellent employer of excellent people.

During the case study *Finco* was committed to a clear corporate approach, encapsulated in a series of statements under 'This is *Finco*' known as TIF. The aim was to make the organization more customer responsive, innovative, entrepreneurial and competitive, by encouraging empowerment and teamwork. Key espoused values were customer responsiveness, and a number of values in relation to staff: trusting staff, caring for them, empowering them, rewarding them. Opinions varied as to its effectiveness. A number of views were expressed that *Finco* did not follow through on its commitments to staff, for instance there was no training or support for the policy of empowerment, and there was confusion about acceptable management style. Women managers said that empowerment had not really been sufficiently explained, or supported by training. They felt there was a gap between the espoused values encapsulated in the TIF statement and what was really happening, which is illustrated in Table 9.1.

There were mixed messages in the organization about management style, particularly in relation to how much one should speak out.

Table 9.1 *Espoused values and underlying assumptions that are ambiguously related –* general issues, **Finco**

Espoused values	Underlying assumptions
Empowering staff	Managers believe in empowerment, the organization does not The company believes that employees do not need explanation, training and support in order to be empowered

Until recently *Finco* offered managers a career for life. The right experience was essential for promotion and included selection for attendance at a top European management school. Career moves were almost impossible without the universally acknowledged informal system of sponsorship, and judicious self-promotion. In *Finco* everyone talked openly about the system of sponsorship, which was more important than formal procedures in gaining promotion. In theory *Finco* had an open, equitable internal system for promotion; in practice it was a mixture of sponsorship and ad hocery, where outlook and approach were more important than specific competence. In *Finco* the role of sponsorship and suitable job assignments were crucial in ascertaining promotion, and the system clearly had not worked as well for women as for men. This can be seen in Table 9.2.

Table 9.2 *Espoused values and underlying assumptions that conflict with each other –* general issues, **Finco**

Espoused values	Underlying assumptions
Open, equitable, internal promotion system	Ad hoc promotion system relying on sponsors and self promotion

Sponsorship also appeared significant as a locally understood symbol. It seemed to be a dynamic attachment between respectively more and less powerful employees, with both parties aware of the relationship. The sponsor invested reputation, power, energy and influence in order to further the career of the person sponsored. The social construction of this particular meaning appeared peculiar to *Finco*, as it was context and organization specific (Schultz, 1995).

The company had an equal opportunity policy and above minimum maternity pay, but had chosen not to join Opportunity 2000, the UK voluntary initiative to promote the quality and quantity of women's contribution in the workplace. It appeared to have an equal opportunity policy for legal/external reasons. There were gendered underlying assumptions that women were not suitable for top positions, and mothers had to prove their commitment. It was a conservative environment about being gay. *Finco* was similar to the gender blind culture of

Maddock and Parkin (1993), in that apart from a few concessions it did not recognize the difficulties women face. Although glass walls (job segregation by gender) were less evident than formerly, a number of managers, both male and female, identified a glass ceiling for women in the company. The few women who had gained substantial middle manager positions in previous restructurings had not progressed further. In addition, a glass elevator probably existed for young men to speed them on their way, first via men's informal networking, and second through the medium of corporate entertaining to which women were not always invited. There was a tendency for certain job roles and sections to be seen as gendered (Roper, 1994). For instance, it was suggested that work dealing with the public which required good interpersonal skills, often done well by women, was undervalued. On the other hand, negotiations with other financial institutions were seen as high profile, and a pre-requisite for promotion to senior manager grade. These were more likely to be undertaken by men. These conflicts between espoused value and underlying assumptions are illustrated in Table 9.3.

Table 9.3 *Espoused values and underlying assumptions that conflict with each other – gender issues,* **Finco**

Espoused values	Underlying assumptions
Equal Opportunities	Women are not suitable for top positions
	Some jobs are better done by men, and some better done by women
	Women are good in support roles and departments

The glass ceiling was confirmed symbolically by the apparent lack of any women's toilets on the top managers' floor. This was repeated categorically by several interviewees, and only latterly did it emerge that there were toilets, but that they were very difficult to find. The significance of this seemed to be not the fact of whether there were women's toilets but rather the widespread understanding that there were not. *Finco's* HQ was a modern building, about 20 years old, so any partiality in the toilet provision could be assumed to be a deliberate ascription of top managerial roles to men. Both the glass ceiling and gendered perceptions of work appeared to be widely held socially constructed meanings in *Finco*.

Finco demonstrates that organizational progression may be subject to gendered influence, as there was a disparity between supposedly meritocratic processes and actual outcomes. This conflict was most acute in the experience of new mothers. On the one hand they benefited from generous maternity provisions, and on the other hand they were treated as less than committed, and less than competent. It can be conjectured that the confusion about management style also reflected gendered concerns; the more participative style proposed being more feminine than the traditional command and control approach (Rosener, 1990). Local meanings and symbols were important, for instance the particular understanding of sponsorship, and the elusive toilets. Gendering can thus be explained both in terms of Schein's (1992) model, and through a symbolic perspective.

Conclusion

This chapter has indicated the pervasiveness of gender as an organizing principle within organizational culture. It is perhaps more helpful to see gender as integral rather than as an independent variable or influence upon culture. The chapter has demonstrated how some popular conceptions of culture, those broadly based on functionalism, have barely touched upon gender and other differences, and fail to incorporate gender. Generally the symbolic perspective is more sympathetic to a gendered perspective, and more easily incorporates gender as one of many aspects of reality. The implication for the organizational researcher is not that every organization should be studied principally from the point of view of gender. Rather she or he should be alive to gendered processes, which may be borne in mind as possible interpretations for other inexplicable events. Gender neutrality is no longer feasible.

References

Aaltio-Marjosola, Iiris (1994) 'Gender stereotypes as cultural products of the organization', *Scandinavian Journal of Management*, 10 (2): 147-62.

Acker, Joan (1990) 'Hierarchies, jobs, bodies: a theory of gendered organizations', *Gender and Society*, 4 (2): 39-158.

Alimo-Metcalfe, Beverly (1993) 'Women in management: organizational socialization and assessment practices that prevent career advancement', *International Journal of Selection and Assessment*, 1 (2): 68-83.

Alvesson, Mats (1993) *Cultural Perspectives on Organizations*. Cambridge: Cambridge University Press.

Alvesson, Mats and Berg, Olaf Per (1992) *Corporate Culture and Organizational Symbolism: An Overview*. Berlin: De Gruyter.

Alvesson, Mats and Due Billing, Yvonne (1992) 'Gender and organization: towards a differentiated understanding', *Organization Studies*, 13 (12): 73-103.

Anthony, Peter (1994) *Managing Culture*. Buckingham: Open University Press.

Bartol, Kathryn (1978) 'The sex structuring of organizations: a search for possible causes', *Academy of Management Review*, 3 (4): 805-15.

Bell, Ella Louise and Nkomo, Stella (1992) 'Re-visioning women managers' lives', in Mills, Albert and Tancred, Peta (eds) *Gendering Organizational Analysis*. London: Sage. pp. 235-47.

Brown, Andrew (1995) *Organizational Culture*. London: Pitman Publishing.

Carr-Ruffino, Norma (1996) *Managing Diversity: People Skills for a Multicultural Workplace*. USA: Thomson Executive Press.

Case, Susan Schick (1994) 'Gender differences in communication and behaviour in organizations', in Davidson, Marilyn and Burke, Ronald (eds) *Women in Management, Current Research Issues*. London: Paul Chapman Publishing. pp.148-60.

Cockburn, Cynthia (1991) *In the Way of Women: Men's Resistance to Sex Equality in Organizations*. Basingstoke and London: Macmillan.

Cornwall, Andrea and Lindisfarne, Nancy (1994) 'Dislocating masculinity: gender, power and anthropology', in Cornwall, Andrea and Lindisfarne, Nancy (eds) *Dislocating Masculinity: Comparative Ethnographies*. London: Routledge. pp. 11-47.

Davidson, Marilyn and Cooper, Cary (1992) *Breaking the Glass Ceiling: The Woman Manager*. London: Paul Chapman.

Deal, Terrence E. and Kennedy, Alan A. (1982) *Corporate Cultures the Rights and Rituals of Corporate Life*. London: Addison-Wesley.

Gherardi, Sylvia (1994) 'The gender we think, the gender we do in our everyday organizational lives', *Human Relations*, 47 (6): 591-610.

Gherardi, Sylvia (1995) *Gender, Symbolism and Organizational Cultures*. London: Sage.

Handy, Charles (1985) *Understanding Organizations*. 3rd Edition. Harmondsworth: Penguin.

Harrison, R. (1972) 'Understanding your organization's character', *Harvard Business Review*, 50 (May-June): 119-28.

Hearn, Jeff, Sheppard, Deborah, Tancred-Sheriff, Peta and Burrell, Gibson (1989) 'The sexuality of organization: a postscript', in Hearn, Jeff, Sheppard, Deborah, Tancred-Sheriff, Peta and Burrell, Gibson (eds) *The Sexuality of Organization*. London, Newbury Park: Sage. pp. 178-81.

Hofstede, Geert (1980) *Culture's Consequences: International Differences in Work-Related Values*. Beverley Hills, California: Sage.

Itzin, Catherine (1995) 'The gender culture in organizations', in Itzin, Catherine and Newman, J. (eds) *Gender, Culture and Organizational Change.* London: Routledge. pp. 30-53.

Kanter, Rosabeth (1977) *Men and Women of the Corporation.* USA: Basic Books.

Maddock, Su and Parkin, Di (1993) 'Gender cultures: women's choices and strategies at work', *Women in Management Review,* 8 (2): 3-9.

Marshall, Judi (1994) *Women Managers Moving On: Exploring Life and Career Choices.* London: Routledge.

Meek, V. Lynn (1988) 'Organizational culture - origins and weaknesses', *Organization Studies,* 9 (4): 453-73.

Meyerson, D. and Martin, J. (1987) 'Cultural change: an integration of three different views', *Journal of Management Studies,* 24: 623-47.

Mills, Albert and Murgatroyd, Stephen J. (1991) *Organizational Rules: A Framework for Understanding Organizational Action.* Milton Keynes: Open University Press.

Morgan, Gareth, Frost, Peter J., and Pondy, Louis R. (1983) 'Organizational symbolism', in Pondy, Louis R., Frost, Peter J. Morgan, Gareth, and Dandridge, Thomas C. (eds) *Organizational Symbolism.* London: JAI Press Inc. pp. 3-38.

Newman, Janet (1995) 'Making connections: frameworks for change', in Itzin, Catherine and Newman, J. (eds) *Gender, Culture and Organizational Change.* London: Routledge. pp. 273-86.

Personnel Management (1994) 'Macho management style can put brake on success', *Personnel Management,* 26 (2): 9.

Personnel Management Plus (1994) 'Macho styles condemned', *Personnel Management Plus,* 5 (4): 8.

Peters, Tom and Waterman, R.H. (1982) *In Search of Excellence.* New York: Harper and Row.

Quinn, R.E. and McGrath, M.R. (1985) 'The transformation of organizational cultures: a competing values perspective', in Frost P.J., Moore, L.F., Louis, M.R., Lundberg, C.C. and Martin, J. (eds) *Organizational Culture.* Newbury Park, California: Sage. pp. 315-34. cited in Brown, Andrew (1998) *Organizational Culture.* London: Pitman Publishing.

Roper, Michael (1994) *Masculinity and the British Organization Man Since 1945.* Oxford: Oxford University Press.

Rosener, J. (1990) 'Ways women lead', *Harvard Business Review,* 68: 119-25.

Schein, Edgar (1992) *Organizational Culture and Leadership.* 2nd Edition. San Francisco: Jossey-Bass.

Scholz, C. (1987) 'Corporate culture and strategy - the problem of strategic fit', *Long Range Planning,* 20 (4): 78-87. Cited in Brown, Andrew (1998) *Organizational Culture.* London: Pitman Publishing.

Schultz, Majken (1995) *On Studying Organizational Cultures: Diagnosis and Understanding.* Berlin: de Gruyter.

Smircich, Linda (1983) 'Concepts of culture and organizational analysis', *Administrative Science Quarterly,* 28: 339-58.

Symons, Gladys (1992) 'The glass ceiling is constructed over the gendered office', *Women in Management Review,* 7 (1): 18-22.

Tannen, Deborah (1995) *Talking from 9 to 5.* London: Virago.

Turner, Barry (1971) *Exploring the Industrial Subculture.* London: MacMillan.

Wilson, Elisabeth and Iles, Paul (1996) *Managing Diversity: Critique of an Emerging Paradigm.* Proceedings of the British Academy of Management Conference, 12-14 September. Aston University, Birmingham.

10 Power

Lorraine Green, Wendy Parkin, Jeff Hearn

This chapter analyses the engendered and genderized nature of organizational power, and how this relates centrally to the way organizations are perceived, experienced, managed and theorized. Key concepts which will be analysed include gender, sex and power, men and masculinities and their relevance for organizations; the difficulties and controversies associated with attempting to differentiate gender and sexuality; the importance of, and interconnections between, public and private spheres; internal networks and organizational dynamics; and organizational values, beliefs and identities. Following the exploration of these key concepts, a short illustrative case study dealing with residential child care organizations will be presented.

Continuing omissions in contemporary organizational literature

Most classic organizational texts and key organizational textbooks written, failed to analyse the significance of gender or the relationships between sex, gender, organizations and power, in any explicit manner (see Hearn and Parkin, 1992; Mills and Tancred, 1992; Acker and Van Houten, 1992). The nature of masculinist, generic power was, however, evidenced within most of these texts by assumptions that organizations were inhabited only by men, or that it was not necessary to differentiate between men and women in examining organizations and the distribution of organizational positions (Hearn and Parkin, 1992). Organizations also tended to be presented not only as agendered but also as undifferentiated with regard to race, culture and even class (Hearn et al., 1989; Mills and Tancred, 1992; Mulholland, 1996a) with the exception of some Marxist/class-based approaches (for example, Clegg and Dunkerley, 1977, 1980). Therefore only a very partial view of organizations was given, even though it was presented as if it was a whole, objective and unbiased evaluation.

In many contemporary organizational behaviour and work psychology texts, gender is increasingly referred to, although not always (see Dawson, 1997). It is, however, often included in a very brief, piecemeal, ad-hoc, marginalized and unanalytic manner. For example, Charles Handy, a high profile organizational theorist who omitted any mention of gender or women in his early work, apologizes for this omission in later revised editions (e.g. Handy, 1993: 9) and claims to redress it but does not. In *Understanding Organizations* (1993) most of the extracts and exemplars Handy cites are from male writers who ignore gender or only refer to men. Regarding motivation and work he poses questions, such as whether biological sex makes a difference, whether men and women decide priorities differently or whether men are dominated by sexuality and aggression (p. 29), but then these issues are left unanalysed. Handy (1993) also remains unapologetic about his predominant use of the male rather than a female or ungendered pronoun in his book because he states it still represents how most organizations operate. Such examples demonstrate not only how little understanding of gender and power still exists, but how small the commitment is to try and challenge the current status quo.

Men in the driving seat: men, masculinity and structural power in organizations

The denial of gender and its relationship with power, in current and past studies of organizations and organizational textbooks seems strange, given that statistics indicate that men hold the majority of formal positions of power in most organizations. Drawing from published statistics, Collinson and Hearn (1996) note that fewer than 5 per cent of managers were female in the UK and the US and that in many other countries it was around 2 per cent. For example, 5 per cent of the UK Institute of Directors and less than 1 per cent of senior executives were women (Hansard Society, 1990). This picture is replicated again and again by numerous other studies such as Equal Opportunities Commission's Annual Reports and research by Colgan and Ledwith (1996). Where women are located within middle management positions, they tend to be 'hived off' into specific, 'niche' areas where they have little strategic power (Crompton and Sanderson, 1990) and are deprived of the wide range of managerial experiences, mentoring and training vital for future promotion (Calas and Smircich, 1993; Collinson and Hearn, 1996; Ohlott et al., 1991).

The proportion of women in the labour market does not explain their under-representation at senior occupational levels, as in the mid-1990s women constituted 47 per cent of the UK employed labour force (Sly, 1993). Even when comparing men and women with equal qualifications, men quickly forge ahead into more and more senior positions (McGuire, 1992; Institute of Management, 1994; Colgan and Ledwith, 1996). While some women clearly do embrace the ideal of a managerial career, this does not necessarily lead to more egalitarian power relationships either in the home or within organizations. In a study of countries within the European Union where affirmative action policies are in place, the number of women in top positions was negligible and the number of women in managerial positions was actually decreasing, although the number of managerial positions was increasing overall (Woodward, 1996). Affirmative or positive action is a radical approach to equal opportunities involving the application of different policies or processes to specific, often disadvantaged groups, such as black people and women, to transform inequalities in condition at the beginning to equalities at the end, that is, equality of outcome or result (Bagilhole, 1997).

Men and women tend to be segregated in different kinds of jobs within the same organization or within different types of organizations (Cockburn, 1983; Woodward, 1996). Women are often concentrated in types of jobs or occupations associated with tending to others, which are often societally and organizationally perceived as having little value, such as those in the catering, servicing and welfare sectors (Hearn, 1982; Adkins, 1992; Davies, 1992). Conversely men are more likely to inhabit higher status jobs where physical strength or technical or instrumental skills are seen to be needed, such as manual labour jobs, computing and engineering, or jobs where they are expected to manage and oversee others (Collinson and Hearn, 1996; Colgan and Ledwith, 1996; Cheng, 1996b).

Women are generally paid less for doing the same job as a man or for doing work that is different but could be regarded as having equal value (Zimmeck, 1992; Cockburn, 1983, 1991). Additionally, even in welfare work such as social work, where women predominate in the lower positions, men still are overwhelmingly over-represented in the higher managerial positions (Howe, 1986; Hugman, 1991; Grimwood and Popplestone, 1993).

Defining the relationships between gender, sex and power

Power

In examining the pivotal and primary importance of gender and its relationship to power in organizations, some initial exploration is needed of what is meant by the terms sex, gender and power. Power is a multifaceted concept that is difficult to define. There is much contestation around whether power is a possession or a resource that can be imposed hierarchically (Lukes, 1986; Clegg, 1988; Hindess, 1996) or whether it is an immeasurable circulatory, capillary and relational phenomenon, enshrined in discourse and only observable in its exercise (Foucault, 1977, 1979; Clegg, 1988; Hindess, 1996).

To simplify the complex arguments around power, four modes or dimensions of power will be briefly described. Power has thus been traditionally construed as a capacity and the ability to dominate or influence others through reward or punishment (Weber, 1958; Dahl, 1957; Wrong, 1979). The second face of power sees some people's interests as never reaching the formal level of decision making or agenda setting (Bachrach and Baratz, 1970). The third dimension of power views people's 'real interests' as being distorted by ideological conditioning devices (Lukes, 1974). Post-structuralist conceptions of power see individuals as constituted by their discursive environments and therefore argue it is impossible to see whether there are 'real', 'objective' interests waiting to be defined (Barbalet, 1987; Foucault, 1977, 1979).

In analysing organizational theory textbooks, power tends to be treated as either one or two dimensional. Weber's concept of organizational rational-legal power is often cited as important, (that is, power that is derived from one's official position in the organizational hierarchy) (Buchanan and Huczynski, 1985; Mullins, 1996), even when criticisms of Weber are mentioned, such as his insufficient attention to informal networks of power. Many organizational theory textbooks also utilize French and Raven's (1968) reward, coercive, legitimate, referent and expert power bases, (Buchanan and Huczynski, 1997; Mullins, 1996; Sims et al., 1993) although rarely are the concepts of gender and power interlinked. Sims et al. (1993) is a rare exception here. Lukes's (1974) third dimension of power via ideological conditioning and the fourth, discursive and circulatory notion of power, are noticeable by their omission. In both the third and fourth dimensions of power individuals may collude with or even actively seek positions or activities that others may see as disadvantaging them.

The discursive and gendered nature of power is, however, evident in the way some organizational theory commentators describe power per se. Buchanan and Huczynski (1985), for example, illustrate reward power by reference to a mother offering a child a reward, coercive power by the father's ability to punish a child, and then describe the other three forms of power only by using male pronouns. The link between gender and power is evident here as men and women's personality characteristics are 'naturalized' and essentialized. Men are implicitly presented as naturally authoritarian and coercive and women as maternal and co-operative. By using solely male pronouns to illustrate power, Buchanan and Huczynski also implicitly inferiorize and diminish the importance of women in organizations.

In this chapter not only concepts of coercive or influential, top-down, gendered power will be used but the concepts of three dimensional and discursive gendered power will be drawn upon. Thus genderic, organizational power can be conceptualized, not only as the ability of men to physically prevent women from entering into organizations on an equal basis and being accorded advancement on merit within organizations, through both covert and overt material means, but also in terms of the part discourses and communication play in dissuading women from resisting or wanting to resist that situation. It will also be shown that ideologies, discourses and material relations merge and influence each other in a self-perpetuating fashion.

Gender

In some organizational texts the terms sex and gender are used interchangeably as if they were one and the same, or the term sex is used to denote gender. However, here, (as in chapter one) sex is seen to be a biological category which defines individuals as males or females according to physiological and chromosomal criteria.   Gender is seen as a socially constructed phenomenon whereby certain personality or other social characteristics are connoted as masculine or feminine and are inaccurately assumed to be 'naturally' related to the possession of a male or female body.

However this bi-polar socially constructed view of gender often implicitly suggests masculinity and femininity to be static, unidimensional and diametrically opposed ways of being or acting.   It also does not deal satisfactorily with the dynamics of social change or with structural, discursive or practice-based aspects of gender.   Such a view is in itself artificially homogenizing, ethnocentric and Eurocentric. It does not acknowledge the existence of plural, multiple masculinities or femininities that may depend on historical and social context, culture and racialization (Eichler, 1980; Carrigan et al., 1985; Connell, 1987, 1995; Hamada, 1996).   Additionally it fails to demonstrate how femininities may be performed by males and masculinities by females, or that one person can be androgynous in the same or different cultural contexts (Cheng, 1996a; Hamada, 1996, Bem, 1974; 1981).

Both Daly (1973) and Hollway (1996) have emphasized how masculinity is constructed both generally and occupationally by the positioning of women as the undesirable and deficient 'other'.   Masculine characteristics have thus tended to be exalted not necessarily because they are commendable in themselves but because they are oppositional to and are construed in direct aversion to feminine characteristics (Chodorow, 1978; Dinnerstein, 1987).

Various commentators have recently explored the proliferation of, differential hegemony of, and competition between, different types of organizational masculinities. In a Japanese company situated in the US, where power was globally held by a distant multi-national Japanese organization, American managers resented and represented Japanese styles of working as 'feminine', because they were more co-operative and gave less power to the individual managers to wield over subordinates (Hamada, 1996). The American managers felt deprived of power, having to do their own administration and not having individual secretaries to do this and additionally resented having to put on overalls and regularly fraternize and co-operate with the shopfloor workers. This seeming shift to more egalitarian styles at lower levels of management was actually autocratically imposed from the top which remains patriarchal. Hamada's findings therefore link closely with Hearn's argument (1982, 1992) that society is becoming more publicly patriarchal than privately patriarchal or fratriarchal, in that the power of individual men is becoming transubstantiated into the male dominated body of the corporations, the state, the professions and the law.

Cheng (1996a) researching 200 almost equal numbers of male and female students on organizational behaviour courses in the US, conducted a study where the students were asked to assess and choose the 'ideal' student manager. No Asian/American or Asian candidates were chosen, 23 out of the 25 selected were Euro/American men and two were Euro/American women. Using Bem's

1974 Sex Role Inventory (BSRI), Cheng showed how characteristics associated with being a good manager were directly related to characteristics deemed masculine on the BSRI. These included assertion, aggression, athleticism, the ability to make decisions easily, competitiveness, self reliance, independence and a strong and individualistic personality – all part of hegemonic Western masculinity. The Asian males were labelled as unsuitable 'nerds' and too feminine to be good managers because they were seen as too polite, deferential, passive and not tough enough. Qualities they did show such as understanding, tolerance and teamwork were not assessed positively because they were discordant with BSRI masculine ascribed characteristics. Notwithstanding the critique of the BSRI (Eichler, 1980), Cheng illustrates that it is not biological sex alone that dictates occupational elevation but also performative gender (Butler, 1990, 1993), in this case hegemonic masculinity.

In terms of Western organizations the ideal of a good manager often embodies the notion of hegemonic masculinity, therefore coinciding with stereotypical notions of masculinity as competitive, aggressive, competent, autonomous, tough psychologically and physically, goal oriented and non-emotional (Hoch, 1982; Carrigan et al., 1985; Connell, 1987). Suggestions of the emergence of the caring, sharing 'new man' who is not dominated by an obsession with work or status seem not to be sustained in reality (Mintel, 1994). Hegemonic masculinity is the culturally dominant and most powerful form of masculinity. Other forms of masculinity such as complicit masculinities which aspire to and collude with hegemonic masculinity and subordinated masculinities such as homosexual and some Asian masculinities are less powerful and femininities are even less valued (Connell, 1995; Pilcher, 1998).

In addition, men in lower occupational positions, although subordinated by other men, often continue to misogynize, harass and devalue women located in equal or lower, or sometimes even higher organizational positions (Gutek, 1989; Cockburn, 1983, 1991). It therefore cannot be presumed that marginalized men, even those that may be seen as feminized in the context of the dominant culture (for example, Hamada, 1996) do not reinforce gendered hegemony through their masculinities or are devalued in the same way as women. Although it might be argued that women can correspondingly perform 'hegemonic masculinity' and that some who perform this attain high level occupational positions (Collinson and Hearn, 1996; Colgan and Ledwith, 1996), it is only very few women who reach the highest echelons of organizations. This suggests it is not only the formal doing of gender (Butler, 1990; Gherardi, 1996) but the culturally assumed biological sex of the performer, more precisely the ascribed presence or absence of being male, that is generally important.

The most salient issue in the sex/gender debate is not that there are different types of masculinities and femininities that are seen as 'natural' and appropriate in different contexts and cultures but that the dominant forms of masculinities associated predominately with male biological sex and hegemony (and construed in aversion to femininity) are those that dictate how organizations are run (Collinson and Hearn, 1996; Hamada, 1996; Cheng, 1996b).

Gendered sexuality or sexualized gender in organizations?

The difficulty of separating gender and sexuality has been much debated in recent organizational analysis. The concept of 'organization sexuality' also became an analytical field in itself in the late 1980s (Hearn and Parkin, 1987, 1995; Hearn et al., 1989). A specific focus on sexuality has since been criticized on the grounds it dilutes the analytical importance of gender (Witz and Savage, 1992). However, far from obscuring the paramount importance of gender in organizations, the concept of organization sexuality shows how inextricable and interlinked the categories of sexuality and gender are. Sexualities are thus often subsumed under, and are core, if not defining qualities, of gendered identities. For example, hegemonic masculinity is often defined by its hierarchically heterosexist masculinist nature. Femininities and alternative masculinities are often subordinated and derogated because they are seen to be linked to women and passive and receptive female sexuality (Reynaud, 1983; Hearn, 1987), which is negatively connoted (Addelston and Stirratt, 1996). Some commentators have even gone as far to suggest that it is the sexing or sexualizing of gender, in particular the sexing of females that actually defines the female gender (MacKinnon, 1982) or leads to their domination through compulsory heterosexuality (Rich, 1983). Others query the binary division and demarcation of male and female, questioning the uncritical acceptance of there being two distinct biological sexes (Laqueur, 1990; Butler, 1990, 1993).

It is therefore difficult to argue that the concept of 'organization sexuality' (Hearn and Parkin, 1987, 1995) obscures or eclipses the central importance of gender, for if gender is not only sexed and sexualized, but sexuality is also gendered, then it may be very difficult to separate out the two concepts, particularly if they are organizationally institutionalized.

The dominance of male-defined, hierarchical heterosexuality is embedded in metaphorical and literal gendered language and action within organizations. In business organizations there is talk of 'penetrating' markets (Collinson and Hearn, 1996); in military organizations recruits and cadets are encouraged to be more 'masculine' or derided by superiors calling them 'poufs' or women (Addelstone and Stirratt, 1996). Both of these terms make an analogy to a 'weak' and passive feminine sexuality and presence. And litigators, the majority of whom are male, use a language of gamesmanship and winning. Good, that is, manly, litigators are seen to 'destroy', 'control' or 'rape' the witnesses, whereas those who do not are seen as 'sissy' or 'feminized' (Pierce, 1996). Thus the language of male control within organizations is often relayed in terms of commodified male sexual conquest (Reynaud, 1983; Evans, 1993). Language is further discussed in Newell (in this volume).

At the same time that the metaphorical language of sex and conquest is genderically and hegemonically employed in institutionalized business and occupational language, women within organizations are actually sexually commodified by men, who ironically present themselves as non-sexual beings, whilst using conquest sexual imagery and metaphor, conducting relationships at work and sexually harassing women in the workplace (Hearn and Parkin, 1987, 1995; Hearn et al., 1989). Gutek (1989) writes of how men use their sexuality more than women and in more diverse and exploitative ways, but how paradoxically male sexuality is made invisible whilst at the same time female sexuality is illuminated and problematized.

Sexual harassment has also been of great issue in some organizational analysis, having been traditionally defined as ranging from unwanted, repeated, sexual innuendoes, jokes, touching or overtures to forcible rape, which is predominantly male/female perpetrated both by superiors and co-workers (Schneider, 1985; Wise and Stanley, 1987; Sims et al., 1993). The situation is, however, complicated as consensual sexual banter is often common in working environments and used by both sexes to break the monotony of the job (Cockburn, 1983; Sims et al., 1993). It may therefore depend on a multiplicity of different factors including the work context and individual personalities as to whether certain behaviour is perceived as harassment by either the potential perpetrator or potential victim.

This ambiguity around what constitutes sexual harassment has often led to 'victims' suffering in silence and often complaints are not taken seriously if the behaviour is perceived as a joke on the man's behalf (Sims et al., 1993). Sexual harassment also has a number of consequences, ranging from women feeling ashamed and humiliated, to them losing their confidence, becoming physically or mentally ill or going off sick or leaving their jobs (Schneider, 1985). 'Sexual' harassment may also not be directly sexual and this has led to some commentators, suggesting substituting the term with '(hetero)sexist harassment'. Epstein (1994), for example, cites many instances of men touching women or talking to women, in a way they perceived as demeaning and infantilizing, but because the behaviour was not perceived of as sexual, these women found they had little recourse to official complaints procedures.

Public/private dichotomies and disjunctions

The importance of private sphere gender ideology has a great impact on how men and women are perceived and treated within organizations. While historically and contemporarily many distinctions have been made between public and private spheres, the intrinsic interrelationships between them have often been left untheorized (Pateman, 1989). The public sphere has been unequivocally associated with the world of men, masculinity, technology, work, politics and organizations (Hearn, 1992), whereas the private sphere has been conceptualized as the world of the family and associated with women, child care, domesticity, sexuality and femininity (Pateman, 1989; Parkin, 1989).

Public/private sphere dichotomies can also be linked to the notion of the male breadwinner. This has played an emotive part in dictating men's salaries and trade union campaigning (Crompton, 1986); it has often been argued that men are working for a family wage, rather than a wage just to support themselves, whereas women are working for supplementary 'pin money' (Reed, 1996). Furthermore the male career ideal has been constructed taking into account not only the notion of a sole male breadwinner, but also the assumption of a complementary, unpaid female servicer in the home. The male career ideal is therefore dependent on the female 'servicer' wife role, even though these roles are often ideologically reversed and thus obscured, with the female seen as dependent on the male rather than vice versa (Crompton, 1986; Crompton and Jones, 1986). The facts that some men are single, many families are by necessity dual-income, and an increasing number of families are lone parent, female-headed families are still often not added into this simple equation. Rarely are private sphere costs, for example, supporting husbands practically and psychologically, and child care, accounted for in terms of the emotional cost or their potential monetary worth (Oakley, 1972, 1974, 1985; Waring, 1988; French, 1995; Mulholland, 1996a; 1996b).

A range of forces from direct controls in both home and work to educational structures and discourses of maternalism may help to explain why women take the majority of the responsibility with child care and support their husbands' careers but are not supported in the same way by their husbands. Discourses of maternalism are propounded and naturalized by lay, media and 'expert' voices, placing the onus for child care on women not men, and blaming women exclusively for any problems they may have with their children (Russell, 1983; French, 1985; Kaplan, 1986).

When women enter the labour market they are concentrated in particular areas, mainly those of the service and caring industries, or within industries where their role is equated with their assumed private sphere role. For example, both Kanter (1977, 1993) and Pringle (1988) saw secretaries as undervalued and doing more than performing an administrative support role. Kanter (1977) spoke of them as 'office wives', performing non-occupational and emotional labour for their bosses and Pringle saw them as embedded in familial and sexual discourses.

Similarly, when women are concentrated in the caring professions often there is little support for them or the room to make mistakes because their roles are assumed to be inherently vocational (Menzies, 1977; Davies, 1992). Whilst women's servicing and caring locations in organizations are often essentialized or judged to be a 'free choice', this is not always the case. Wilkes's (1995) study of women and caring careers distinguished between 'being caring' and 'doing caring' and many of her respondents had chosen a caring profession because it would be seen as an acceptable 'female' career choice.

Internal networks and organizational dynamics

Kanter (1977), drawing on Weberian views about bureaucracy, delineated the 'sexed' way in which corporations and organizations operated in order to reproduce a majority of men in positions of power. She attributed these unequal differentials and opportunity structures existing within organizations solely to the possession of power, thus suggesting women would behave similarly to men if they were located within seats of power. Her analysis has since been critiqued on the grounds that she denies specifically gendered modes of behaviour and suggests that power differentials obliterate or wipe out sex and gender (Witz and Savage, 1992; Collinson and Hearn, 1995), thus ignoring the implications of social constructionist views of gender.

Kanter (1977, 1993) also talked about metaphorical male 'organizational homosexuality' in terms of how men attempted to reproduce their dominant power relations by only mixing with and sharing the same occupational space and privilege with those males they deemed similar in image and behaviour, thus cloning themselves in their own image. Witz and Savage (1992) regard her use of the term male 'homosexuality' as 'clumsy' and replace it with the term male 'homosociability' because of the assumed homo-erotic connotations associated with 'homosexuality'. However, Roper (1996) reclaims and argues for the validity and use of the term 'homosexual' as well as 'homosocial' in terms of male managerial same-sex relations, bonding and reproduction. Roper maintains, echoing Sedgwick (1985), that male bonding involves often unconscious homo-erotic elements and cites examples of how some men emulate and subtly eroticize the verbal language, bodily gestures and styles of dress of other men managers that they admire.

Martin's research (1996) shows how homosocial male networks not only preclude women from high status jobs by sex segregation and selecting in their own image but also actively seek to discredit women whilst elevating men. Martin cites the example of a group of men in a chemistry department decrying a competent but not brilliant woman being awarded a chemistry prize, but simultaneously supporting a man in their department whose work they knew was flawed on the spurious grounds that he was charismatic. Martin also discusses how in selection processes some men will immediately find criticisms of women candidates but look for positive aspects about male candidates. She also documents a tendency for some men to maliciously and unjustifiably publicly criticize females in senior positions, for which they themselves had applied.

Long working hours tend to be equated with managerial jobs but groups of predominantly male managers have also been shown to deliberately and artificially extend the hours of meetings and then criticize or marginalize women who cannot stay because of child care commitments (Bittman, 1991; Watson, 1994; French, 1995). Many top level jobs are also organized around long and antisocial hours that preclude women with children unless they have the resources, willingness and organizational capacity to employ round the clock childminders or have a partner prepared to take on work and care. In many societies there appears to be a tendency for high level positions to be occupied mainly by married men with children while those women who do reach such posts tend to be single, divorced and childless (Popplestone, 1980; Alban Metcalfe, 1984; Davidson and Cooper, 1984; Howe, 1986; Woodward, 1996).

Collinson and Hearn (1995) also showed that Kanter's (1977) conception of male homosociability in terms of exclusion of women from top jobs was still relevant. They showed that men tended to recruit, promote and privilege male candidates, whilst at the same time often mismanaging sexual harassment cases and being sexual harassers themselves (Collinson and Collinson, 1996).

A number of studies have highlighted men's domination of assessment, selection and promotion processes (Collinson et al., 1990; Alimo-Metcalfe, 1993, 1994; Martin, 1996). Zuboff (1988) also showed how male managers protected their status and attempted to consolidate their power by mystifying their knowledge and exaggerating their abilities rather than by sharing knowledge. This may be because of a combination not only of fragile gender identity (Collinson, 1992; Hollway, 1996) but also because the nature of the managerial task is in itself not objective, but is ambiguous with clear prediction of events not always possible (MacIntyre, 1981). Josefowitz (1988) also showed how women were marginalized in meetings because men would refuse to hear or ignore the contribution they were trying to make or attribute it to a male participant (see also Case, 1994).

Women in senior management or jobs traditionally viewed as male jobs have also had to contend with a great deal of male hostility and misogyny because men have felt they are taking their jobs (Gutek, 1989). One senior female manager spoke of being subject to a great deal of vitriolic anger and intimidation by a male subordinate at the end of his contract because he could not find a job and was unjustifiably blaming her for it (Martin, 1996). A further gender subtext in this scenario became clear when he said to her that if he did not find a job soon his wife was 'threatening' to get one.

Women in traditionally working class, physically tough 'male' jobs also report being subject to unrelenting sexual harassment, ridicule and discrimination from some of their male colleagues who continually express unjustified and uncorroborated doubt about their competence (Cockburn, 1983, 1991; Gutek, 1989). This behaviour may be related to the 'they are taking our jobs' argument as well as the fact that men in jobs where they are controlled by and subordinate to other men create an image of masculine toughness and bravado and being physically superior to their managers to compensate for this masculine 'mutilation' (Cockburn, 1983, 1991). However, if women are demonstrating they are capable of doing such 'physically tough' jobs the view that women and male managers are weak, is no longer sustainable.

Organizational beliefs, values and identities

Hegemonic masculinity performed by women is in itself a contradiction in terms. By performing hegemonic masculinity women invalidate their femininity and identity as women (Martin, 1996) and are looked on suspiciously as if they were impostors, women emulating men, 'pseudo men' or organizational 'drag kings', rather than 'real men'. There is also a concerted effort by men to inhibit women's attempts at performing hegemonic masculinity and/or attaining top jobs, often by criticizing their appearance or behaviour as unfeminine, or by attempting to draw them into conversation about private sphere or familial issues when the women concerned are trying to talk about work (Martin, 1996). Women also often find the aggressive and competitive interactional style they are expected to convey in certain jobs such as engineering as uncomfortable and list this as the reason they did not like the job rather than the actual content or technical demands of the jobs themselves (Burris, 1996).

Men and women are metaphorically endowed or imbued with certain naturalized characteristics; this plays a large part in how organizations perceive and treat men and women. Men are often projected as being rational, controlled automatons who have no subjectivities or vulnerabilities and can therefore make straightforward, objective decisions which are untainted or uncorrupted by the messiness of feelings (Kerfoot and Knights, 1996). Women, on the other hand, are perceived as emotional and closer to nature then men and therefore as unsuitable for positions where they have to make important 'objective' managerial decisions.

Men therefore tend to control, devalue and dominate women, through their positioning of them as being constructed by sexual and related emotional qualities (MacKinnon, 1982; Hearn, 1987; Hearn and Parkin, 1987, 1995; Hearn et al., 1989). Women thus tend to be pigeonholed in certain stereotypical boxes such as that of a sex object or a mother figure or those who do not fit either side of these poles are often relegated to the ranks of man-haters or lesbians, regardless of sexual identity or actual behaviour (Pringle, 1988; French, 1995; Brooks-Gordon, 1995). 'Organization sexuality' is very important here, emphasizing time and time again women are only identified by their perceived and projected sexual and related reproductive qualities. This is compounded by the view that women are likely to have children and may therefore leave the job or be out of the labour market so that they will be defined as too expensive to train up and put in positions of importance (Cockburn, 1991).

While there are certainly dangers in essentializing gendered behaviour, Gilligan's research (1982) presents an interesting alternative approach. From a moral developmental perspective she looks at how girls and boys from a very young age are encouraged to think about, perceive and attempt to solve problems in divergent ways. Gilligan argues women are therefore more likely to look at a problem in a wider and more holistic way than men and consider the consequences both longitudinally and in terms of a much wider range of actions. Men in contrast have a tendency not only to formulate problems in a linear and parochial manner but to try and respond to those problems in a short term and limited way. This may be because by objectifying women and by splitting and denying parts of themselves in order to conform to stereotypical definitions of hegemonic masculinity men also objectify themselves and are unable to see the subjectivity inherent in their view of the world (MacKinnon, 1982; Hollway, 1996).

Such processes do not occur in abstract but through the specific arrangement of work in time and space. Many men define their masculine identities largely in terms of different forms of occupational identity and work. Workaholism has reached epidemic proportions with many men showing little resentment and sometimes an active commitment to working long hours which give little time for life outside work (French, 1995). Some commentators have suggested that men use work as a haven as they flee from the private and emotional sphere to the public sphere, where they define goals as technical and instrumental and are serviced and have their needs provided for in an artificial, sanitized environment. For example, masculinity is often perceived of as disembodied and self-estranged requiring constant affirmation through conquest. Seidler (1994) locates this within a western rationalist, Cartesian culture where men use their bodies as machines and learn to control, silence and deny their feelings because expressing feelings invalidates their claims of reason and patriarchal power. This then leads to a compulsive urge in organizations to control self and others which becomes the only means of relating to others (Kerfoot and Knights, 1996).

Such processes can be disadvantageous to organizational performance, as the pursuit of organizational goals may be subordinated to individual searches for status, self identity and conquest. Jackall (1988) in his study of mainly male managers, graphically exemplifies this when he demonstrates how most managers were dishonest, competitive, self-serving and exploitative, regardless of organizational goals, and few showed concern about ethical goals and standards. Men's frequent proving of and striving to prove their masculinity and the need to be seen as strong and self-reliant however does not only affect work standards at higher levels of organizational hierarchies but also at lower levels where there may be efforts to conceal mistakes to protect masculine identity. Martin (1996) gives the example of a male lineworker at a telephone company refusing for days to ask for help with a problem he could not solve, yet ironically ridiculing a woman who sought help after only half a day.

Women are dominantly constructed by men as being emotional within a negative context of irrationality yet the behaviour of men in organizations is also emotional (Hearn, 1993). Men, when in positions of control, organize and control emotions yet are seen to be unemotional in themselves (Hearn, 1982; Hochschild, 1993). This suggests certain types of male emotions are seen as acceptable, particularly those not involving vulnerability, yet these emotions are often not seen as emotions. Male aggression and anger continue to be considered desirable in managerial jobs but are not labelled as emotional behaviour.

Women are saturated with emotion through generic power discourses and thus labelled as unfit for certain jobs that require rationality. In many jobs they are also required as part of the job to 'dramaturgically' perform emotional and/or sexual labour. Hochschild's (1983) classic study of flight attendants showed how women were expected to look sexually glamorous and be alluring to male passengers as well as servicing them with manufactured charm on their flights. Similarly Adkins' (1992) research on women in the tourist industry found men just had to appear to be smart whereas women were instructed to dress in a sexually 'provocative' manner (for example, off the shoulder dresses, stockings and short skirts). The women were also expected to deal with the sexual advances of the males in a way that did not cause them to complain, for example, by laughing them off. In this particular way they were being paid not just for their physical and mental abilities and labour but for being sexually objectified and commodified fetishistic objects (Evans, 1993).

Case study: social work organizations and residential child care settings

This case study will illustrate and give substance to some of the arguments that have been outlined above, showing that although the relations between gender and power is complex, shifting and multifaceted, men in the main 'hold' and wield power in the particular case study organizations, both at lower and higher levels of occupational hierarchies. This disadvantages and subordinates women both individually and as a class, whilst simultaneously advantaging men (Cockburn, 1991; Mills and Tancred, 1992; Collinson and Hearn, 1996). It often also works against the attainment of organizational goals (Jackall, 1988; Messerschmidt, 1996).

Women sometimes contributed both actively and passively to their diminished occupational power as well as finding it very difficult to resist or challenge the power of men within organizations. This occurred most noticeably through their acceptance and internalization of discourses that position women within an essentialized and naturalized femininity, even when they are located within the public world of work.

The material for this case study was drawn from research conducted between 1994 and 1996 in and about residential child care organizations (children's homes). Although the research was concerned primarily with issues of gender, sexuality and sexual abuse within the settings, information about the wider context of organizations was gained both from within residential child care and from interviews with external managers and workers not directly located within children's homes. Two settings were ethnographically researched, and the research methods used within the ethnography included formal interviews, participant observation and documentary analysis. A large number of other interviews were also conducted outside the ethnographic fieldwork with managers, residential workers, ex-residents and other agency workers. Overall information was gained about past and present practices in over a hundred different settings covering many different social work organizations and local authorities. Quotations used are from the research interviews.

Children's homes are short-term or long-term 'last resort' residential settings where children, predominantly teenagers, are placed by local authorities. They are placed there because of behavioural problems and/or past abuse and because they are unable to be cared for by their families of origin, foster parents or in any other environment (Aymer, 1992; Madge, 1994). There is little forward planning or child and parental involvement regarding these placements (Roach, 1991), and the majority of staff within these homes are untrained (Utting, 1991; Warner 1992). There has also been a stream of inquiries about and media exposés of the physical, sexual and psychological abuse of children in these settings over the last ten years (Levy and Kahan, 1991; Wardhaugh and Wilding, 1993; Berridge and Brodie, 1996).

Gender, power and management

Although women numerically predominated within these organizations, they were disproportionately concentrated either within the lower echelons of social work (Abbott and Wallace, 1990; Grimwood and Popplestone, 1993), as residential workers, ancillary workers and secretaries. Where women did hold managerial positions these tended to be at lower levels, as in managers of specific units and they had little overall power within the organizations (Crompton and Sanderson, 1990). Women were disproportionately located within positions where they were concerned with caring for or servicing others (mainly men or children), for example, basic grade residential workers caring on a day to day basis for children in care, or secretaries to managers, roles accordant with their sexual, domestic or maternal presumed location within the private sphere (Pateman, 1989; Seidler, 1989).

At higher managerial levels outside the residential care settings much of the data suggested the ongoing and immediate presence of male homosociability. Women tended to be excluded from higher positions not only by tokenistic or ineffective equal opportunities and selection processes, but within managerial circles by the sexually discriminatory and exclusionary behaviour of their male colleagues.

> I was a lone female in an all male management group and I found that quite difficult because of 'men speak' if you like. ... They would talk about things that I was excluded from. There would be men jokes that weren't exactly

crude but bordering on that. They might swear a lot or say things I found particularly uncomfortable. Sometimes I would just end up by telling them to shut up (female manager).

In the quote above the female manager is already isolated by being a lone female manager but is isolated further from the managerial group by the use of sexist, sexual language which offends her to the extent she chooses to self exclude as well as being simultaneously excluded (see also French, 1995).

Examples given of discrimination included harassment through gendered bullying, and being marginalized and treated as less important than equivalent, male colleagues. In meetings this was visible when women managers were expected to make the tea, were frequently interrupted or not listened to, or were not given important information which was given to equivalent male colleagues. In the following quotation it is shown not only how male managers subtly and manipulatively discriminate against female managers but also how that discrimination is so hard to challenge because it is rationalized and embedded within the organizational culture. The discrimination in this instance is also filtered through another female manager so it would be difficult for those women targeted to identify it as discrimination.

If two units had similar problems and one was ran by a woman and one by a man I would get more resources from my [male] manager for the one ran by a man and less for the woman. It was very difficult to argue with him and if I tried to push it any further he would come up with all sorts of excuses, the subtext of which were based in reality but I don't think they were genuine reasons (female manager).

Examples of male homosociability and collusion with abuse included men being unprepared to intervene when other men harassed women and ignoring the situation, or alternatively men in power trivializing the issue or blaming or punishing the women if they complained.

One case included a series of physical/sexual assaults on one young woman and the male manager had a history of sexually harassing women and everyone in the building knew about it but the women had been too frightened to complain before. Other men came to me afterwards and said 'I'm disgusted by his behaviour. He's been doing this for years. It's about time something was done about it'. So I said 'what have you done about it?' They'd known for years and done nothing (equal opportunities worker).

Some relationships were consensual but exploitative and in such situations, older men in positions of power, used their position and mismanaged organizational resources to gain sexual advantage. However it would almost always be the female subordinates that would be subject to punishment in consensual situations, not the male managers, as recognized in previous research (see Schneider, 1985; Hearn et al., 1989).

Last year the manager was having an affair with a young night care assistant and he used to bring in wine for them to drink. And he would send her on courses the older female staff who had been there for years were not allowed to go on. Eventually somehow her husband found out and he and his sister later wrote to the principal officer to complain. The principal officer was a great friend of the managers so he got off with it and she lost her job. I couldn't believe it! I thought it was his first affair but it's happening again with the new, female night care assistant he appointed (residential worker).

There is a very clear message here internalized by the respondent that it is not advisable to complain because if you are a female in a subordinate position then you will lose your job, even though she is aware this situation is abusive and unfair.

Female workers located in children's homes were often constructed by male managers as sexual and liable to overexcite adolescent boys if the women did not fit a maternal type image. They would therefore try to persuade them to adopt a maternal and 'non sexual' look. However in contrast secretaries working for the managers were encouraged to wear short skirts, high heels and stockings, clothing which could be perceived as commodified and fetishistic sexual clothing (Evans, 1993). Both male workers and male managers were almost never perceived as sexual in appearance and they appeared to evade dealing with sexuality in any formal capacity. The male residential workers were never seen as sexualized or potentially alluring to the teenage girls in their care even if they were only wearing shorts. The male managers often power dressed in uniform grey suits that superficially desexualized and disembodied them despite the fact some harassed females or mismanaged sexual harassment cases. Sexuality was also not an issue managers would address formally (through policies, training, procedures) with regard to children's homes, although many of the children had been sexually abused, were very sexually active and were adolescents, for whom sexuality was a major personal developmental concern (Moore and Rosenthal, 1993).

Managerial ineffectiveness reinforced by male homosociability and collusion was also demonstrated by the hierarchical and distanced manner in which external managers worked. They communicated normally dictatorially through memo or telephone conversations with internal managers and had little real contact with the residential settings and those who lived and worked in them. This had the result when children were being sexually or physically abused in such settings external managers were rarely aware, particularly since abuse was sometimes conducted by the internal managers themselves. This hierarchical distancing also had the effect of both workers and children feeling alienated and objectified. This corresponds closely with Kerfoot and Knights' (1996) concept of managerial disembodiment and objectification through the inferiorization of the 'other' (Hollway, 1996).

Often the children are just black and white writing on a piece of paper and not real people when it omes to meetings. The managers don't see the children's emotions and what's important to them. They just need to satisfy certain legal requirements and then they go on to the next child so they can get the meeting over and done with as soon as possible (residential worker).

Managers overtly concerned with their own personal careers (Jackall, 1988) and associated organizational reputation also had a tendency to cover up, and minimize the extent of abuse of children within these settings, sometimes over many years. External managers were also unlikely to publicly admit to problems or difficulties even if they were not of their own doing. This again pays heed to a gendered fear of being judged incompetent (Martin, 1996).

A guy who had done temping in residential care spoke to the newspapers about the girls in one home being picked up by their pimps at 9.a.m and dropped back at the children's home early in the morning. The managers played that down, saying they have solved the problem but they haven't, they've just moved the girls out to another area (HIV/AIDS worker).

The first unit I was in the manager used pin-down (violent restraint) type methods and the kids got frightened to death so they either didn't step out of line or they did a runner. In other units children might be expressing their feelings in the only way they could – by for example putting a table through the window. The managers wouldn't see that, they'd just see the children as disruptive and as costing them a lot of money. So the first unit with the dictatorial manager was costing less money and seemed to have fewer problems so it became the role model for all the other units despite noises being made about how it was run (residential worker).

The employment by managers of predominantly female, untrained residential workers based on a mistaken essentialized organizational/societal assumption that caring for children is a woman's vocation, often led to very poor care for these children. In conjunction with little support and implicit managerial condoning of controlling, rather than caring and therapeutic staff practices, these settings often became highly, institutionalized and repressive (Goffman, 1969; Parkin and Green, 1997a, 1997b). The staff did not have the resources, knowledge or support to deal appropriately with children in their care and turned to punitive, stigmatizing and containing methods to try and deal with their difficulties. An institutionalized climate was also conducive to a range of abuses, including sexual abuse, perpetrated by both staff, adults and young people from within and outside the settings.

Grassroots residential workers, gender and power

Male residential workers located in positions commonly associated with maternalism and the caring role often reconstructed their role to preserve their constructions of masculinity and differentiate themselves from the female staff.

This was done in a way that would also elevate their occupational status and increase promotional opportunities.

> A classic example of men putting the women down was if the female members of staff had been having any problems they would think the women couldn't handle it and say there should be a male on duty at all times. And it was about if any of the lads get violent the women can't handle it (residential worker).

Sometimes women also colluded with their perceived dependent situation by calling on the men when situations with the children became potentially volatile. The women were therefore continually cast back into an inferior and maternal role by their equivalent male co-workers.

> It was an all male resident group and most of the staff were men. Me and this other female member of staff offered to teach the lads to cook one day and the male staff wouldn't have it because they saw that as 'women's work'. And the women staff were always expected to do all the cooking. We'd get back after being out somewhere and the male worker would plonk themselves in front of the TV and say to the kids I was going to make them chips or cups of cocoa (residential worker).

Women workers were additionally gender-stereotyped by being seen to be a calming influence in general while men were simultaneously seen as wild but ironically able to physically control situations.

> The place was riot torn and it was 'Get the lads in' and it became a male dominated place. And after the place was calm again I wanted the femaleness of it to come out as well. It's not just the riot shield boys are here, it's let's get it calm again and how do you do that - you get some females in (male manager).

Women in higher organizational positions than men were also often resented.

> I can think of one person in particular who thinks women should be staying at home. He keeps quiet about that because he's shouted at every time he says it. He also has a problem with female staff who are more experienced than him. If he has done something and it could have been done differently and more efficiently and a female tries to tell him that he doesn't like it very much (residential worker).

However some women firmly located themselves within and identified positively with maternal and domestic discourses of femininity and womanhood and would not have perceived themselves as being oppressed in any way.

> They were sewing the curtains, were always in the kitchen and that sort of thing and were happy doing that. Also when male members of staff were

sleeping in these women would get in early or before their shift and make the men breakfast and take it up to the sleeping in room (residential worker).

These discourses of maternalism and essentialized femininity also reflected on how the children in the homes were treated. Even abused girls requiring care were seen as appropriate to look after younger children or to be a calming influence on their male peers and their needs remained unconsidered.

> There was a view it was a good thing to put little children with older girls because it drew on their maternal responsibility - fascinating thinking. And it was really good for the kids because they got this extra mothering from the girls and it was really good for the teenage girls because it steadied them up (residential manager).

> The cottages (in the residential settings) were originally single sex but we had horrendous problems as the boys were really wild. So we split them up, two girls and six boys in each unit to calm things (residential worker).

Women were also subject to sexual objectification and harassment by male co-workers and male subordinates but the harassment was often subtle and not perceived as such at the time or just seen as a habitual part of the job.

> This care assistant asked me out and I refused but he carried on asking me out. I felt sometimes that if he was feeling vindictive about it or I hadn't spent another time with him, he could rally the staff on my shift, pick up on something that had happened, and cause a real furore. So I'd spend a lot of time calming them all down (deputy internal manager).

Often the women would self organize to try and prevent a particular member of
staff being harassed but rarely would the harassment be challenged or complained about.

> It wasn't overt as such, but he would always put her on shift when he was on and he would keep giving her lifts everywhere she didn't want. So we organised it so we swapped shifts and arranged to give her lifts home before he asked (residential worker).

> He would keep on brushing against you and coming up really close, too close and making sexual jokes. So we warned all the new staff and tried to avoid being alone with him as much as possible (residential worker).

This case study clearly illustrates how different types of masculinities and femininities can organizationally co-exist within the same organization. Many men, however mould their masculine identities to position themselves hierarchically above women, whom they both covertly and overtly project into subordinate materialiszd and sexualized roles. Some women in the organization, notably some in the lower echelons, clearly positively identified with and unequivocally embraced such discourses. However, for others who attempted to subvert such discourses, both overt and insidious means of control were available to try and prevent this. The predominantly male managers also seemed more concerned with career and personal reputations than ethical standards and wider organizational goals and were homosocial in their self organization.

Conclusion

This chapter has demonstrated that gender and its relationship with who holds and exercises power in organizations are vital in understanding how organizations are perceived, experienced, managed and theorized. Notions of hegemonic masculinity guide and dictate how most Western organizations operate and many men in organizations appear to collude with and be complicit with such hegemony, deriding, discriminating against and harassing men who perform alternative subordinated masculinities as well as women and femininities. Some non-Western organizations operate differently by not according individual men a great deal of personal organizational power but their locus of power, although distant and condensed, is still inherently patriarchal and male-dominated.

Women are frequently pigeonholed into objectified and subordinate maternal or sexual roles and it is not uncommon for women to collude with such positioning. Attempts to subvert the masculinist status quo are frequently unsuccessful, with men attempting to re-feminize, sexualize and maternalize 'careerist' women in order to devalue their work competence and construct them through private sphere ideology, or institutionalized, structural discrimination. This devaluation and diminution of women in the workplace is affected not only overtly and structurally through discriminatory selection, mentoring and training processes, a concentration of homosocial men at the top of organizational hierarchies, generalized sexist or sexual harassment and differential treatment, but additionally by much more subtle and often unrecognized forms of indoctrination and conditioning. Such male homosociability not only keeps women out of key organizational roles, but also polices and controls the behaviour of other men. Thus through overt threats, insidious controls and discursive entrapments, as outlined, the relationships between gender and power in organizations is continually reproduced.

References

Abbott, P. and Wallace, C. (eds) (1990) *The Sociology of the Caring Professions.* London: Falmer.

Acker, J. and Van Houten, D. (1992) 'Differential recruitment and control: the sex structuring of organizations', in Mills, A.J. and Tancred, P. (eds) *Gendering Organizational Analysis.* London: Sage. pp. 15-30.

Addelston, J. and Stirratt, M. (1996) 'The last bastion of masculinity: gender politics at the citadel', in Cheng, C. (ed.) *Masculinities in Organizations.* Thousand Oaks, California: Sage. pp. 54-76.

Adkins, L. (1992) 'Sexual work and the employment of women in service industries', in Savage, M. and Witz, A. (eds) *Gender and Bureaucracy.* Oxford: Blackwell. pp. 207-28.

Alban Metcalfe, B. (1984) 'Current career concerns of female and male managers: an analysis of free response comments to a national survey', *Equal Opportunities International,* 3: 11-18.

Alimo-Metcalfe, B. (1993) 'Women in management: organizational socialization and assessment practices that prevent career advancement', *International Journal of Selection and Assessment,* 1 (2): 68-83.

Alimo-Metcalfe, B. (1994) 'Gender bias in the selection and assessment of women in management', in Davidson, M.J. and Burke, R.J. (eds) *Women in Management: Current Research Issues.* London: Paul Chapman. pp. 93-109.

Aymer, C. (1992) 'Women in residential work: dilemmas and ambiguities', in Langan, M. and Day, L. (eds) *Women, Oppression and Social Work.* London: Routledge. pp. 186-200.

Bachrach, P. and Baratz, M. (1970) *Understanding Poverty: Theory and Practice.* New York: Oxford University Press.

Bagilhole, B. (1997) *Equal Opportunities and Social Policy: Issues of Gender, Race and Disability.* New York: Longman.

Barbalet, J.M. (1987) 'Power, structural resources and agency', *Perspectives in Social Theory,* 8: 1-24.

Bem, S.L. (1974) 'The measurement of psychological androgyny', *Journal of Consulting and Clinical Psychology,* 42 (2): 152-62.

Bem, S.L. (1981) 'Gender schema theory: a cognitive account of sex-typing', *Psychological Review,* 88 (4): 354-64.

Berridge, D. and Brodie, I. (1996) 'Residential care in England and Wales: the inquiries and after', in Hill, M. and Allgate, J. (eds) *Child Welfare Services, Developments in Law, Policy, Practice and Research,* London, Jessica Kingsley. pp. 180-96.

Bittman, M. (1991) *Juggling Time: How Australian Use Time.* Canberra: Office of the Status of Women.

Brooks-Gordon, B. (1995) 'Struggling in the city: the subordination of women traders in the London oil broking market and their coping strategies', paper presented to the British Psychological Society's Psychology of Women Section Conference, Leeds University, 9 July 1995.

Buchanan, D. and Huczynski, J. (1985) *Organizational Behaviour: an Introductory Text.* London: Prentice Hall.

Buchanan, D. and Huczynski, J. (1997) *Organizational Behaviour: An Introductory Text*. 3rd Edition. London: Prentice Hall.

Burris, B. (1996) 'Technocracy, patriarchy and management', in Collinson, D.L. and Hearn, J. (eds) *Men as Managers, Managers as Men: Critical Perspectives on Men, Masculinities and Management*. London: Sage. pp. 61-77.

Butler, J. (1990) *Gender Trouble: Feminism and the Subversion of Identity*. New York: Routledge.

Butler, J. (1993) *Bodies that Matter: On the Discursive Limits of Sex*. London: Routledge.

Calás, M. and Smircich, L. (1993) 'Dangerous liaisons: the "feminine-in-management" meets "globalization"', *Business Horizons*, 36 (2): 71-81.

Carrigan, T., Connell, R.W. and Lee, J. (1985) 'Towards a new sociology of masculinity', *Theory and Society*, 14 (5): 551-604.

Case, S.S. (1994) 'Gender differences in communication and behaviour in organizations', in Davidson, M.J. and Burke, R.J. (eds) *Women in Management: Current Research Issues*. London: Paul Chapman. pp. 144-67.

Cheng, C. (1996a) '"We choose not to compete": the "merit" discourse in the selection process and asian and asian american men and their masculinity', in Cheng, C. (ed.) *Masculinities in Organizations*. Thousand Oaks, Ca: Sage. pp. 177-200.

Cheng, C. (ed.) (1996b) *Masculinities in Organizations*. Thousand Oaks, Ca: Sage.

Chodorow, N. (1978) *The Reproduction of Mothering: Psychoanalysis and the Sociology of Gender*. London and Berkeley, Ca: University of California.

Clegg, S.R. (1988) *Frameworks of Power*. London: Sage.

Clegg, S. and Dunkerley, D. (1980) *Organization, Class and Control*. London: Routledge and Kegan Paul.

Clegg, S. and Dunkerley, D. (eds) (1977) *Critical Issues in Organization Theory*. London: Routledge and Kegan Paul.

Cockburn, C. (1983) *Brothers: Male Dominance and Technological Change*. London: Pluto Press.

Cockburn, C. (1991) *In the Way of Women: Men's Resistance to Sex Equality in Organizations*. Basingstoke: Macmillan.

Colgan, S. and Ledwith, S. (eds) (1996) *Women In Organizations: Challenging Gender Politics*. Basingstoke: Macmillan.

Collinson, D.L. (1992) *Managing the Shopfloor*. Berlin: de Gruyter.

Collinson, D.L. and Hearn, J. (1995) 'Men managing leadership: men and women of the corporation revisited', *International Review of Women and Leadership*, 1 (2): 1-24.

Collinson, D.L. and Hearn, J. (eds) (1996) *Men as Managers, Managers as Men: Critical Perspectives on Men, Masculinities and Management*. London: Sage.

Collinson, D.L., Knights, D. and Collinson, M. (1990) *Managing to Discriminate*. London and New York: Routledge.

Collinson, M. and Collinson, D.L. (1996) '"It's only Dick": the sexual harassment of women managers in insurance work', *Employment and Society*, 10 (1): 29-56.

Connell, R.W. (1987) *Gender and Power*. Cambridge: Polity.

Connell, R.W. (1995) *Masculinities*. Cambridge: Polity.

Crompton, R. (1986) 'Women and the service class', in Crompton, R. and Mann, M. (eds) *Gender and Stratification*. Cambridge: Polity. pp. 119-36.

Crompton, R. and Jones, G. (1986) *A White Collar Proletariat? Deskilling and Gender in Clerical Work*. Basingstoke: Macmillan.

Crompton, R. and Sanderson, K. (1990) *Gendered Jobs and Social Change*. London: Unwin Hyman.

Dahl, R.A. (1957) 'The concept of power', *Behavioral Science*, July, 2: 201-5.

Daly, M. (1973) *Beyond God the Father*. London: Women's Press.

Davidson, M. And Cooper, C. (1984) 'Occupational stress in female managers: a comparative study', *Journal of Management Studies*, 21 (2): 185-205.

Davies, C. (1992) 'Gender, history and management style in nursing: towards a theoretical synthesis', in Savage, M. and Witz, A. (eds) *Gender and Bureaucracy*. Oxford: Blackwell. pp. 229-52.

Dawson, S. (1997) *Analysing Organizations*. 3rd Edition. Basingstoke: Macmillan.

Dinnerstein (1987) *The Rockng of the Cradle and the Ruling of the World*. London: Women's Press.

Eichler, M. (1980) *The Double Standard*. New York: St. Martins.

Epstein, D. (1994) 'Keeping them in their place: (hetero)sexist harassment, gender and the enforcement of heterosexuality', paper presented to BSA Conference, Sexualities in Social Context, University of Central Lancashire, March.

Evans, D.T. (1993) *Sexual Citizenship: The Material Construction of Sexualities*. London: Routledge.

Foucault, M. (1977) *Discipline and Punish*. London: Allen Lane.

Foucault, M. (1979) *A History of Sexuality: Volume One*. London: Allen Lane.

French, K. (1995) 'Men and locations of power: why move over?', in Itzin, C. and Newman, J. (eds) *Gender, Culture and Organizational Change: Putting Theory into Practice*. London and New York: Routledge. pp. 54-67.

French, M. (1985) *Beyond Power: On Men, Women and Morals*. London: Abacus.

French, J.R.P. and Raven, B. (1968) 'The bases for social power' in Cartwright (ed) *Studies in Social Power*. Ann Arbor, Michigan: University of Michigan Press.

Gherardi, S. (1996) 'Gendered organizational cultures: narratives of women travellers in a male world', *Gender, Work and Organization*, 3 (4): 187-201.

Gilligan, C. (1982) *In a Different Voice*. Cambridge, Mass: Harvard University Press.

Goffman, E. (1969) *Asylums*. Harmondsworth: Penguin.

Gramsci, A. (1981) *Selections from the Prison Notebooks*. London: Lawrence and Wishart.

Grimwood, C. and Popplestone, R. (1993) *Women, Management and Care*. Basingstoke: BASW/Macmillan.

Gutek, B. (1989) 'Sexuality in the workplace: key issues in social research and organizational practice', in Hearn, J. Sheppard, D. L., Tancred-Sheriff, P. and Burrell, G. (eds) *The Sexuality of Organization*. London: Sage. pp. 56-70.

Hamada, T. (1996) 'Unwrapping Euro-American masculinity in a Japanese multinational corporation', in Cheng, C. (ed.) *Masculinities in Organizations*. Thousand Oaks, Ca: Sage. pp. 160-76.

Handy, C. (1993) *Understanding Organizations*. 4th Edition. London: Penguin.

Hansard Society (1990) *Women at the Top*. London: The Hansard Society.

Hearn, J. (1982) 'Notes on patriarchy, professionalisation and the semi-professions', *Sociology*, 16 (2): 184-202.

Hearn, J. (1987) *The Gender of Oppression: Men, Masculinity and a Critique of Marxism*. Sussex: Wheatsheaf.

Hearn, J. and Parkin, W. (1987) *Sex at Work: the Power and Paradox of Organization Sexuality*. Brighton: Wheatsheaf and New York: St. Martins.

Hearn, J. (1992) *Men in the Public Eye: The Construction and Deconstruction of Public Men and Public Patriarchies*. London: Routledge.

Hearn, J. and Parkin, W. (1992) 'Gender and organizations: a selective review and critique of a neglected area', in Mills, A.J. and Tancred, P. (eds) *Gendering Organizational Analysis*. London: Sage (first published 1983). pp. 46-66.

Hearn, J. (1993) 'Emotive subjects: organizational men, organizational masculinities and the (de)construction of emotions', in Fineman, S. (ed.) *Emotion in Organizations*. London: Sage. pp. 148-66.

Hearn, J. and Parkin W. (1995) *Sex at Work: The Power and Paradox of Organization Sexuality*. Revised edition. Brighton: Wheatsheaf and New York: St. Martins.

Hearn, J., Sheppard, D. L., Tancred-Sheriff, P. and Burrell, G. (eds) (1989) *The Sexuality Of Organization*, London: Sage.

Hindess, B. (1996) *Discourses of Power: From Hobbes to Foucault*. Oxford: Blackwell.

Hoch, P. (1982) *White Hero, Black Beast*. London: Pluto Press.

Hochschild, A. (1983) *The Managed Heart: Commercialization of Human Feeling*. Berkeley, Ca: University of California Press.

Hochschild, A. (1993) 'Preface', in Fineman, S. (ed.) *Emotion in Organizations*. London: Sage.

Hollway, W. (1996) 'Masters and men in the transition from factory hands to sentimental workers', in Collinson, D.L. and Hearn, J. (eds) *Men as Managers, Managers as Men: Critical Perspectives on Men, Masculinities and Management*. London: Sage. pp. 25-42.

Howe, D. (1986) 'The separation of women and their work in the personal social services', paper presented to 6th Annual Critical Social Policy Conference, The Future of Welfare: Visions and Strategies, Sheffield City Polytechnic, Sheffield, April.

Hugman, R. (1991) *Power in Caring Professions*. London: Macmillan.

Institute of Management (1994) *Management Development in the Millennium*. Corby: IM Books.

Jackall, R. (1988) *Moral Mazes: The World of Corporate Managing*. New York: Oxford University Press.

Josefowitz, N. (1988) 'Paths to power in high technology organizations', in Zimmerman, J. (ed.) *The Technological Woman*. New York: Praeger. pp. 191-200.

Kanter, R.M. (1977) *Men and Women of the Corporation*. New York: Basic Books. (Also 2nd edition, 1993.)

Kaplan, P. J. (1986) 'Take the blame off mother', *Psychology Today*, 20 (10): 70-71.

Kerfoot, D. and Knights, D. (1996) 'The best is yet to come?: the quest for embodiment in managerial work', in Collinson, D.L. and Hearn, J. (eds) *Men as Managers, Managers as Men: Critical Perspectives on Men, Masculinities and Management*. London: Sage. pp. 78-98.

Laqueur, T. (1990) *Making Sex: Body and Gender from the Greeks to Freud*. London: Harvard University Press.

Levy, A. and Kahan, B. (1991) *The Pindown Experience and Protection of Children*. Stafford: Staffordshire County Council.

Lukes, S. (1974) *Power: A Radical View*. Basingstoke: Macmillan.

Lukes, S. (ed.) (1986) *Power*. Oxford: Blackwell.

MacIntyre, A. (1981) *After Virtue: A Study in Moral Theory*. London: Duckworth.

MacKinnon, C.A. (1982) 'Feminism, marxism, method and the state: an agenda for theory', in Keohane, N. Rosaldo, M. and Gelpi, B. (eds) *Feminist Theory: a Critique of Ideology*. Brighton: Harvester. pp. 1-30.

MacKinnon, C.A. (1992) 'Sexuality', in Crowley, H. and Himmelweit, S. (eds) *Knowing Women: Feminism and Knowledge.* Cambridge: Polity Press in association with OUP. pp. 114-16.

Madge, N. (1994) *Children and Residential Care in Europe.* London: National Children's Bureau.

Martin, P.Y. (1996) 'Gendering and evaluating dynamics: men, masculinities and managements', in Collinson, D.L. and Hearn, J. (eds) *Men as Managers, Managers as Men: Critical Perspectives on Men, Masculinities and Management.* London: Sage. pp. 186-209.

McGuire, S. (1992) *Best Companies for Women, Britain's Top Employers.* London: Pandora.

Menzies, I. (1977) *The Functioning of Social Systems as a Defence against Anxiety.* Greenwich: Search Publications.

Messerschmidt, J. (1996) 'Managing to kill: masculinities and the space shuttle Challenger explosion', in Cheng, C. (ed.) *Masculinities in Organizations.* Thousand Oaks, Ca: Sage. pp. 29-53.

Mills, A.J. and Tancred, P. (1992) (eds) *Gendering Organizational Analysis.* London: Sage.

Mintel, A. (1994) *Men 2000.* London: Mintel.

Moore and Rosenthal (1993) *Sexuality in Adolescense.* London: Routledge.

Mulholland, K. (1996a) 'Entrepreneurialism and the self made man', in Collinson, D.L. and Hearn, J. (eds) *Men as Managers, Managers as Men: Critical Perspectives on Men, Masculinities and Management.* London: Sage. pp. 123-49.

Mulholland, K. (1996b) 'Gender, power and property relations within entrepreneurial wealthy families', *Gender, Work and Organization*, 3 (2): 78-82.

Mullins, L. (1996) *Management and Organizational Behaviour.* 4th Edition. London: Pitman.

Oakley, A. (1972) *Sex, Gender and Society.* London: Temple Smith.

Oakley, A. (1974) *Housewife.* London: Allen Unwin.

Oakley, A. (1985) *Sex, Gender and Society.* Revised edition. Aldershot: Gower.

Ohlott, P., Ruderman, M. and McCauley, C. (1991) 'Gender differences in managers developmental job experiences', *Academy of Management Journal*, 37 (1): 47-67.

Parkin, W. (1989) 'Private experiences in the public domain: sexuality and residential care organizations', in Hearn, J., Sheppard, D.L., Tancred-Sheriff, P. and Burrell, G. (eds) *The Sexuality of Organization.* London: Sage. pp. 110-24.

Parkin W. and Green, L. (1997a) 'Kickboxing the system: divisive cultures and counterproductive resistances in residential child care', paper for Annual BSA conference Power and Resistance, York.

Parkin W. and Green, L. (1997b) 'Cultures of abuse within residential child care', *Early Child Development and Care*, 133: 73-86.

Pateman, C. (1989) *The Disorder of Women.* Cambridge: Polity Press.

Pierce, J. (1996) 'Rambo litigators: emotional labor in a male dominated occupation', in Cheng, C. (ed.) *Masculinities in Organizations.* California: Sage. pp. 1-28.

Pilcher, J. (1998) 'Hormones or hegemonic masculinity: explaining gender and inequalities', *Sociology Review*, 7 (3): 5-9.

Popplestone, R. (1980) 'Top jobs for women - are the cards stacked against them?', *Social Work Today*, 12 (4): 12-15.

Pringle, R, (1988) *Secretaries Talk: Sexuality, Power and Work.* London: Verso.

Reed, R. (1996) 'Entrepreneurialism and paternalism in Australian management: a gender critique of "self-made" man', in Collinson, D.L. and Hearn, J. (eds) *Men as Managers, Managers as Men: Critical Perspectives on Men, Masculinities and Management.* London: Sage. pp. 99-122.

Reynaud, E. (1983) *Holy Virility: The Social Construction of Masculinity.* London: Pluto.

Rich, A. (1983) *Compulsory Heterosexuality and Lesbian Existence.* London: Onlywomen. p. 5.

Roach, D. (1991) 'The implications for residential care', *Children and Society*, 5 (1): 87-95.

Roper, M. (1996) 'Seduction and succession: circuits of homosocial desire in management', in Collinson, D.L. and Hearn, J. (eds) *Men as Managers, Managers as Men: Critical Perspectives on Men, Masculinities and Management.* London: Sage. pp. 210-26.

Russell, G. (1983) *The Changing Role of Fathers.* London: Open University Press.

Schneider, B. (1985) 'Approaches, assaults, attractions, affairs: policy implications of the sexualization of the workplace', *Population Research and Policy Review*, 4 (2): 93-113.

Sedgwick, E.K. (1985) *Between Men: English Literature and Male Homosocial Desire.* New York: Columbia University Press.

Seidler, V. (1989) *Rediscovering Masculinity: Reason, Language and Sexuality.* London: Routledge.

Seidler, V. (1994) *Unreasonable Men: Masculinity and Social Theory.* London: Routledge.

Sims, D., Fineman, S. and Gabriel, Y. (1993) *Organizing and Organizations.* London: Sage.

Sly, F. (1993) 'Women in the labour market', *Employment Gazette*, 101 (11): 483-92.

Utting, W. (1991) *Children in the Public Care.* London: HMSO.

Wardhaugh, J. and Wilding, P. (1993) 'Towards an explanation of the corruption of care', *Critical Social Policy Issue*, 37: 4-32.

Waring, M. (1988) *If Women Counted: a New Feminist Economics.* San Francisco: Harper Collins.

Warner, N. (1992) *Choosing With Care - The Report of the Committee of Inquiry into the Selection, Development and Managment of Staff in Children's Homes*, London: HMSO.

Watson, T. (1994) *In Search of Management: Culture, Chaos and Control In Managerial Work.* London: Routledge.

Weber, M. (1958) *The Protestant Ethic and the Spirit of Capitalism.* New York: Charles Scribner and Sons.

Wilkes, J. (1995) 'The social construction of a caring career', in Burc, C. and Speed, B. (eds) *Gender, Power and Relationships.* London: Routledge. pp. 232-47.

Wise, S. and Stanley, L. (1987) *Georgie Porgie: Sexual Harassment in Everyday Life.* London: Pandora Press.

Witz, A. and Savage, M. (eds) (1992) *Gender and Bureaucracy.* Oxford: Blackwell.

Woodward, A. (1996) 'Multinational masculinities and European bureaucracies', in Collinson, D.L. and Hearn, J. (eds) *Men as Managers, Managers as Men: Critical Perspectives on Men, Masculinities and Management.* London: Sage. pp. 167-85.

Wrong, D. (1979) *Power: Its Forms, Bases and Uses.* Oxford: Blackwell.

Zimmeck, M. (1992) 'Marry in haste, repent at leisure: women, bureaucracy and the Post Office 1870-1920', in Savage, M. and Witz, A. (eds) *Gender and Bureaucracy.* Oxford: Blackwell. pp. 65-93.

Zuboff, S. (1988) *In the Age of the Smart Machine.* New York: Basic Books.

11   Organizational Change

Judith Foreman

Introduction

Contemporary literature on the management of organizational change rarely discusses the issue of gender. The absence of gender from most mainstream analyses and discussions of managing change is notable in the light of a number of developments in the study of management and organizations generally. First, the broader disciplinary and theoretical foundations which underpin approaches to the management of organizational change have been subject to critical examination from a gender perspective for some time, resulting in a significant literature focusing on the gendered nature of organization/s and the ways in which they operate and are managed, as well as critiques of the gender bias and gender-blind nature of organizational theory and analysis. Second, many areas of organization behaviour central to understanding the management and effective implementation of change have also been subject to critical reappraisal through the inclusion of gender as an aspect of analysis (see other chapters in this book). Third, changing the gender order and changing gender relations in organizations are major focuses of organizational change and pose many challenges in terms of effective management. Fourth, there is much historical and accumulating contemporary evidence of the gendered impact of organizational change on the women and men who use or work in organizations.

Locating gender in the management of change is complex. Problems of definition and focus are evident. The management of organizational change draws on a broad range of academic disciplines and embraces a variety of different theoretical and conceptual approaches to understanding organizations and organizational change, and approaches to management. This means that the task of identifying key theoretical foundations and core concepts underpinning the topic and relating these to the issue of gender is complex and runs the risk of becoming a very general critique of management and organizational theory.

At the more practical level, understanding gender as an aspect of the management of change is made difficult by the breadth of the topic, its implications in terms of the practices and processes involved in achieving change and the different ways in which change is experienced by organizational members. The management of change embraces a wide range of managerial work and organizational behaviour. This may involve planning change at a strategic level, and/or devising and implementing the changes necessary to achieve strategic objectives, or implementing the day-to-day decisions which enable the organization to adapt to and cope with ongoing externally generated change. For those involved in the management of change, the change may be small or large-scale, the focus may be the whole organization or a small part of it; change may be simple or more complex and may include a wide range of types of intervention as for example changes in technology, structure, personnel practices, systems, culture, attitudes and behaviour. Managing change may involve people as enthusiastic change agents and champions, more reluctant change minders, or unwilling recipients of other people's decisions.

What follows, therefore, is an attempt first, to examine briefly current theoretical, analytical and practical perspectives in the area of managing change and link these to developments in organization theory and analysis more generally; and second to explore some key issues in which the links between gender and organizational change are highlighted. This is necessarily selective and not an exhaustive account of what is potentially a huge field of investigation.

Organization theory, gender and the management of organizational change

Approaches to the management of organizational change have, for a long time, assumed a model of organization as a purposive, rational entity, subject to manipulation, and change itself as resulting from rational planning and decision-making activities. Contained in this approach is the belief that managers can identify future goals for the organization and the changes necessary to get there; that initiatives can be undertaken in order to introduce and implement the necessary changes; that managers can acquire the necessary skills to implement change; and that change will occur in a linear fashion. Lewin's (1951) 'three step' model of change provides a classic, enduring and influential example of this kind of approach. An additional element in approaches to the management of change in the last few years has been the emergence of 'programmed approaches to organizational change', such as Total Quality Management (TQM) based on so-called new organizational paradigms (Wilson, 1992).

Until recently, the majority of approaches to understanding and managing organizational change have drawn on two main theoretical influences in social science which dominated organization theory and analysis for almost half a century; structural-functionalism and general systems theory (Hassard, 1993). Translated into organization theory, organizations are understood as systems of functionally differentiated, yet interdependent, parts. Like biological organisms, organizations are assumed to have needs which must be satisfied if they are to survive. In order to survive and achieve its primary task, an organization must possess functional unity, with each part, or sub-system, functioning to produce and reproduce the whole.

From the perspective of analysing organizations, the focus has largely been on the identification and exploration of the constituent organizational sub-systems and clarification of the imperatives which enable organizations to survive, adapt to the wider environment of which they are also parts, and achieve their primary task. A major thrust of organizational studies until very recently, has been to uncover the 'preferably one but possibly more best ways' of managing organizations (Mills, 1992: 2). In terms of the management of change, much work has focused on identifying the 'constituent parts of managerial behaviour' and the particular managerial skills necessary to effectively manage change (Wilson, 1992: 50).

Other approaches to organizational theory, including more complex interpretations of systems thinking, have challenged the orthodoxy of structural functionalism as the basis for understanding organizations and raised questions regarding the nature of change and how it can be managed. The problem of reifying the notion of organization and thus obscuring the complex and conflictual processes by which organizational goals and policy are determined and achieved has long been recognized. The Human Relations school of the 1920s and 1930s recognized that as social systems organizations are complex, composed of informal structures and processes as well as formal practices and procedures, and that people in organizations have emotional as well as economic needs. In the 1970s, more sociologically informed approaches such as those associated with social action and negotiated order perspectives questioned the ontological status of organizations as independent concrete forms and asserted that organization/s could only be understood as socially produced, maintained and reproduced through the intersubjective experience of members and processes of social interaction. Thus conceived, the focus of organizational analysis should be on the definitions of situations and views held by organizational members and the ways in which these definitions informed their actions and understanding of their actions (see Silverman, 1970). Since then, much research and writing exploring the area of organizational politics and processes associated with policy formulation and implementation, and processes of resistance, have been influenced by these social action and negotiated order perspectives (e.g. Pettigrew, 1973, 1985; Clegg, 1989).

From the mid-1970s more radical structuralist approaches also added to understandings of the nature of control, conflict and resistance within organizations through exploring organizations as systems of oppression within the broader framework of dominant social, economic and political interests of which they are a part (Mills, 1992). More recently a view of organizations as symbolic constructions and cultural orders has become increasingly popular and visible within organizational analysis. During the 1980s, developments in postmodernism raised fundamental questions regarding the theory and analysis of organizations (Clegg, 1990), positing a break with organizational forms associated with 'modernism' and the end of bureaucracy.

Despite changes in organization theory and analysis and moves away from the orthodoxies of structural functionalism and systems theory, the issues of gender and its relationship to organization/s was largely ignored until the 1980s. In the 1980s, however, organization theory and feminist theory began to engage in dialogue and gender became a focus of study in organizations. Since then an increasing number of writers and researchers have highlighted gender as central to organizational reality, to understanding culture, structure and organizational behaviour, and as integral to organizational processes which can only be properly understood through an analysis of gender (Acker, 1990, 1992; Hearn and Parkin, 1987; Hearn, et al., 1989; Ferguson, 1984; Mills and Tancred, 1992;

Savage and Witz, 1992; Halford, Savage and Witz, 1997; Wilson, in this volume, chapter 1). Understanding of gender and organization/s has also been enriched by research addressing sexuality, emotions and bodies, and exploration of the connections between gender and race, ethnicity, class and age in shaping organizations and the experience of those who use and/or work in organizations.

Some of the changes in understanding and analyzing organization/s, outlined above, are also evident in the managing change literature. In recent years, analysts and practitioners in the field of managing change have been concerned to explore the processes, contexts and complexities involved in devising and implementing change. This has entailed a critique of recipe-driven approaches, a challenge to rational models of change and associated scientific management techniques, and a rejection of notions of linearity and progress in the change process (Mabey and Mayon White, 1993; Kirkbride et al., 1994). The view of organization/s in this literature is as complex social, cultural and political systems operating under a range of internal and external constraints and within turbulent, dynamic, and unpredictable environments. In terms of the direction of change this may be contradictory and multidirectional rather than experienced in linear or cyclical conceptions of temporality (Burrell, 1992). Organizations are seen as contested terrains, characterized by different and sometimes conflicting interest groups, by different cultures, by political behaviour and by informal structures and processes as well as formal procedures. The existence of multiple rationalities is acknowledged (Carnall, 1995) as are the implications of a more complex understanding of organizational life and decision making for the ways in which change is managed. According to Senior (1997) for example:

> change in this scenario, will only be possible and effective if it is accompanied
> by processes which address, in particular, the feelings, needs and aspirations of
> individuals, the group processes which bind them together and the structures
> and systems which are the forces for stability rather than change (p. 257).

For some writers working within a postmodernist framework, fundamental questions are raised about the change process and whether this can be managed using any of the existing change models and practical tools associated with a so-called 'modernist' view of the world (Kirkbride et al., 1994).

Despite these developments, however, much of the literature on the management of organizational change, especially those texts intended specifically for business and management courses, remain silent on issues of gender. Where gender is touched on, it tends to be incorporated into discussion in limited ways, as for example, in brief references to equal opportunities issues, or acknowledgement of gender divisions in employment. Recently the 'challenge of diversity' has become more visible in texts on the management of change. Senior (1997), for example, concludes her discussion of organizational change with a brief exploration of diversity and its implications for the effective management of change. In the following section an attempt is made to link gender and the management of organizational change by drawing on research examining a variety of aspects of gender and organizational practices and processes.

Locating gender in the management of organizational change

This section attempts to locate gender as a social process within a more general framework of practices and processes associated with the management of organizational change. The first half of the discussion outlines two areas in which gender and the management of organizational change are linked: the relationship between gender and corporate strategies; and the implications of organizational change and restructuring for gender relations at work, and upon the operation of established equal opportunities policies and practices. As a strategic resource available to managers, gender is complexly and intimately related to the making of organizations and work, historically and in the current context of organizational change and restructuring. At the same time, however, the 'embedded' (Halford et al., 1997) nature of gender in the internal formal and informal political and cultural dynamics of organizations, and in the external environment in which organizations are located, means that gender plays a significant role in shaping the processes and outcomes of organizational change. In the second half of the discussion in this section, the significance of gender in relation to internal organizational processes such as culture, political behaviour and resistance, and their links to organizational change, are explored through a focus on gender and organizational cultures, and the role of women as organizational change agents.

Gender and corporate strategy

In his analysis of the management of organization change, Wilson (1992) states that 'corporate strategy appears at best a sexually neutral world, at worst a virtually all-male world of managerial and executive action' (p. 59). Despite the under-representation of women from empowered decision-making positions in organizations, accounts and analyses of the history and development of organization/s are saturated with examples of the ways in which gender has shaped organizations. More particularly there are many examples of the manipulation of gender for instrumental reasons in the construction of modern bureaucratic forms. Gender, as well as sexuality and bodies, can be thought of as an organizational resource, implicated in, and utilized by, organizations in the pursuit of corporate and managerial goals (Acker, 1990, 1992).

Many writers have recognized the diverse roles that gender may play in corporate strategy and human resource utilization as part of processes associated with managerial control and production. Currently there is much research interest in the relationship between gender and corporate strategies in the context of developments in human resource management, and in the restructuring and expansion of the service sector. The utility and benefits of gendered labour to patriarchal and capitalist interests, both inside and outside the workplace have been recognized and explored over many years in feminist research (Beechey, 1987; Cockburn, 1983, 1985; Walby, 1986). More recently, feminist research has also highlighted the issue of sexuality in relation to gender, and the embodied nature of gendered and sexualized labour as central to understanding the employment contract and the labour process (Cockburn, 1991; Acker, 1992; Brewis and Kerfoot, 1994; Witz et al., 1994; Adkins, 1995; Hearn and Parkin, 1987; Hearn, et al., 1989). In outlining the connection between embodied labour, sexuality and the employment contract, Brewis and Kerfoot (1993), for example, suggest that in some jobs, particularly in the service sector, the gender and sexual identities of workers, manifested in embodied characteristics such as appearance, demeanour and manner, form the basis of the contractual relationship between employer and employee and are central to the processes of production, appropriation and exploitation. A study of women in the service industries (a hotel and a leisure park) by Adkins (1992, 1995) provides an example of the ways in which the provision of sexual services for both male customers and male employees was part of the employment contract for women. In this case, sexual work was also 'body work' (Shilling, 1993) since female employees were expected to 'look right' in order to do the job properly. Other studies also highlight the ways in which the gendered and sexualized characteristics of women's embodied labour, including their capacity to perform 'emotional labour', the management of human feelings as part of the labour process (Hochschild, 1983) are commodified in the performance of particular occupational roles (James, 1989; Pringle, 1988; Filby, 1992; Tyler and Hancock, 1998). Gherardi (1995) also notes the ways in which the gendered and sexualized characteristics of the body are co-opted through the employment contract and utilized in the production process. She suggests, however, it is not only female bodies and gendered characteristics which are co-opted, as the male body is also, increasingly, caught up in the process (Gherardi, 1995). McDowell (1997) highlights the significance of the performance of 'body work' for men in a study of professional financial service workers.

Gender can also be understood as a resource for, and important contributor to, organizational change and restructuring and there are many historical and contemporary examples of the ways in which the manipulation and exploitation of gender has been used by managers/owners, and other groups of workers, in the process of organizational development, and in the processes whereby men retain control of organizational hierarchies.

An interesting historical example of the utilization of gender, and gender divisions in the pursuit of organizational development is the employment of women as clerks by the newly formed Post Office after 1869. Employers' reasons for preferring women focused on their cheapness, their higher skills and their perceived manageability. In addition, since women were expected to retire from work on marriage, this was seen to be beneficial in terms of the numbers of Post Office employees who would have claims to maximum salaries and to retirement pensions, while leaving promotion and career development open for men (Walby, 1986; Zimmeck, 1992). The links between organizational strategy and gender are also evident in literature exploring economic restructuring in Britain in the 1970s and 1980s (Massey, 1984). Gender has been a resource for multinationals and globalizing firms as they seek out new sources of low-wage labour on the grounds that women work for lower wages and, in addition, have more 'nimble fingers' than men. In Britain, employer strategies over many years to increase labour-force flexibility have often utilized gender difference as a way of achieving the different kinds of flexibility required by organizations.

Recent studies of change in a number of industries have highlighted a variety of other links between corporate strategy, human resource utilization and gender. For example, in a complex case-study of a divisionalized financial services company, Morgan and Knights (1991) document the ways in which pre-existing gender divisions associated with selling financial services in the organization became implicated in the process of developing new strategies in relation to human resources and management control, as male senior managers struggled to make the company profitable and maintain their own positions within the divisionalized structure in the face of competition from other men. According to their analysis, the use of female bank staff to sell some insurance products, previously sold by the men employed by the insurance division of the company, was regarded by managers in the bank as bringing a variety of benefits in terms of the utilization of staff and reducing costs. This ensured the continuation of a largely male management and professional banking hierarchy at bank level, and resisted the competition posed by the presence of the male insurance sellers (Morgan and Knights, 1991).

In another recent study of change in banking, local government and nursing Halford et al. (1997) identify the emergence of what they term 'productive heterosexuality' (p. 244) as an important part of new workplace cultures, used by managers as a way of policing workplace life and contributing to a productive working environment. According to their research, the dynamic and sexualized nature of the interaction between women and men in mixed work environments was tolerated and encouraged at times by managers as a way of improving working relationships and morale, and 'curbing the excesses of unruly single-sex groups' (Halford et al., 1997: 244). (Of course, this positive view of sexuality in the workplace has to be considered in alongside much research documenting the problematic nature of sexuality in the workplace, see Green et al. in this volume.)

Nevertheless, managerial interest in the strategic utilization of the gendered and sexualized characteristics of labourers has been largely ignored and unacknowledged in managerial literature, analysed and discussed only by those concerned with understanding the production and reproduction of gender divisions and inequalities, or those concerned with so-called 'women's issues' in organizations. Recently, however, some researchers have suggested that managers are taking a more 'explicit' interest in the gender characteristics of their workforce in the context of developments in human resource management and pressures on managers to utilize human resources in the pursuit of profit (Morgan and Knights, 1991).

Precisely how, why and in what circumstances, gender may become a component of labour and part of corporate strategy is complex, as Morgan and Knights' (1991) case study demonstrates. In this case, the extent to which this is a new aspect of management thinking, and exactly how this is linked to current developments in human resource management, perhaps needs more explanation. Arguably, however, there are current developments in managerial discourses and approaches to labour and corporate strategy that do open themselves for scrutiny in relation to gender.

For example, initiatives such as TQM, with its emphasis on the customer, are making more explicit the significance of the 'character' of individuals, in addition to education, training and skills, as the basis for selection, promotion and appraisal (Townley, 1998). 'Character' may include such attributes and capacities as motivation, flexibility, initiative, self-discipline, ability to get on with others and willingness to please the customer. The focus on 'character' as a resource for processes of control and production, can perhaps be linked to wider debates regarding economic restructuring and developments in service economies, and what Lash and Urry (1994), for example, see as the increasing value being placed on the 'emotional' and 'aesthetic' aspects of labour in comparison with more technical components. The importance of 'emotional labour' in the service sector, and its relationship to quality initiatives such as TQM, has been increasingly recognized by researchers investigating contemporary workplaces as has the distinctly gendered nature of emotional labour (Filby, 1992).

The focus on the 'whole person' as an organizational and occupational resource is also evident in current debates regarding managing diversity and some arguments associated with the development of the so-called 'business case' for equal opportunities. In these debates the focus is on using the differences of employees strategically for the benefit of the organization. This may entail mobilizing aspects of the self, including cultural and social identity, previously left unacknowledged or marginalized in approaches to people management. Managing diversity explicitly acknowledges the contribution that individual personal differences such as gender experience and identity can make to organizational effectiveness. The emphasis is on the full utilization of the person in pursuit of organizational goals. According to the IPD (1996) for example, managing diversity encourages innovative ideas, different perceptions, increased creativity and hence improved competitiveness.

The idea of gender as an organizational asset is also evident in recent debates regarding approaches to management. Since the 1980s a number of writers have articulated an approach to management based on traits and orientation traditionally associated with women (e.g. Rosener, 1990). These traits include qualities stereotypically assumed to be feminine such as the ability to nurture and empower staff as well as the capacity to communicate effectively. Such arguments have been used to strengthen the 'business case' for the progression of women as managers by emphasizing the distinctive skills which women can bring to the workplace. These arguments are discussed more fully in Metcalfe and Altman (in this volume).

It is interesting to note, however, that over the last 20 years debate and political action on achieving gender inequality has emphasized that gender and sexuality are *irrelevant* to production and the performance of work by individuals. Within this view, discrimination in, for example, recruitment and selection, which is based on perceptions of assumed gender differences in personality, as well as knowledge and skills, is interpreted as irrational from an organizational perspective, and inefficient and wasteful in terms of the utilization of human resources. Managing diversity is presented as an extension to developments in equal opportunities and a way of combating 'prejudice, stereotyping, harassment and undignified behaviour' (IPD, 1996, p. 1). Nevertheless, there must surely be some questions regarding the possibly contradictory effects of explicit managerial interests in the social character and identity of labour and the pursuit of gender equality and changes in the gender order of work. Morgan and Knights (1991) for example 'can see implicit and explicit ideologies of gender being reproduced, but also, potentially restructured' (p. 182) in the context of managerial interest in the gender characteristics of their employees, giving rise possibly to transformational change in gender relations, patterns of job segregation, and the self-identities of women and men. Other writers are more sceptical of the likely effects of an increased managerial focus on gender and other aspects of identity and 'character' as organizational resources, particularly for women. For example, in her analysis of the implications of the 'business case' for women in management Cassell (1997) points out that although the links between valuing women's skills and business success tend to be made unproblematically and are assumed to be of benefit to women, it is important to remain cautious about the potentially contradictory effects of the ideology on women's progression in organizations. She cites examples from the service industry in which women are selected for jobs because they are perceived to be physically attractive and, therefore, more likely to attract male customers. Cassell (1997) concludes that 'taking a purely business case, therefore, legitimized the status quo, rather than creating opportunities for women workers' (p. 15). The danger that such thinking implies essentialist claims about so-called 'female' characteristics and may lead to stereotyping women as 'caring' managers and further gender segregation of management roles is widely commented on (see for example, Hall-Taylor, 1997; Webb, 1997). Cassell (1997) also raises the question of what will happen to women if there is no 'business case', or when cost-cutting become key business imperatives and threaten positive initiatives.

Gender and the impact of organizational change

As has been demonstrated above, gender is intimately connected with corporate strategy and processes of control and production. The following outline attempts to highlight a variety of ways in which current organizational change and restructuring may be implicated in changes in gender relations and the gender organization of work. Research into the human resource consequences of organizational restructuring and change has tended to be gender blind. However, recent research on gender, work and organization has increasingly focused on the gendered impact of organizational change. It is clear from this research that the gender outcomes of organizational change are complex, and closely bound up with the histories and specific conditions of different economic sectors, organizations and occupations; and that women and men are not passive in the process of organizational change.

The impact of organizational changes on gender relations at work

For organizations in the private and public sectors macro level changes such as the development of global markets, fluctuations in the economy, the development of new areas of productive activity, deregulation of labour markets, and technological change have led to increased competition, as well as changes in the nature and organization of work, in the content of many jobs, and the skills and people required for them.   In the public sector political intervention and pressure on public expenditure have led to changes in the way in which the sector is financed, and the ways in which services are organized and provided. In both private and public sectors there have been moves towards downsizing, delayering, decentralizing and centralizing, with the aim of reducing costs and creating more responsive and efficient organizations. There has also been a search for more flexibility in terms of the utilization of the workforce, the organization of production, and in the provision of services. Within this broader context a variety of aspects of organizational change have been highlighted in terms of their impact on the women and men who work in them and in particular their impact on women's employment opportunities. Here, a selection of aspects of change will be briefly explored: the growth in flexible work; the effects of 'downsizing' and 'delayering' on career structures and opportunities; the emergence of new management practices and cultures in the context of organizational change; the introduction of Compulsory Competitive Tendering (CCT) and market testing in UK local government (recently replaced by Best Value).

  It could be argued that contemporary changes in organizations and the organization of work may alter the conditions that have contributed to gender inequality and segregation. For example, increases in flexible types of work might offer possibilities for shaping organizations to accommodate non-paid aspects of life, opening up opportunities for employees to combine work and family life and reducing the disadvantages for women in paid employment. Recent research initiated by the UK Equal Opportunities Commission, however, shows evidence of the poor quality of much flexible work and the perpetuation of job segregation and gender inequalities. Research by Dex and McCulloch (1995) on trends in flexible employment in Britain shows that non-standard employment has increased since the 1970s. The number of men's flexible jobs increased by 834,000 and the number of women's flexible jobs by 703,000 between 1986 and 1994. The study reveals important differences in the types of non-standard jobs done by women and men and considerable variation by age, marital status, family circumstances, and ethnic origin. Despite increasing numbers of men taking part-time jobs and pressure on them to take lower paid jobs, the study shows that women are still 'disproportionately located in flexible jobs, particularly the worst sort of flexible jobs' (p. xii) not covered by employment protection legislation. The study also concludes that trends in job segregation and gendered patterns of working and working time are being maintained (Dex and McCullough, 1995).

  The combined effects of 'downsizing' and 'delayering' in organizations has prompted questions regarding the implications of change for career structures and opportunities. Some commentators have argued that less hierarchy and more emphasis on team working may provide opportunities for women to work as equals with men and contribute to the removal of gender stereotypes. Research tends to highlight a variety of effects of change including, however, the perpetuation of gender differences and other likely effects. In a study of organizational change in five organizations in the private and public sector, Coyle (1996) suggests that the flattening of organizational hierarchies has led to the truncation of career structures and to increasing competition between women and men for promotion to a diminishing number of jobs. Other writers are less convinced of the general disappearance of the organizational career or the development of increased competition between women and men for promotion. In their study of banking and local government for example, Halford et al. (1997) conclude that 'the organizational career continues to have some vitality, even though it has undeniably changed in nature' (p. 262). They also conclude that the gains women have made in management do not appear to have been made at the expense of men but through the expansion of professional and managerial jobs in Britain. The changes they note are the fragmentation of careers as professional and managerial employment has become more specialized, and the re-segregation of careers between women and men 'with women being concentrated either as operations managers or lending managers in banking, and in secondary hierarchies in local government' (p. 263). Other writers have also noted the likelihood of new forms of gender segregation emerging in the context of change with the maintenance of male domination in higher status, more powerful and higher paid positions (Wilson, 1994; Rubery and Fagan, 1994; Maile, 1995).

Some discussions regarding the future shape and management of organizations have been critical of traditional management practices for being overly hierarchical and bureaucratic, and have argued that so-called 'female ways of managing' will be more appropriate in a future of less hierarchical organization characterized by teamwork and consensus management. As has already been noted, among some writers this new management thinking is seen as a way for women to break into male-dominated hierarchies. Evaluating the validity of these claims is empirically difficult and this is discussed further in Metcalfe and Altman (in this volume). Furthermore, there is much uncertainty regarding the nature and extent of actual structural change taking place in organizations and the implications of these changes for styles of management and leadership emerging in the process. Some recent research on organizational restructuring does highlight the importance of gender as integral to managerial discourse in the context of change. However, the research findings tend to describe a picture of complex and ambiguous implications for both female and male employees. For example, a study of management style in five male-dominated multi-national corporations conducted by Judy Wajcman (1996) concluded that 'macho management' and traditional hierarchical structures were still very much in evidence, sustained by a culture of fear and uncertainty generated by continuous change:

> The business context of almost continuous restructuring and job losses has greatly intensified pressures for senior managers and means that insecurity

> about the future is pervasive. The traditional career-for-life model, based on employment security and promotion prospects, has been replaced by a climate of fear about the very real prospect of redundancy in many organizations ... the logic of survival results in heightened individualistic competition for a dwindling number of job opportunities. In this economic climate, both men and women feel the need to conform to the male stereotype of management because it is still, in practice, the only one regarded as effective (Wajcman, 1996: 345).

Other researchers have noted changes in management style in the context of organizational change. Their conclusions, however, tend to indicate the continuity of gender differences in managerial work and the possibility of male domination. For example, in their study of change in financial services in Britain, Kerfoot and Knights (1993) describe the transition from what they term 'paternalistic' management practices, based on nineteenth century middle class conceptions of masculinity, to a model of strategic management characterized by 'competitive masculinity'. In their study of change in banking, nursing and local government, Halford et al. (1997) note a move away from managerial cultures associated with familial and gendered notions towards what they describe as new 'performative management' cultures based around values of competitiveness, specialist skills, dedication and 'getting things done' (p. 264). According to the authors, the change is linked to the wider context of organizational restructuring in each organization which 'has replaced familial and gendered discourses of management and organization with an ostensibly gender-neutral management based on performativity' (p. 262). Theoretically, this 'decoupling' of gender from organizational position should make it more possible for women to move into more senior positions. The authors are sceptical, however, of its likely effects, seeing the new culture as essentially based around an ethos of 'competitive individualism' and endorsing a largely masculine life style and life cycle:

> It is ... a culture that depends on a particular configuration of the relationship between home and work, and which valorises the independent, lone individual with no other commitments. This has the *de facto* effect of making it difficult for people, especially women, who value other aspects of their lives, or who have domestic responsibilities they do not wish to, or are not able to avoid, from playing a leading role in the organizations concerned (pp. 264-265).

Similar observations are made by Newman (1995) in her consideration of the emergence of 'competitive' cultures in parts of the public sector as a response to internal and external competition. The new culture is described as 'less familial' than the traditional bureaucracy, with many of the 'old patriarchs and benevolent paternal figures' having been 'dethroned' (p. 16). In this case, however, Newman (1995) stresses the unforgiving 'macho' nature of the new regime wherein 'women are allowed to join if they can prove that they can deliver, and are tough enough to stand the pace' (p. 17).

The gender impact of CCT and market testing on employment and pay in local authorities also received attention. Research carried out for the Equal Opportunities Commission in 39 case study local authorities in 1993 and 1994 showed that the extension of CCT into manual services had a differential impact on women and men. There was evidence of a decline in the average number of hours worked, particularly in female job areas such as catering and cleaning. Consequently, women were more frequently excluded from employment protection, were more often involved in multiple job holding and a greater number of women had weekly earnings below the National Insurance Lower Earnings Limit. There was also evidence that pay levels in predominantly male areas, such as refuse collection, had increased, while pay rates did not increase in any of the case studies in the predominantly female catering and cleaning fields. The report concludes that a:

> two-tier workforce has become prevalent within local authorities, driven by a combination of economic pressures and CCT. Existing differences between permanent and casual work, between full-time and part-time jobs and between male and female employment have been accentuated (EOC, 1995: 3).

The impact of organizational change and restructuring on equal opportunities policies and practice

Equal opportunities policies have been a major focus for achieving gender equality in organizations for nearly 20 years. Arguably there are a great many changes taking place in organizations which may have implications for the development and pursuit of equal opportunities policies and initiatives. For example, the need for greater competitiveness and cost effectiveness, as well as changes in corporate strategy, may result in the subordination of human resource policies to economic considerations (Purcell, 1993). This in turn may lead to a reduction of resources directed towards sustaining equal opportunities and loss of commitment to equality issues in the face of competition from other imperatives. Changes to the shape of organizations and changes in employment practices may also have important implications, making the need for monitoring and assessing the effectiveness of equal opportunities policies in the new situation more urgent, and raising questions regarding the development of more appropriate initiatives and systems for the implementation of equal opportunities in the context of change.

A variety of specific aspects of change have been highlighted as possibly problematic in terms of sustaining equal opportunities policies. Recent research on the public sector has shown that the drive to reduce the cost of services as well as the introduction of market testing and CCT can have a detrimental effect on equal opportunities policies and initiatives as discussed above (Escott and Whitfield, 1995; Wainwright Trust, 1997). Concern has also been expressed regarding the abolition in some local authorities of separate equality structures such as gender and race equality units, and the incorporation of equality issues into HRM structures and managerial discourses (Newman, 1995; Maile, 1995). Changes in the management of organizations such as decentralization and devolution, have also prompted questions and investigations regarding their impact on equal opportunities policies and practices, as discussed in the Case Study below.

Gender, culture and organizational change

The subject of organizational culture has received a lot of attention in management theory and practice concerned with organizational change in recent years. The assumed potency of culture in facilitating corporate change and renewal evident in some contributions to the debate is likened by Wilson (1992) to an 'elixir' capable of bringing life back to organizations and curing all organizational ills. Within the literature and various debates concerning the role of culture in organizational transformation a number of different ways in which the two are assumed to be linked are evident. For example, the idea that culture and organization performance are linked and that 'strong cultures make a strong organization' (Handy, 1986) has been influential over many years. Second, there is concern that culture will have to change if other aspects of organizational change are to be successful. This idea can be clearly linked to the Culture-Excellence view outlined above, but also has wider support among those who believe that changing structures and processes is not enough if attitudes and values among organizational members do not also shift. Third, given 'the pervasive nature of organizational culture' it is 'likely to affect virtually all aspects of organizational life' (Wilson and Rosenfeld, 1990: 237), facilitating change but also impeding or altering the intended impact of change.

The role and importance of culture in understanding organizations is well established in organization theory and analysis. The different ways of conceptualizing and analysing culture are discussed in Wilson (chapter 9, in this volume). How organizational culture is viewed will lead to very different interpretations of the process of organizational change and whether culture should, or should not, can or cannot, be managed as part of that process (see for example, Wilson, 1992; Burnes, 1996; Senior, 1997). Despite the rather uncertain status of 'culture' within current debates on managing change, a broad and analytically informed approach to culture is a useful way of understanding what happens in organizations, highlighting the informal as well as the formal aspects of organizational life, and illuminating some of the dynamics of organizational behaviour, such as resistance, which are an important part of the change process. Wilson (1992), for example, highlights the ways in which the adoption of an 'interpretive' approach to organizational culture and an explicit focus on the ways in which individuals define and interpret situations have been utilized by researchers in analysing and understanding the process of change.

The idea that organizational cultures are gendered is well established (Gherardi, 1995). Potentially interesting connections between gender, culture and organizational change are not difficult to find. The gendered, often masculinized, characteristics of corporate cultures are well established (e.g. Wajcman, 1996). In addition, an exploration of the literature on workplace and occupational subcultures provides insight into the links between culture, resistance and conflict in organization, as well as the ways in which gender forms part of these subcultures. There are many detailed studies of organizations examining the ways in which women and men construct gendered subcultures, characterized by rituals and particular linguistic and behavioural practices, which defy the formal and official regime of their workplaces to make boring and dead-end jobs bearable, to resist rules and control, to solidify work groups and mobilize against others (Lupton, 1963; Beynon, 1975; Willis, 1977; Pollert, 1981; Cavendish, 1982; Cockburn, 1983; Westwood, 1984; Pringle, 1988; Benson, 1992; Collinson, 1992; Filby, 1992; Gottfried and Graham, 1993; Ackroyd and Thompson, 1999).

'Resistance' may, of course, be a response to a variety of aspects of organizational life, including change and the imposition of managerial authority. Writers have, over many years, highlighted gender and sexuality as an aspect of workplace identity, with implications of masculine and feminine identities in the process of conflict between 'managers' and 'workers', and between different occupational groups. Cockburn (1983) provides a graphic account of the complex interplay between gender identity, occupational culture and resistance to change in her account of male printworkers threatened with the introduction of new technology and the introduction of women into the workplace.

The gendered nature of organizational cultures has also been highlighted recently as a significant barrier to change by writers and activists explicitly concerned with attempting to change gender relations in organizations through the development of equal opportunities policies and initiatives (Cockburn, 1991; Itzin and Newman, 1995). Understanding the characteristics of the 'gender culture' of organizations is, therefore, a vital part of the process of implementing and managing gender change.

The emergence of new organizational cultures in the broader context of organizational change may have important implications for gender relations and the shaping of gender identities. This aspect of organizational change is receiving much attention as writers (e.g. Halford, et al., 1997; Maddock, 1999) attempt to grapple with and unravel the impact of recent change on the women and men who work in and use organizations.

Women as organizational change agents

Despite recent improvements in the number of women in managerial and professional occupations, the continued absence of women from empowered decision-making positions as leaders or managers clearly reduces women's influence over change in terms of policy making and restructuring processes. Although it is argued that new models and cultures of management, including change management, are emerging in the context of economic restructuring and organizational change, the tendency to associate particular conceptions of 'masculinity' with 'manager' is still widespread, particularly in uncertain and competitive environments where perceptions of effective management are linked to characteristics such as aggressiveness, independence and the ability to take 'hard' decisions. Much of the literature on the management of change has also reflected this view by using images of masculinity and male stereotypes when referring to change champions, 'cowboy' (Kanter, 1997) and 'trouble shooter' (Television series featuring Sir John Harvey-Jones).

The factors which encourage gender imbalances and the exclusion of women from decision making have been widely discussed. Nevertheless, and despite the difficulties and problems encountered by women in relation to access to corporate power and influence, women have been active in organizational change over many years. This is evident in historical and contemporary studies of women's involvement in challenging gender politics in organizations, and more recent work on the role of women managers in mainstream corporate change and restructuring.

Women's collective and individual struggles have had an important effect on opening up organizations to women and pushing back the barriers to women's progression in the pursuit of equal opportunities and citizenship rights. In recent years there has also been a rise of 'gender work' in organizations: jobs and careers in equal opportunities and gender change, often based on specialist knowledge in such areas as industrial relations, the law and personnel management (Shaw and Perrons, 1995). Examination of examples of collective and individual equality strategies by women which aim to bring about change in organizations reveal diversity in terms of aims and sorts of action. Women are involved in working within mainstream organizations and attempting to create the changes necessary for women to participate and to progress in those structures, and they are working on the creation of alternative and independent organization/s outside of the existing structures (Cockburn, 1991;   Griffin, 1995; Ledwith and Colgan, 1996; Shaw and Perrons 1995; Savage and Witz, 1992; Itzin and Newman, 1995).

Although studies of women's involvement and activism in gender change programmes have increased over recent years, women's approach to and influence on corporate change management more generally is less well documented. Within the women in management literature, there has been little recognition or exploration of the role that women managers play in organizational change. As more women are appointed to middle and senior management posts, however, and as debate continues regarding the best way to manage organizational change, more attention is being paid to women's role as innovators. As outlined in the introduction, recent discussion on the management of change has tended to stress the need to move away from a systems or structural approach to change towards a perspective which is more people and process focused. In some contemporary accounts of gender and management style, women are seen as more likely than men to possess the skills of leadership and empowerment, as well as the ability to 'read' organizational processes and dynamics, necessary for the successful management of change and the transition to new organizational forms (Helgesen, 1990; Rosener, 1990).

A recent study by Maddock (1999) explores the role of women managers and their approach to change in the public sector. Maddock's thesis is that in the context of public sector transformation and the increase of women managers in local government during the 1980s, women have a positive and distinctive role to play in managing change. According to Maddock the women managers who participated in the research were:

> ... passionate about the public services and their desire to transform management practices. They were innovators, leaders and confident of

alternatives; they were accustomed to discussion and supported each other. Their views were not merely representative of women's experience but demonstrated the extent to which these particular women were innovators capable to thinking through many of the obstacles to partnership, collaboration and new organizational agencies (Maddock, 1999: 4).

Maddock's findings support the idea that women have a key role to play in the change process and have the skills required to management change. At the same time, however, the study also documents the extent to which women managers were met with resistance and were 'frustrated and thwarted by the male gender culture' (Maddock, 1999: 4) in their efforts to challenge traditional practices. As far as women's ability to use their skills to manage change Maddock (1999) identifies a contradiction between the theorists and senior managers who claim that a collaborative culture is necessary in order to transform public services, and the continuation of cultures which characterize 'challenging women' as 'difficult'.

Case-study: the impact of devolution on equal opportunities policies and practices

This research examined the effects of changes in the operation of personnel management on the development and implementation of equal opportunities policies and initiatives. The particular focus of change in personnel management was the devolution of tasks in key areas of personnel practice, formerly undertaken by personnel specialists, to line managers. A variety of organizations in the private sector were chosen for the research. The experience of a large high street bank is discussed here.

Background: devolution and equal opportunities practice

In general terms, devolution can be understood as part of a much wider process of organizational restructuring and change in the management of organizations, as companies have sought to increase their flexibility and responsiveness to environmental change and survive economic uncertainty. Key aspects of these changes have been, for example, business divisionalization, 'de-layering', job-shedding, trends toward decentralization, the introduction of new technologies, and changes in the organization of work.

Within this wider context of organizational change, many organizations have also reorganized the personnel function, and redefined the role of personnel specialists and line managers. This has often resulted in the reduction of the personnel function, greater integration of its activities with corporate planning, and personnel specialists working for and providing support for business managers. At the same time, line managers are expected to take more responsibility for attracting, retaining, motivating and developing the staff they supervise.

Differing views have been expressed regarding the consequences of devolution in relation to personnel practice. Some commentators have suggested that giving line managers more responsibility for the staff they supervise will improve personnel practice, since it is these managers who are in the best position to motivate and develop staff, especially if they are held accountable, through staffing budgets or performance appraisal, for their decisions.

On the other hand, concern has been expressed regarding a possible reduction in the quality of personnel performance. Possible problems such as the inadequate training and skills of line managers in personnel practice, role overload and role conflict, diversity and inconsistency in the implementation and application of policy 'down the line', have been highlighted. In relation to equal opportunities issues specifically, there is concern that the implementation of company equal opportunity policies, and good practice in relation to established personnel procedures, may be weakened by decentralization, the slimming down or abolition of central personnel services, and the allocation of personnel tasks to line managers (see, for example, CRE, 1995). Particular concern has been expressed regarding the possibility that decentralization and devolution may erode formality and consistency in relation to the specification of procedures and practices in such areas as recruitment, promotion and staff development, as recommended by bodies such as the Comission for Racial Equality, Equal Opportunities Commission and Institute for Personnel and Development.

The case study

The Bank is a PLC within a group of financial services companies. The focus of the research was the Retail Banking Division which is one of the UK's major high street banks.

During the time of the research the Bank was devolving more people management responsibilities and tasks to line managers within the Branch Network. This included local planning and resourcing, performance management and appraisal, staff development, recruitment and selection. At the same time, line personnel management was being re-formulated to provide support, advice and guidance to line managers in personnel planning and practices, and to be more involved in general business functions.

Equal opportunities management was located in the Corporate Personnel function which provided services to all divisions within the Group. An Equal Opportunities Manager was appointed in the mid 1980s. Prior to the changes the Bank had a good track record with regard to equal opportunities, especially in relation to gender.

The research findings indicate that the formulation of equal opportunities policies had been retained at the centre, supported by specialist staff. The danger that equal opportunities expertise and policies would be lost in the changes was not evident in the research although there was little evidence that equal opportunity specialists were represented or fully involved in processes of strategic decision making at corporate level. There were, however, problems in the implementation of policies 'down the line'. The two main sources of the problems were inadequate training in personnel practice and lack of commitment to equal opportunities at line manager level. There were clear indications that the priorities for many line managers were their immediate business results, and that personnel professionals had difficulty making a business case for more attention to equality issues. Equality aims and objectives were not included in managers' performance targets or appraisals. In addition, the research found evidence in recruitment and selection procedures of many practices at variance with, for example, EOC guidelines for generating job applications and interviewing potential staff which had the potential of contributing to biased selection decisions. Interviews with non-managerial staff indicated widespread perception that internal promotion systems were subject to unfair manipulation by managers.

Discussion

Devolution has had no effect on equal opportunities policy making but the implementation of policy now has to be effected through the devolved organization. Although devolution was in an early stage during the period of the research, the apparent lack of commitment from line managers to equal opportunities, and in some cases lack of understanding, presents challenges for the development of equal opportunity strategies and outcomes in the new situation.

Conclusion

The developing focus on gender in organizational theory and analysis provides insight into many aspects of organization and management. Mainstream literature on the management of organizational change has been slow to respond to wider developments in the study of organizations and incorporate gender into discussion regarding the process of managing change. This chapter has explored some key issues in which the links between gender and organizational change are highlighted. The chapter suggests that gender is integral to organizational change processes and that our understanding of organizational change and the ways change is managed is enriched by an analysis of gender.

Note: the case presented here is part of a larger survey of organizations undertaken by Judith Foreman and Rachel Bedingfield for the Wainwright Trust (Wainwright Trust, 1997).

References

Acker, J. (1990) 'Hierarchies, jobs, bodies; a theory of gendered organizations', *Gender and Society*, 4 (2): 139-58.

Acker, J. (1992) 'Gendering organizational theory', in Mills, A.J. and Tancred, P. (eds) *Gendering Organizational Analysis*. London: Sage. pp. 248-60.

Ackroyd, Stephen and Thompson, Paul (1999) *Organizational Misbehaviour*. London: Sage.

Adkins, L. (1992) 'Sexual work and the employment of women in the service industries', in Savage, Mike and Witz, Anne (eds) *Gender and Bureaucracy*. Oxford: Blackwell Publishers. pp. 207-28.

Adkins, L. (1995) *Gendered Work: Sexuality, Family and the Labour Market*. Buckingham: Open University Press.

Beechey, V. (1987) *Unequal Work*. London: Verso.

Benson, S.P. (1992) 'The clerking sisterhood: rationalization and the work culture of saleswomen in American department stores, 1890-1960', in Mills, A.J. and Tancred, P. (eds) *Gendering Organizational Analysis*. London: Sage. pp. 167-84.

Beynon, H. (1975) *Working for Ford*. Harmondsworth: Penguin.

Brewis, J. and Kerfoot, D. (1994) 'Selling our selves? Sexual harassment and the intimate violations of the workplace', paper presented to the British Sociological Association, Annual Conference, University of Central Lancashire, Preston, March.

Burnes, Bernard (1996) *Managing Change. A Strategic Approach to Organizational Dynamics*. London: Pitman Publishing.

Burrell, G. (1992) 'Back to the future: time and organization', in Reed, M. and Hughes, M. (eds) *Rethinking Organization: New Directions in Organization Theory and Analysis*, London: Sage.

Carnall, C. (1995) *Managing Change in Organizations*. London: Prentice Hall.

Cassell, Catherine (1997) 'The business case for equal opportunities: implications for women in management', *Women in Management Review*, 12 (1): 11-16.

Cavendish, Ruth (1982) *Women on the Line*. London: Routledge and Kegan Paul.

Clegg, S. (1989) *Frameworks of Power*. London: Sage.

Clegg, S. (1990) *Modern Organizations: Organization Studies in the Postmodern World*. London: Sage.

Cockburn, Cynthia (1983) *Brothers: Male Dominance and Technological Change*. London: Pluto.

Cockburn, C. (1985) *Machinery of Dominance: Women, Men and Technical Know-How*. London: Pluto

Cockburn, C. (1991) *In the Way of Women: Men's Resistance to Sex Equality in Organizations*. London: Macmillan.

Collinson, D.L. (1992) *Managing the Shopfloor: Subjectivity, Masculinity and Workplace Culture*. Berlin: William de Gruyter.

Coyle, Angela (1996) *Women and Organizational Change*. Manchester: EOC Research Series.

Dex, Shirley and McCulloch, Andrew (1995) *Flexible Employment in Britain: A Statistical Survey*. Manchester: Equal Opportunities Commission.

Equal Opportunities Commission (1985) *Code of Practice for the Elimination of Discrimination on the Grounds of Sex and Marriage and Promotion of Equality of Opportunity in Employment*. London: HMSO.

Equal Opportunities Commission (1995) *The Gender Impact of CCT in Local Government: Summary Report*. Manchester: Equal Opportunities Commission.

Escott, K. and Whitfield, D. (1995) *The Gender Impact of CCT in Local Government*. Manchester: Equal Opportunities Commission.

Ferguson, K.E. (1984) *The Feminist Case Against Bureaucracy.* Philadelphia: Temple University Press.

Filby, M. (1992) 'The figures, the personality and the bums: service work and sexuality', *Work, Employment and Society*, 6 (1): 23-42.

Gherardi, Silvia (1995) *Gender, Symbolism and Organizational Cultures.* London: Sage.

Gottfried, H. and Graham, L. (1993) 'Constructing difference: the making of gendered sub-cultures in a Japanese assembly plant', *Sociology*, 27 (4): 611-28.

Griffin, G. (1995*) Feminist Activism in the 1990's.* London, Taylor and Francis.

Halford, S., Savage, M. and Witz, A. (1997) *Gender, Careers and Organizations: Current Developments in Banking, Nursing and Local Government.* Basingstoke: Macmillan Press.

Hall-Taylor, B. (1997) 'The construction of women's management skills and the marginalization of women in senior management', *Women in Management Review*, 12 (7): 255-63.

Handy, Charles (1986) *Understanding Organizations.* Harmondsworth: Penguin.

Hassard, J. (1993) *Sociology and Organization Theory. Positivism, Paradigms and Postmodernity.* Cambridge: Cambridge University Press.

Hearn, J. and Parkin, W. (1987) *'Sex' at 'Work'. The Power and Paradox of Organization Sexuality.* Brighton: Wheatsheaf Books.

Hearn, J., Sheppard, D. L., Tancred-Sheriff, P., and Burrell, G. (eds) (1989) *The Sexuality of Organization.* London: Sage.

Helgesen, S. (1990) *The Female Advantage - Women's Ways of Leadership.* New York: Doubleday.

Hochschild, A.R. (1983) *The Managed Heart: the Commercialization of Human Feeling.* Berkeley: University of California Press.

Institute of Personnel and Development (1996) *A Vision for the Development of Equal Opportunities: Managing Diversity. An IPD Position Paper.* London: IPD.

Itzin, Catherine and Newman, Janet (eds) (1995) *Gender, Culture and Organzational Change: Putting Theory into Practice.* London: Routledge.

James, N. (1989) 'Emotional labour: skill and work in the social regulation of feelings', *Sociological Review*, 37 (1): 15-42.

Kanter, R.M. (1997) *Men and Women of the Corporation.* New York: Basic Books.

Kerfoot, D. and Knights D. (1993) 'Management, masculinity and manipulation: from paternalism to corporate strategy in financial services in Britain', *Journal of Management Studies*, 30 (4): 659-77.

Kirkbride, Paul S., Durcan, Jim and Obeng, Edward D.A. (1994) 'Change in a chaotic post-modern world', *Journal of Strategic Change*, 3, June: 151-63.

Lash, S. and Urry, J. (1994) *Economies of Signs and Space.* London: Sage.

Ledwith, S. and Colgan, F. (1996) *Women in Organizations: Challenging Gender Politics.* London: Macmillan Press.

Lewin, K. (1951) *Field Theory in Social Science.* New York: Harper and Row.

Lupton, T. (1963) *On the Shop Floor: Two Studies of Workplace Organization and Output.* Oxford: Pergamon Press.

McDowell, L. (1997) *Capital Culture: Gender at Work in the City.* Oxford: Blackwell.

Mabey, C. and Mayon-White, B. (1993) *Managing Change.* London: Paul Chapman Publishing in association with The Open University.

Maddock, S. (1999) *Challenging Women: Gender, Culture and Organization.* London: Sage.

Maile, S. (1995) 'The gendered nature of managerial discourse: the case of a local authority', *Gender, Work and Organization*, 2 (2): 76-87.

Massey, D. (1984) *Spatial Divisions of Labour: Social Structures and the Geography of Production.* London: Macmillan.

Mills, A. and Tancred, P. (eds) (1992) *Gendering Organizational Analysis.* London: Sage.

Morgan, Glenn and Knights, David (1991) 'Gendering jobs: corporate strategy, managerial control and the dynamics of job segregation', *Work, Employment and Society*, 5 (2): 181-200.

Newman, Janet (1995) 'Gender and cultural change', in Itzin, Catherine and Newman, Janet (eds) *Gender, Culture and Organzational Change: Putting Theory into Practice.* London: Routledge. pp. 11-29.

Pettigrew, A. (1973) *The Politics of Decision Making.* London: Tavistock.

Pollert, A. (1981) *Girls, Wives and Factory Lives.* London: Macmillan.

Pringle, Rosemary (1988) *Secretaries Talk: Sexuality, Power and Work.* London: Verso.

Purcell, J. (1993) 'The impact of corporate strategy on human resource management', in Storey, J. (ed.) *New Perspectives on Human Resource Management.* London: Routledge: 67-91.

Rosener, J.B. (1990) 'Ways women lead', *Harvard Business Review*, November-December: 119-25.

Rubery, J. and Fagan, C. (1994) 'Occupational segregation: plus ca change . . .?', in Lindley, R. (ed.) *Labour Market Structures and Prospects for Women.* Manchester: EOC Research Series: 29-42.

Savage, M. and Witz, A. (eds) (1992) *Gender and Bureaucracy.* Oxford: Blackwell Publishers/The Sociological Review.

Senior, Barbara (1997) *Organizational Change.* London: Pitman Publishing.

Shaw, J. and Perrons, D. (eds) (1995) *Making Gender Work: Managing Equal Opportunities.* Buckingham: Open University Press.

Shilling, C. (1993) *The Body and Social Theory.* London: Sage.

Silverman, D. (1970) *The Theory of Organizations.* London: Heinemann.

Townley, Barbara (1998) 'Beyond good and evil: depth and division in the management of human resources', in McKinlay, Alan and Starkey, Ken (eds) *Foucault, Management and Organization Theory.* London: Sage Publications. pp. 191-210.

Tyler, M. and Hancock, P. (1998) 'Flight attendants and the management of gendered "organizational bodies"', paper presented at the annual conference of the British Sociological Association, University of Edinburgh, April.

Wainwright Trust (1997) *Decentralisation and devolution: the Impact on Equal Opportunities at Work.* Hertfordshire: The Wainwright Trust.

Wajcman, J. (1996) 'Desperately seeking differences: is management style gendered?', *British Journal of Industrial Relations*, 34 (3): 333-49.

Walby, S. (1986) *Patriarchy at Work.* Cambridge: Polity.

Webb, J. (1997) 'The politics of equal opportunity', *Gender, Work and Organization*, 4 (3): 159-69.

Westwood, Sally (1984) *All Day Every Day: Factory and Family in the Making of Women's Lives.* London: Pluto.

Willis, P. (1977) *Learning to Labour.* Aldershot: Saxon House.

Wilson, David (1992) *A Strategy of Change, Concepts and Controversies in the Management of Change.* London: Routledge.

Wilson, R. (1994) 'Sectoral and occupational change: prospects for women's employment', in Lindley, R. (ed.) *Labour Market Structures and Prospects for Women.* Manchester: EOC Research Series: 14-28.

Wilson, D.C. and Rosenfeld, R.H. (1990) *Managing Organizations.* Maidenhead: McGraw-Hill.

Witz, A., Halford, S. and Savage, M. (1994) 'Organised bodies: gender, sexuality, bodies and organizational culture', paper presented to the annual conference of the British Sociological Association, March.

Zimmeck, M. (1992) 'Marry in haste, repent at leisure: women, bureaucracy and the post office, 1870-1920', in Savage, M. and Witz, A. (eds) *Gender and Bureaucracy.* Oxford: Blackwell Publishers. pp. 65-93.

Index

perception 38
teamworking 143
guilt, working women 93

Handy, Charles 26, 170–1
Hawthorne Studies 4, 25, 155
health care, collaboration 144
hegemonic masculinity 6, 44, 198
helpmeet roles 45
heroes 138, 172
heroism 25, 26
heterarchy, organizational 70
hierarchies
    flattening of 225
    in organizations 28–9, 70, 133
    and power 139
homophobia 44
homosexual reproduction 114–15
homosociability 197, 203, 204
homosocial male networks 197
homosocial reproduction 115
Human Relations school 217
Human Resource Management, The New Agenda 87
human resource utilization, and gender 221
humanism, organizational 132

identity
    gender 18, 21
    organizational 198–200
Imperial Airways 48
individualism, male gender 26
individuals, corporate culture 176
industrial subculture 168, 179
inequality, everyday life 88
informal communication, in organizations 70
informal networks 72
informalism 115
information exchange 63
Information Systems/Information Technology (IS/IT) 79–80
information technology
    reduced workloads 161
    working from home 158
insensitivity, gender 9
instrumental approach 173
integration, organizations 69
integrity, corporate culture 175–6
intellectual antecedents, feminist research 7
inter-group dynamics, collaborative 143
interaction
    communication 76
    perception 38
    sexual stereotyping 41
internal networks, power 196–8
interpersonal barriers 72
intonation 66
intra-group dynamics, collaborative 143

job evaluation 45–6
jobs, definition of 154
jokes, behaviour reinforcement 44

Kennedy, Alan A. 171–2
knowledge
    discourse and 75
    feminist research methodology 8

labour, division of 4, 45, 152–3
laddish behaviour 45
language 75–6
    gendered 65–7, 194
    IS/IT 79
    organizational 29, 73
    and perception 37–8
language game 76
Language in Society 65
Language and Women's Place 65
Leaders 106
leaders, team-based organizations 139
leadership 104–24
    communication styles 73
    corporate 138
    Deborah and Barak 118–21
    feminization of management 116–17
    gender differences 110–14
    masculinity and management 114–17
    team-based organizations 139
    theories of 107–10
    women and 104–7
Leading Self Directed Work Teams 116
learned helplessness 67
Least Preferred Co-Worker (LPC) Scale 109
linear models, communication 61
lip service/feminist pretenders culture 181
literature (OB)
    attention to gender 5–6
    communication 64–73
    focus of 17
    gender stereotyping 41
    male emphasis in 25
    personality theories 18, 21–4
    power in 188–9
locker room cultures 107, 181
lower status groups 46

macho management 181, 225
male sexuality, in workplace 45
male/female dichotomy 3, 131
management
    feminization of 116–17
    and masculinities 114–17
    origins of 151
    psychoanalytic theory 27
    social process 159
    social services organizations 201–5
    women in 6
management style 225–6